Chicago's
Sweet Tooth

Chicago's Sweet Tooth

Five Hundred Prominent Chicagoans
Divulge Their Favorite Dessert Recipes

Ann Gerber

Chicago Review Press

First edition

First printing

Published by Chicago Review Press, Chicago

Library of Congress Cataloging in Publication Data

Gerber, Ann.
  Chicago's sweeth tooth.

  Includes index.
  1. Desserts. 2. Celebrities—Illinois—Chicago.
I. Title.
TX773.G38   1985   641.8′6   85-11705
ISBN 0-914091-77-8

This book is dedicated to The Candyman,
my husband BJK; my children Jeff and Blair,
Marcy, Brian and Lisa, who have made my life sweet.

Foreword

There are eight million sweet tooths in and around this hungry city of Chicago. Eight million mouths watering at the thought, the sight, the suggestion of some special seductive dessert.

Ann Gerber asked the 500 most important Chicagoans, from all walks of life, to reveal their favorite desserts. Public officials like President Ronald Reagan and First Lady Nancy, Gov. James and Jayne Thompson, Mayor Harold Washington; sports stars Carlton Fisk, Walter Payton, Ryne Sandberg; show biz types Jim Belushi, Daryl Hannah, Lindsay Crouse, Mr. T, Ann Jillian; TV personalities Linda Yu, Walter Jacobson, Oprah Winfrey; and just regular guys like Mike Royko, Ald. Ed Vrdolyak, Sir Georg Solti and Wally Phillips admitted what turned them on. The results are a testimonial to the tantalizing temptations that each has found satisfying and addictive.

Rumors that chocoholics live openly (and secretly) among us are true! Of the 500 dessert choices admitted by these confiding eaters, more than 125 are chocolate! This book contains the recipes for more than 25 different chocolate mousses, more than 15 cheesecakes, not to mention fudge, brownie and truffle recipes to indulge the cravings of confirmed, industrial-strength chocolate lovers.

You'll learn the recipes for Better Than Sex Chocolate Bars, Fat Man's Misery, and an easy fudge pie so decadent that it won the Culinary Institute of America Regional Cuisine Award in 1984. There are lemon meringue pies, souffles, meringues, rum cakes, myriad mousses, tarts, chocolate cakes, custards, eclair cakes, carrot cakes, coffee cakes and cookies like mother never made.

But Chicago is not all sugar-coated. There are strong, brave, reformed sweet teeth among us. Cardinal Joseph Bernardin, playwright David Mamet, have rejected gooey palate pleasers for cheese and fruit. This book duly notes a few other unique citizens who choose fresh raspberries or grapes at the end of a meal or as a snack. Their invulnerability is suspect, but this cookbook is not meant to cast doubts on them or what may be smuggled home from bakeries or candy stores. This is a volume dedicated to sharing recipes that will keep your sweet tooth satisfied in the most pleasant way—tasting and sampling as you pursue the unending search for the ultimate dessert sensation.

My sincerest thanks to the 500 V.I.P.s who in their own words and according to their own methods have shared their favorites with us.

Ann Gerber
May 1985

Contributors

x

PRESIDENT RONALD AND NANCY REAGAN

The First Lady is a former Chicagoan. She reports this is her husband's favorite dessert.

Pumpkin Pecan Pie

4 slightly beaten eggs
2 cups canned or mashed cooked
 pumpkin
1 cup sugar
½ cup dark corn syrup

1 teaspoon vanilla
½ teaspoon cinnamon
¼ teaspoon salt
1 unbaked 9-inch pie shell
1 cup chopped pecans

Combine ingredients except pecans. Pour into pie shell. Top with pecans. Bake at 350 degrees for 40 minutes, or until set.

1

GOV. JAMES AND JAYNE THOMPSON

Illinois' leader and his lawyer wife are both antique buffs, maintaining homes in Chicago and in Springfield.

Quick Chocolate Mousse

1 6-ounce package chocolate chips
2 eggs, slightly beaten
2 tablespoons strong hot coffee

3 tablespoons rum
¾ cup milk, almost boiling

In a blender, blend all but the eggs, for two seconds. Add eggs and blend for two minutes more. Pour into dessert dishes and chill for eight hours. Serves 4.

MAYOR HAROLD WASHINGTON

He and Mary Ella Smith baked this for the March of Dimes recipe competition in 1984.

Lemon Lights

Crust:
1 cup butter
½ cup sifted confectioners sugar

2 cups sifted flour

Filling:
4 eggs
2 cups sugar
¼ cup sifted flour

1 teaspoon baking powder
¼ cup lemon juice
2 tablespoons grated lemon peel

Glaze:
2 cups cups sifted confectioners sugar

3 tablespoons hot water

To prepare crust, beat butter and sugar until creamy. Stir in the flour until evenly blended. Spread into an ungreased 13 by 9-inch baking pan. Bake in a 350 degree oven for 15 minutes, or until lightly browned.

While the crust is in the oven, prepare the filling. Beat eggs and sugar until very light and fluffy. Stir in the remaining ingredients. Pour over the hot crust. Return to oven and continue baking for 30 minutes or until filling is set. Remove from the oven and cool for 10 minutes.

Make a glaze by mixing the sugar and hot water, stirring until the sugar is dissolved. Spread over top and finish cooling. Cut into squares.

HOPE ABELSON

Patron of the arts, active with Stratford's Shakespearean Festival.

Folie Du Chocolat

In bottom of large and heavy champagne glasses, place a meringue cookie made as follows:

2 egg whites
2 drops white vinegar
1 teaspoon vanilla

pinch salt
pinch cream of tartar mixed with
¾ cup super-fine granulated sugar

Beat egg whites until stiff, adding vinegar, vanilla, salt and cream of tartar-sugar mixture as you beat.

Drop meringue by spoonfuls onto a waxed-paper-covered baking sheet. With a spoon, make an indentation in each meringue to help hold the ice cream in place. Bake meringues for ½ hour—no longer—in a 250 degree oven, and cool.

When ready to serve, place one large scoop of Haagen-Dazs chocolate ice cream over meringue, pressing lightly to secure in the glass. For topping, pass chocolate sauce and/or fresh raspberry sauce of your choice. Serves 6.

KATHERINE ABELSON

Patron of the arts, supporter of Hubbard Street Dance Co., Art Institute, local ballet companies.

Raspberry and Orange Meringue

1 teaspoon cornstarch
1 teaspoon vanilla
1 teaspoon white vinegar
3 egg whites
7 ounces confectioners sugar
2 ounces butter

4 ounces icing sugar
grated rind 1 orange
1 teaspoon orange juice
¼ pint heavy cream
8 to 12 ounces fresh raspberries

Blend the cornstarch, vanilla, and vinegar in a cup. Whisk egg whites until stiff, whisk in a little sugar, then fold in the remainder with the blended cornstarch. Cover a baking sheet with oiled waxed paper and sprinkle it with some sugar. Shape meringue mixture into a circle about 1½-inch thick on the baking sheet and cook it for one hour at 275 degrees. Switch off oven and leave meringue to cool in oven for 1 hour. Remove from oven, cool and tear off paper.

Cream butter and icing sugar, add the grated orange rind and beat in the juice. Whisk the heavy cream until softly stiff and fold it into the butter cream. Spread this over the meringue and finally cover the top with the raspberries. Serves 6.

MARJORIE ABRAMS

Publicist, world traveler.

Garnished Oriental Oranges

4 oranges
2 tablespoons Grand Marnier

1 tablespoon grenadine syrup

Peel and segment oranges. Sprinkle with mixture of Grand Marnier and grenadine syrup. Refrigerate for several hours, stirring occasionally. If desired, garnish with a little grated orange peel and with bittersweet chocolate shavings, toasted coconut or toasted almonds. Serves 4.

AUDRI ADAMS

Publicist.

Ginny's No Bake Bars

1 16-ounce package chocolate chips
1 16-ounce package butterscotch chips
¾ cup peanut butter

2 cups miniature marshmallows
½ cup chopped walnuts

Melt both kinds of chips and peanut butter in double boiler. Mix in marshmallows and nuts. Pour into 9 by 13-inch greased pan. Chill and cut into squares. Bars keep in refrigerator for weeks.

"My aunt Ginny White, before marrying my uncle, was Dan Topping's right hand at the Hollywood Canteen (WWII). Now she has a Minnesota farm where they raise Black Angus cattle."

DIETER AHRENS

Restaurateur, owner of Jovan.

Russian Creme with Berries in Wine Sauce

Creme:

1 envelope unflavored gelatin
½ cup water
¾ cup sugar

1 cup heavy cream
1½ cups sour cream
1 teaspoon vanilla

Sprinkle gelatin over water in medium saucepan. Let soften about 5 minutes, add sugar and put on heat. Stir constantly until it boils, remove from heat and whisk in heavy cream.

In a separate bowl mix together sour cream and vanilla. Whisk hot gelatin/sugar mixture into sour cream. Fill to half-full 10 regular-sized coffee cups or molds. Set in refrigerator for 5 hours.

Sauce:

¾ cup sugar
1 cup red wine
½ stick cinnamon

4-5 teaspoons cornstarch
1½ cups blackberries, raspberries
    combined (or berries of your choice)

To make sauce, place sugar, red wine and cinnamon in medium saucepan over medium heat. Stir until mixture boils. Place cornstarch in a bowl, add some hot wine mixture and stir. Then pour this into the wine mixture, stir and bring back to a boil. Cook until mixture becomes clear and thickens (but not too thick). Let cool to room temperature. Add berries and refrigerate.

When ready to serve run knife around edge of each cream, hold cup in hot water for about 10 seconds and turn out onto individual plates. Place sauce around the Russian Creme. Serves 10.

GRACE ALDWORTH

Socialite, active in charitable endeavors.

Pears in Cointreau

18 firm Bartlett pears
9 cups water (bottled)

6 cups light brown sugar
2 cups Cointreau

Peel the pears, leaving them whole on their stems. Put immediately in cold tap water with a few drops of lemon juice to prevent discoloration. Make a syrup of 6 cups light brown sugar and 9 cups water (bottled). Boil for a few minutes, add pears, and cook until tender, not mushy. Fill a tea cup with Cointreau and when the pears are done, saturate each one thoroughly with the Cointreau by dipping it into the cup. Pile the pears in a pyramid in a large glass dish. Continue to cook the juice until moderately thick and then add the Cointreau in which the pears were dipped. Pour the syrup over the pears and chill.

Cocoa Cream Fluff:
1 pint heavy cream, whipped　　　　**2 tablespoons confectioners sugar**
6 tablespoons cocoa

To whipped cream add cocoa and confectioners sugar. Fold together gently and serve over pears. Pass Fluff in a separate bowl.

"Best made night before, except for fluff."

DR. GEORGE AND JANICE ALLEN

Both are active on the social, charitable scene. She is a former model.

Prunes in a Pitcher

3 dozen dried prunes　　　　　　**½ vanilla bean**
16 ounces ruby port　　　　　　　**scant cup of sugar**
16 ounces red bordeaux wine　　　**heavy cream**

Soak prunes in ruby port for 24 hours. Add red bordeaux wine, vanilla bean, and sugar. Simmer for 5 minutes, then allow them to cool. Place them in a crystal bowl or pitcher and cover with heavy cream. Serve very cold with toasted slices of brioche.

"This was a favorite dessert of the Aga Khan III, grandfather of the present Aga Khan. It was prepared for him at La Pyramide restaurant. The Aga Khan had given a magnificent terracotta vase, decorated with Islamic motifs, to Fernand Point, the owner and chef. M. Point served him this dessert in the vase which he familiarly called "le pichet" (the pitcher)."

JAMES AND MARILYNN ALSDORF

Patrons of the arts, art collectors.

Jim's Rum Cake

Cake:
1 package yellow cake mix
1 package instant vanilla pudding
½ cup oil

½ cup rum
4 beaten eggs

Mix above together for 3 minutes. Bake at 350 degrees for 55 to 60 minutes. While cake is cooling in pan, prepare glaze.

Glaze:
1 cup sugar
1 stick margarine

½ cup rum

Boil all together. Let stand 5 minutes and pour over cake.

JOANNE ALTER

Metropolitan Sanitary District Commissioner.

Chocolate Mousse

1 6-ounce package chocolate chips
2 whole eggs
3 tablespoons strong coffee

1 to 2 tablespoons orange liqueur
¾ cup scalded half & half

Blend in blender for two minutes at high speed. Pour into cups (or a bowl) and chill at least 4 hours. Serves 4.

"Recipe may be doubled, but not booze."

DR. RENE AND DENISE AMON

He is professor of structural engineering at U. of I. and she is a fashion consultant.

Flan(Creme Caramel)

10 eggs
1 quart milk

3 cups sugar
rind of 1 lemon

In a metal mold, place 1½ cups sugar with one-half cup water and heat until sugar becomes caramelized. Let mixture cool.

In a blender, place eggs, milk, 1½ cups sugar, and the lemon rind (grated). Blend well.

Pour egg and milk mixture into the carmelized mold and place mold into a shallow pan of hot water. Bake 45 minutes in an oven preheated to 350 degrees.

Refrigerate overnight and unmold.

ABRA PRENTICE ANDERSON

Socialite, writer, philanthropist.

Open French Strawberry Tart

1 quart large, ripe strawberries (raspberries, blueberries, etc. may be substituted)
1 jar black raspberry jelly

1 home-baked or store-bought 9-inch pie shell
2 tablespoons kirsch
whipped cream and/or sour cream

Bake pie shell and set aside.

About an hour before serving, wash, drain and hull strawberries, being careful not to drown them. Place them bottoms down on pie shell with largest berries toward the center. Just before serving heat jar black raspberry jelly with kirsch. Spoon on top of berries. Run under the broiler for a few minutes to glaze the berries. Watch carefully as it will burn quickly. Serve immediately and pass separate bowls of whipped and sour cream. Serves 4 to 6.

KAREN ANDREAE

Personal management executive.

Karen's Delight

1 stick butter
1 cup graham cracker crumbs
1 10-ounce package chocolate chips
1 6-ounce package (or 1 cup)
   butterscotch chips

1 cup pecan pieces
1 14-ounce can sweetened condensed
   milk

Preheat oven to 350 degrees. Melt butter in a 9 by 13-inch pan in the oven. Add in layers the cracker crumbs, chocolate chips, butterscotch chips and pecan pieces. Pour milk over all. Bake at 350 degrees for 35 minutes. Cool and cut into tiny squares.

JOHN ANDRICA

Management consultant, active in local politics.

Grand Marnier Mousse

1 egg white
⅔ cup heavy cream
3 tablespoons confectioners sugar

3 tablespoons Grand Marnier
¼ cup chopped, toasted nuts of your
   choice

Whisk egg white until stiff. In a separate bowl whisk cream until beginning to thicken. Add sugar and continue whipping until thick but not solid. Fold in egg white and Grand Marnier. Spoon into individual glasses and sprinkle with nuts. Place in freezer until firm. Let stand 5 to 10 minutes before serving. Serves 3 to 4.

ANTHONY AND IRENE ANTONIOU

He is a real estate developer and both support the arts.

Honeyed Green Grapes

2 pounds seedless green grapes, rinsed,
  stems removed
1 cup sour cream
½ cup honey

2 tablespoons brown sugar
juice of 2 lemons
2 ounces Puerto Rican rum

Place grapes in a large mixing bowl. Add all other ingredients and gently fold with spatula until grapes are coated. Add more rum if necessary. Refrigerate at least two hours and serve cold in large glass bowl for a buffet, or individual servings for a sit-down dinner. Serves 8.

BENNETT AND MARGOT ARCHAMBAULT

He is head of Stewart-Warner, she is active in charitable, social work.

Lemon Pudding Cake

¾ cup sugar
¼ cup all-purpose flour
dash salt
3 tablespoons butter, melted
1½ teaspoons finely shredded lemon
   peel

3 beaten egg yolks
1½ cups milk
3 egg whites
¼ cup lemon juice

In a large mixing bowl combine sugar, flour and salt. Stir in melted butter, lemon peel and lemon juice. In a small bowl combine egg yolks and milk; add to flour mixture. In a mixer bowl beat egg whites to stiff peaks. Gently fold egg whites into lemon batter. Turn into an ungreased 8 by 8 by 2-inch baking pan. Place in a larger pan on oven rack. Pour hot water into larger pan to a depth of 1 inch. Bake in a 350 degree oven for 35 to 40 minutes or till top is golden and springs back when touched. Serve warm or chilled in individual dessert dishes. Makes 6 to 8 servings.

MICHELE ARCHAMBAULT

Office of White House Liaison to State Department.

Applesauce Cake

Cake:
1 cup brown sugar
1 cup white sugar
1 cup butter, softened
2 eggs, beaten
2 cups applesauce
2 teaspoons baking soda
3½ cups flour

2 teaspoons cinnamon
1 teaspoon ground cloves
½ teaspoon nutmeg
2 cups raisins, chopped
1 cup dates, chopped
1 cup walnuts, chopped
¼ cup sherry

Cream together brown sugar, white sugar and butter. Beat in eggs. Warm applesauce with baking soda. Add to sugar mixture. Sift together flour, cinnamon, cloves and nutmeg. Stir in sugar mixture and blend thoroughly. Lightly flour raisins and dates. Add with walnuts to batter. Divide mixture between 2 greased tube pans. Bake in preheated 325 degree oven for about 1½ hours. While cake is still warm pour equal amounts of sherry over top of each cake. Yield: 2 cakes.

Frost with buttercream icing when cool.

Butter Cream Icing:
⅓ cup shortening
1 pound confectioners sugar

⅓ cup water
1 teaspoon vanilla

Cream shortening and sugar. Add water slowly. Add vanilla, beat until creamy.

HOWARD AND MARGARET ARVEY

He is an attorney. Both are active supporting the Arts.

Pavlova Cake

3 egg whites
pinch salt
6 ounces very fine sugar
1 teaspoon cornstarch

1 teaspoon vinegar
½ teaspoon vanilla
whipped cream, raspberries or sliced
   kiwi fruit

Line an 8 or 9-inch layer cake pan with greased paper. Beat in egg whites and salt until stiff. Beat in half the sugar a little at a time. Mix cornstarch with the rest of the sugar and fold in gently. Add vanilla and vinegar and mix. Spread in pan and bake at 250 degrees for 1 to 1½ hours. It should be firm outside and soft inside. Top with whipped cream, raspberries or kiwi fruit.

"A lot of people claim this was first made in Australia, but all New Zealanders would fight that claim to the death, since this is a national treasure."

DOROTHY ASH

Socialite, supporter of the arts, charity leader.

Mango Pie

1 9-inch pastry shell
2 8-ounce packages cream cheese
1 cup granulated sugar
½ teaspoon vanilla

2 eggs
2 mangos, pitted, coarsely chopped
chopped walnuts

Combine all ingredients except walnuts in bowl of food processor and puree. Pour mixture into pie shell and bake in 375 degree oven 20 minutes or until top sets around edges. Remove and let cool. Sprinkle with chopped walnuts and serve with whipped cream, if desired. Serves 8.

CALVIN ASHFORD

Interior designer.

Chocolate Pie Deluxe

1¼ cups graham cracker crumbs (16
  crackers)
2 tablespoons sugar
¼ cup butter or margarine, melted
16 large or 1½ cups miniature
  marshmallows

1½ cups milk
1 9¾-ounce bar milk chocolate
1 cup heavy cream, whipped
roasted slivered almonds

Heat over to 350 degrees. Mix graham cracker crumbs and sugar in bowl. Add butter; mix thoroughly. Press crumb mixture firmly and evenly on bottom and sides of 9-inch pie pan. Bake 10 minutes. Cool.

In saucepan, combine marshmallows, milk and chocolate; cook over low heat, stirring constantly, until chocolate and marshmallows are melted and blended. Chill until mixture mounds slightly when dropped from spoon. Fold chocolate mixture into whipped cream. Pour into crumb-lined pan; sprinkle with almonds. Chill several hours or until set. To serve, cut into small wedges. 12 servings.

For an added touch, pass a bowl of red-and-white peppermint candies to enhance the chocolate flavor.

MARVIN ASTRIN

WBBM account executive.

Angie's Chocolate Cheesecake

Crust:

8 ounces chocolate wafers

3 ounces sweet butter (¾ stick)

Preheat oven to 375 degrees. Adjust rack ⅓ up from bottom of oven. Separate bottom from sides of a 9 by 3-inch springform pan; butter the sides only, then replace the bottom in the pan and set aside.

Place crumbled cookies in food processor a blender to make fine crumbs. Place in mixing bowl. Melt the butter and stir into the crumbs until thoroughly mixed. Pour about ⅔ of the mixture into the prepared pan. Tilt the pan at about a 45 degree angle and press a layer of the crumbs against the sides. Leave a rim of uncrumbed pan ¾ of an inch deep around the top. Rotate the pan gradually as you press on the crumbs. Then turn the pan upright on its bottom, pour in the remaining crumbs and, with your fingertips, distribute them evenly around the bottom of the pan. Then press down firmly to make a compact layer.

Filling:

12 ounces semi-sweet chocolate
24 ounces cream cheese at room temperature
1 teaspoon vanilla extract

⅛ teaspoon salt
1 cup granulated sugar
3 eggs (large or extra large)
1 cup sour cream

Place the chocolate in the top of a double boiler over hot water on low heat. Cover until partially melted, then uncover and stir until completely melted and smooth. Remove from hot water and set aside to cool slightly.

In the large bowl of an electric mixer, cream the cream cheese until smooth. Add the vanilla, salt and sugar and beat well until very smooth. Add the chocolate and beat to mix. Add the eggs one at a time, beating until thoroughly blended after each addition. Add the sour cream and beat until smooth. Pour the filling into the crumb crust and smooth the top. Bake for one hour. Let stand on a rack until completely cool. Cover the top of the pan with foil and refrigerate overnight. The cheesecake may be removed from the pan just before serving or days before.

MRS. BEAUMONT ATWATER

Socialite and theater buff.

Chocolate Mousse

¼ cup sugar
⅓ cup water
1 6-ounce package semi-sweet chocolate pieces
3 egg yolks

½ cup toasted almonds
1½ cups heavy cream, whipped
3 tablespoons dark rum or Grand Marnier

Combine water, sugar and chocolate in small saucepan and cook 3-5 minutes. Place in blender and add egg yolks and almonds. Process by turning on and off until almonds are coarsely chopped. Place in large bowl and carefully fold in whipped cream and liqueur. Freeze or chill before serving.

THOMAS AND MARY AYERS

He is a business leader best known for work with Commonwealth Edison. Both are active in civic and social organizations.

Three Layer Cookies

First Layer
½ cup melted butter
¼ cup sugar
⅓ cup cocoa
1 teaspoon vanilla

1 egg slighly beaten
2 cups graham cracker crumbs
1 can flaked coconut
½ cup chopped pecans

Mix. Press in 9 by 13-inch pan and cool.

Second Layer:
½ cup melted butter
3 tablespoons milk

2 tablespoons instant vanilla pudding
  mix
2 cups confectioners sugar

Spread on first layer and cool.

Third Layer
1 package (6 ounces) chocolate chips

4 tablespoons butter

Melt and spread. When cool, cut into bars.

BABACHO

Award-winning fashion designer.

The Few Minutes Chocolate Ultimatum

1 box vanilla wafers
1 small box instant coconut pudding,
  prepared according to package
  directions
1 large box instant chocolate pudding,
  prepared according to package
  directions

½ cup vermouth, or to taste
1 pint chocolate or vanilla ice cream,
  softened
½ cup slivered almonds
1 small package grated coconut

Cover the bottom of an oblong glass dish with one layer of vanilla wafers. Mix chocolate pudding with vermouth, pour ⅓ of this mixture over vanilla wafers, and let stand till firm. Add another layer of vanilla wafers, cover with the second third of chocolate pudding. Sprinkle ½ the grated coconut over chocolate and again let stand or chill until firm. Spread coconut pudding over coconut, add another layer of vanilla wafers and the last third of chocolate pudding. Let stand until set. Spread softened ice cream over pudding and cookie mixture, smoothing evenly. Sprinkle almonds and the rest of the coconut over all. Freeze 10 or 15 minutes before serving. Serves 6.

GEORGE BADONSKY

Restaurateur; owner of Maxim's, Tango, George's, Bastille.

Tango Flourless Chocolate Cake

14 ounces semi-sweet baking chocolate
14 ounces granulated sugar
7 ounces sweet butter

10 eggs (yolks and whites separate)
½ ounce Cointreau or Grand Marnier
½ teaspoon vanilla extract

Melt the chocolate in a double boiler with vanilla, liqueur and a tablespoon of water. Cut the butter in small pieces, warm to room temperature; when the chocolate is melted add the butter and sugar. Mix with a wire whip.

Take the pot off the heat; add egg yolks, mix well, put to side. Begin to mix egg whites, add 3 tablespoons sugar, continue whipping until very stiff; fold into chocolate mixture. Pour the mixture into a buttered round 12 by 2-inch pan. Bake at 350 degrees for 50 minutes. When baking, the mixture will rise (like a souffle), and then drop; at that point the cake is ready. If the cake is cooked properly it will not move when the pan is shaken.

To remove, knock the bottom of the pan with a spoon while still warm and lift carefully. Turn the cake over so top is up. Sprinkle with confectioners sugar. Serves 12.

IRIS BAER

Caterer.

Hershey Chocolate Bundt Cake

2 teaspoons vanilla
2 sticks butter
2 cups sugar
4 eggs
1 16-ounce can Hershey's syrup

½ cup buttermilk
2½ cups flour
½ teaspoon baking soda
8 1.45 ounce milk chocolate Hershey
   bars, melted

Cream vanilla, butter and sugar. Add eggs, one at a time. Add can Hershey syrup. Sift in flour and baking soda together. Alternately add buttermilk and Hershey's melted chocolate bars. Bake 45 to 55 minutes at 350 degrees in greased bundt pan.

"Middle is best when gooey."

DR. G. MARIE BAKIARES

Podiatric physician and surgeon.

Twin Lakes Country Cake

Cake:

3 dessert apples
juice of one lemon
2 eggs
¼ cup sugar

dash salt
½ cup flour
¼ cup melted butter

Caramel:

5 ounces cube sugar

¼ cup water

To make the caramel, place the sugar cubes in a saucepan and moisten with the water. Dissolve the sugar over low heat until a light caramel is formed.

Grease sides of an 8-inch cake tin. Coat the base of the tin with the caramel and leave to cool.

Peel, core and thinly slice the apples. Sprinkle with the lemon juice. Mix the eggs with the sugar and salt in a bowl and beat until the mixture becomes pale and creamy. Then fold in the flour and melted butter alternately in small quantities.

Carefully arrange the apples on the cooled caramel in 2 or 3 layers. (When placing the first layer on the caramel arrange the apples neatly as they will form the top of the cake when turned out of the tin.) Pour the cake mixture over the apples. Bake in a moderately hot oven for 30 to 40 minutes and turn out of the tin immediately. Serve hot or cold.

JEAN BANCHET

World-class owner-chef of Le Français.

Lemon Tart

6 whole eggs
5 egg yolks
1 pound sugar (450 grams)

6 lemons (juice and zest)
10½ ounces butter (300 grams)
2 pre-baked tart shells

Place eggs, yolks, sugar, lemon zest, lemon juice in top of double boiler or in stainless steel bowl set over boiling water. Cook, beating constantly with wire whisk until mixture is thick enough for some to remain inside the wires of the whisk when it is lifted. Remove from heat and immediately whisk in butter. Pour into pre-baked tart shells and brown lightly under broiler.

MARJI BANK

Actress.

Pumpkin Pie Perfection

1 9-inch pie shell
2 beaten eggs
1 can pumpkin
1 cup firmly packed light brown sugar
½ teaspoon salt

1 tablespoon pumpkin pie spice
1 tablespoon flour
1 14-ounce can sweetened condensed
  milk
sweetened whipped cream

Add pumpkin to beaten eggs. Mix well. Add dry ingredients all at once. Mix well. Slowly add milk, mixing as you go. When completely smooth and blended, pour into prepared pie shell.

Bake in pre-heated oven at 425 degrees for 15 minutes. Lower heat to 350 degrees for 35 to 40 minutes. Cool and refrigerate. Ice with sweetened whipped cream, avoiding the "ultra-pasturized"; ultra-pasturized cream won't whip as firmly.

WARREN AND HAZEL BARR

Socialites, patrons of the arts.

Champagne Mousse

5 large eggs
½ cup sugar
¾ cup champagne
1 cup heavy cream

pinch cream of tartar
pinch salt
sliced, blanched almonds, lightly
    toasted, or fresh raspberries

In top of double boiler whisk egg yolks until they are frothy and whisk in sugar, a little at a time. Set the top of the boiler over boiling water and whisk the mixture, adding champagne, a little at a time, for 7 minutes, or until it is thickened. Remove the pan from the heat, whisk the mixture until it is cool, and transfer it to a large bowl.

In a chilled bowl, beat heavy cream until it holds stiff peaks. In another bowl, beat egg whites with cream of tartar and salt until they hold soft peaks. Fold the whites and the whipped cream into the yolk mixture gently, but thoroughly.

Spoon the mousse into stemmed glasses and chill it for at least 2 and up to 6 hours. Garnish each serving with sliced blanched almonds, lightly toasted, or fresh fruit. Serves 6.

LILA BASS

Interior decorator.

Apple and Peach Special Crust Pie

Crust:
1 stick sweet butter
1 3-ounce package Philadephia cream
  cheese

1½ cups sifted all-purpose flour

Filling:
6 apples
3 peaches
1 cup sugar

1 teaspoon cinnamon
1 teaspoon lemon juice

Soften butter and cream cheese to room temperature. Mix well in large bowl. Add flour, blend well. Divide into two batches and refrigerate 20 minutes.

Pare and core apples and peaches, slice. Mix with sugar, cinnamon and lemon. Sprinkle 1 teaspoon flour into mixture.

Roll one ball of pie crust mixture between sheets of waxed paper until it will fit pie plate. Remove waxed paper and line pie plate. Fill with filling. Don't use liquid from fruit.

Roll out second ball of pie crust mixture between waxed paper until it will cover fruit. Slash and prick upper crust. Sprinkle a bit of sugar on top.

Bake in hot oven (450 degrees) for 12 minutes. Reduce heat to 350 degrees and bake 40 minutes longer. Remove from oven and cool. Serve with whipped cream or ice cream.

MARSHALL AND MARGARET BAUER

He manufactures pizza crusts and both are antique experts.

Poached Purple Pears

6 or 8 firm pears (preferably Comice or Anjou)

Peel pears, being careful not to remove stems. Core bottoms and place them in casserole just large enough to hold them upright.

In a large saucepan, bring to boil:

½ or ⅓ bottle Cabernet Sauvignon wine	**2 slices lemon**
¾ cup sugar	**15 whole black peppercorns**
2 cloves	**2 teaspoons powdered cinnamon**
2 slices orange	**dash of powdered cloves**

Pour this syrup over pears and poach them covered until they are tender when pierced with a knife. Greener pears require longer poaching time. Let them cool slowly in liquid overnight. Remove pears from poaching liquid and chill. Serve cold garnished with whipped cream and a green leaf next to stem.

(The poaching liquid makes a great punch base. Add additional wine to correct sweetness to taste; whole allspice may also be added.)

GEORGE BAY

Bay's English Muffins executive, award-winning chef.

Apple Brown Betty

2 medium apples
2 whole Bay's English muffins
½ cup light brown sugar, firmly packed
1½ teaspoons ground cinnamon
¼ teaspoon ground nutmeg

grated rind of ½ lemon
½ cup chopped walnuts
5 tablespoons sweet butter, melted
¾ cup water

Preheat oven to 350 degrees. Grease a 9-inch baking dish with 1 tablespoon butter. Set aside.

Peel, core, and thinly slice apples. Set aside. Grind muffins in blender or food processor until fine in texture. In bowl, combine crumbs, brown sugar, spices, and lemon rind. Stir well. Reserve ½ cup of mixture for topping. To the remaining crumbs, add sliced apples and toss well to coat. Turn apple mixture into prepared pan. Add walnuts to reserved crumb mixture and sprinkle over apples. Pour water over mixture; drizzle butter over all. Bake for 45 minutes or until brown and bubbling. Serve warm with ice cream or whipped cream. Serves 6.

JAMES AND KAREN BAY

He is a Bay's English Muffins executive and both are patrons of the arts.

Snotarta (Swedish Snow Cake)

7 egg whites
1⅓ cups granulated sugar
1 cup plus 1 tablespoon all-purpose
   flour (sifted)

1 tablespoon potato flour
1 stick butter, less ½ tablespoon
   (reserve for greasing pan)
½ cup blanched almonds, slivered

Butter a 9-inch cake pan and sprinkle with slivered almonds. Set aside. Melt butter in saucepan and let cool. Sift both flours together. In a separate bowl, beat egg whites until they are firm and hold peaks. Add the sugar a little at a time. Fold flour mixture into beaten egg whites and then add cooled butter. Pour batter in cake tin and bake for approximately 30 minutes in a 375 degree preheated oven.

Place paper lace doily on top of cake and sift confectioners sugar on doily to create a pattern. Gently remove doily. Or, frost cake with a white butter frosting, and sprinkle shredded white coconut on top.

ROBERT AND SALLY BECKER

He's an artist, ad agency exec; she's a real estate developer.

Winners' Squash Pie

3 cups winter squash
¼ cup honey
1 tablespoon molasses
¼ teaspoon ginger

¼ teaspoon allspice
2 teaspoons cinnamon
2 eggs, beaten
whipped cream

Steam squash until very soft and mash in blender. Combine remaining ingredients except cream; mix well with squash. Pour in large square pan, bake at 325 degrees for one hour. Cool and cut in pie shaped wedges. Top with a dollop of whipped cream. Serves 6.

LEE PHILLIP AND BILL BELL

She's a TV personality and with Bill writes TV soaps.

Baked Custard

3 eggs, slightly beaten
2 tablespoons sugar
¼ teaspoon salt
⅛ teaspoon nutmeg

2 cups skimmed milk
½ teaspoon vanilla
dash cinnamon

Preheat oven to 325 degrees.

Combine eggs, sugar, salt and nutmeg. Slowly stir in milk and vanilla. Set six 5-ounce custard cups in shallow pan. Pour hot water in pan to a level of about one inch. Pour custard into cups, sprinkle with cinnamon. Bake for 40 minutes or until knife inserted into custard comes out clean.

MIKE BELL

Antique dealer.

Chocolate Chip Mandel Bread

4 eggs
1 cup sugar
1 cup oil
1 teaspoon vanilla

2¼ cups flour
1½ teaspoon baking powder
1 cup chopped nuts
1 cup chocolate chips

Mix together all of the above. Spread on a 15½" cookie sheet (ungreased). Bake in a 350 degree oven for 45 minutes. While hot, slice into narrow bars. Stand cut side down, sprinkle with cinnamon and sugar and bake 15 to 20 minutes longer to dry.

SALLY AND MILES BERGER

She's an authority on health care and he's a real estate developer.

White Chocolate Mousse Cake Mayfair Regent

Cake:

Any white box sponge cake. Cake to be baked as box directs, in a 10-inch pan. When cake is cooled, slice horizontally into three rounds, and sprinkle each round with Grand Marnier.

Mousse:

8 egg yolks
8 egg whites
½ pound confectioners sugar

1 pound Swiss white chocolate
2 pints heavy cream

Mix egg yolks with the powdered sugar in a cool bowl; whip until thick. Melt down white chocolate in a double boiler and pour into egg yolk and sugar, slowly. Mix until cool. Whip cream until it makes stiff peaks and put to the side. Whip egg whites until they make a meringue. Fold egg whites into egg yolk/sugar slowly, then fold in the whipped cream. Let set and cool one minute. Mousse is to be spread between the layers, and as frosting. White chocolate can be shaved on top.

EDWIN AND BETTY BERGMAN

Art Collectors, civic leaders.

Fruit Torte

1 cup sugar
½ cup butter
1 cup flour, sifted with dash of salt
1 teaspoon baking powder

2 eggs
1 pint blueberries, sliced apples or
   Italian plums

Cream sugar and butter. Add baking powder to flour and add eggs. Add to creamed butter. Place in a 9-inch springform pan. Cover with the fruit of your choice.

Sprinkle top with a little sugar, lemon juice and cinnamon, to your taste. Bake at 350 degrees for one hour. Best when slightly warm and served with vanilla ice cream. (It freezes perfectly.)

NANCY AND BENNETT BERMAN

She's a publicist, he's a lawyer.

Bananas Flambe

3 tablespoons sweet butter
¾ cup brown sugar
¼ cup dark rum

4 medium bananas, sliced
3 tablespoons brandy
vanilla ice cream

Melt butter and brown sugar together in chafing dish. Add rum and bananas; heat and stir. Place brandy in a heat-proof carafe and heat on stove. Bring heated brandy to chafing dish. Using heatproof glove, light brandy in carafe and toss brandy over banana mixture. Spoon bananas over vanilla ice cream and serve immediately.

NOTE: I find it easier to place ice cream in sherbet glasses before dinner. I store the glasses in the freezer and bring them to the table after the banana mixture is all made.

CAROL LAVIN BERNICK

Vice-president, director of new business division of Alberto-Culver.

German Chocolate Magic Cake

1 cup flaked coconut
½ cup chopped pecans
⅓ cup packed light brown sugar
3 tablespoons butter, melted
3 tablespoons evaporated milk
2 tablespoons light corn syrup
½ cup butter, softened
1 cup plus 2 tablespoons sugar

1 egg
1 teaspoon vanilla
1¼ cups plus 2 tablespoons flour
⅓ cup unsweetened cocoa
1 teaspoon cinnamon
1 teaspoon baking soda
½ teaspoon salt
1 cup buttermilk

Line two 8-inch round layer pans with foil; butter foil well. Mix coconut, pecans, brown sugar, 3 tablespoons melted butter, all the evaporated milk and corn syrup in small bowl. Spread half the mixture over bottom of each pan.

Mix ½ cup butter and all the sugar in large mixer bowl until light and fluffy. Add egg and vanilla; blend well. Combine flour, cocoa, cinnamon, baking soda and salt; add alternately with buttermilk to creamed mixture. Spread half the batter into each prepared pan; do not mix with coconut topping. Bake at 350 degrees for 30 to 35 minutes. Invert immediately; carefully remove foil and discard. Cover layers loosely with foil to keep topping soft. Cool completely; place one layer on top of other. Keep well covered.

KENNETH AND ANNETTE BERRY

He's a furniture executive and she's a travel agent.

Quick Cherry Crisp

1 1-pound 6-ounce can cherry pie
  filling
1 ¾ cups white or yellow cake mix

½ cup melted butter
½ cup chopped pecans

Turn contents of cherry can into an 8 by 8 by 2-inch pan. Sprinkle mix on top. Pour ½ cup melted butter over cake mix. Top with ½ cup chopped pecans. Bake at 350 degrees for 45 minutes. Serve warm or cold, plain or topped with whipped cream or ice cream. Serves 8.

MONIKA AND DR. HENRY BETTS

She's an interior decorator and he heads the Rehabilitation Institute.

Upside Down Apple Tart

6 Granny Smith apples, peeled, cored
   and sliced
zest of ½ lemon
1 cup sugar

1 stick sweet butter
1 shot Calvados
pastry dough

Generously butter a 9-inch pie pan, sprinkle with half the sugar and the lemon zest. Arrange sliced apples in pan, sprinkling every layer with remaining sugar and dotting them with butter. Top all with pastry dough that is rolled out to ⅛-inch thick and cut into a round a bit larger than the pie dish to allow for a slight amount of overhang. Cut vents into dough. Put into preheated 425 degree oven for 25 minutes, unmold immediately after it is done. Pour Calvados over tart and serve hot with vanilla ice cream.

JUDGE MICHAEL AND HEATHER BILANDIC

He's a former mayor of Chicago and she's a socialite, patron of the arts.

Honey Cheese Pie

Pastry Dough:
1½ cups flour
1½ teaspoons baking powder
½ teaspoon salt

2 tablespoons sugar
8 tablespoons frozen butter
¼ cup ice water

Filling:
3 8-ounce packages cream cheese
6 eggs
¾ cup sugar

¾ cup honey
2 teaspoons cinnamon

For dough, using food processor steel blade, put flour, baking powder, salt, sugar and butter into bowl. Process until crumbly and butter is cut into flour. With machine on, add ice water through feed tube and process until dough forms a ball. Roll out dough and line a 10-inch pie plate; flute pastry edge.

For filling, using steel blade, add 1 package of cream cheese and 2 eggs to the bowl. Process until smooth. Add another package of cream cheese and 2 more eggs and process until smooth. Add remaining cream cheese and eggs and process. Add sugar, honey and cinnamon and process until creamy. Pour mixture into lined pie plate.

Bake at 350 degrees about one hour, or until golden brown. Serve warm or cooled. Serves 12.

HAROLD BINSTEIN

Owner of Gold Standard Liquors and Cheese Chalets.

Janice's Eclair Cake

Cake:
1 package graham crackers
2 packages french vanilla instant
   pudding

1 8-ounce container Cool Whip
3½ cups milk

Place a layer of whole graham crackers on bottom of 9 by 13-inch greased pan. Combine pudding and milk and beat according to package directions. Fold in Cool Whip. Pour ½ mixture over crackers. Put another layer of graham crackers and then balance of pudding mix. Add third layer of graham crackers.

Frosting:
2 packages of liquid bitter chocolate
2 teaspoons white corn syrup
1 teaspoon vanilla

1½ cups confectioners sugar
3 tablespoons butter
3 tablespoons milk

Mix together and frost. Refrigerate cake for two days.

MARTIN AND MARJORIE BINDER

He is chairman of Abbott/Interfast, on Fine Arts and Tourism Councils. She is president of Atlas Travel Agency.

Port and Fruit

2 pints blueberries
4 ripe purple plums

1 bottle port

Place rinsed berries and halved, pitted plums in 8 serving dishes. Pour port wine over fruit and marinate at least two hours. Leftover port may be served in after-dinner glasses with this dessert.

MRS. P.D. BLOCK JR.

Socialite, active in civic and charitable affairs.

Frozen Fudge Pie

Crust:
4 egg whites
1 teaspoon vanilla

1 cup sugar

Filling:
1 14-ounce can sweetened condensed
  milk
2 ounces unsweetened chocolate
1 teaspoon vanilla

½ teaspoon salt
½ cup hot water
1 cup heavy cream, whipped

Beat egg whites and vanilla until whites are stiff. Beat sugar in gradually, about 2 tablespoons at a time. Spread on bottom and sides of a greased 9-inch pie pan. Bake at 275 degrees for 1 hour. Cool.

Mix milk, chocolate, vanilla and salt in top of double boiler. Cook, stirring constantly until very thick. Add water gradually and continue cooking until mixture is smooth. Cool.

Spread half of whipped cream on bottom of meringue. Cover with chocolate mixture and top with remaining whipped cream. Freeze for several hours or overnight. Serves 8.

DENNIS BOOKSHESTER

Chairman of the board, CEO of Carson, Pirie, Scott & Co.

Carson's Heather House Pie

Graham Cracker Crust:
1¼ cup graham crackers, crushed fine
½ cup sugar

6 tablespoons butter, melted

Mix the above ingredients thoroughly. Press firmly into a 9-inch pie plate. Bake at 375 degrees until edges are brown, about 8 or 9 minutes. Cool.

Ice Cream Filling:
1½ pints vanilla ice cream, softened
(Other flavors may used, and you may add fresh or drained canned fruits.)

Press the softened ice cream into the pie shell. Do not leave air gaps. Put back into the freezer to thoroughly harden the ice cream.

Meringue:
3 egg whites   **6 tablespoons sugar**
¼ teaspoon cream of tartar

Beat the egg whites with the cream of tartar until frothy. Gradually add the sugar to the frothy egg whites. Beat until the egg whites are stiff and glossy. Put the egg whites on the frozen pie and put under the broiler until the peaks are brown.

Topping:
2 ounces (or more) butterscotch topping   **rum or rum flavoring to taste**

Combine well. Other toppings may be substituted.

Slice pie and serve with Butterscotch-Rum Sauce drizzled over each slice. Serves 6.

BEN BORENSTEIN

Contractor/patron of the arts.

Benny's Salt-Free/Sugar-Free Frozen Fruit Pie Delite

1 cup salt-free mixed nuts   **2 bananas**
1 cup raisins   **1 lime**
1 pint strawberries   **1 pint Sweet & Low blueberry yogurt**

Mince raisins and ½ cup of nuts. Press into 9" pyrex pie pan to form pie crust. Puree strawberries and bananas in blender. Add juice of lime. Fold in yogurt. Pour onto pie crust. Chill. When firm, sprinkle balance of minced nuts to form topping. Add whole nuts and decorate with sliced fruit. Freeze and serve frozen. Serves 6 to 8.

DR. EUGENE BORZSONY

Physician and musician.

Cheese Dome Cake a La Borzsony

16 ounces creamy cottage cheese
2 teaspoons vanilla extract
2 teaspoons almond extract
pinch cinnamon
2 or 3 tablespoons sugar (depending on
taste)

1½ small envelopes unflavored gelatin
½ teaspoon lemon juice
6 tablespoons strawberry or orange
preserves

Put all of the above ingredients in bowl and stir with spoon, only to mix. Heat mixture on top of stove on high for about one minute. (Do not cook mixture, as this will change taste.) Blend in food processor until smooth and creamy, about one minute. Pour into four champagne glasses, cover with plastic wrap and put in refrigerator until cold and set, about 20 minutes. Lift out with edge of knife from glasses and put the cheese "domes" in center of small dessert plates. Heat preserves until warm and put some over each dome and serve with fresh, cut-up strawberries if desired. Serves 4.

SUSAN BOWEY

Socialite, supporter of civic, charitable events.

Chocolate Brandy Cake

½ pound Carr's wheatmeal biscuits
½ pound Maillard's sweet chocolate
½ pound butter
2 eggs
6 tablespoons sugar

2 ounces almonds, blanched, toasted
and chopped
4 tablespoons brandy (or rum)
whole blanched almonds
whipped cream

Process biscuits in a food processor to coarse crumbs. Melt chocolate and butter over low heat. In bowl beat eggs and sugar together and beat in chocolate/butter mixture until creamy. Fold in almonds, crushed biscuits and brandy. Pour batter into an 8-inch spring-form pan that has been well greased and lined with buttered wax paper. Store in refrigerator overnight. Unmold and decorate with whole almonds. Serve small slices with whipped cream. Serves 8.

WILLARD BOYD

President of the Field Museum.

Susan's Chocolate Bread Pudding

1 cup fine dry bread crumbs (put
   through blender)
1 cup sugar
⅓ cup cocoa (unsweetened is best but if
   you must use sweetened, adjust for
   less sugar)

2 cups milk
2 eggs
1 teaspoon vanilla

Mix dry ingredients and add milk. Bring to boil together for one minute. Beat eggs and add to above mixture after boiling. Add vanilla and bake in a casserole to 350 degrees for 30 minutes. Be sure center is "set." Serve hot or cold, with cold milk.

BOB BRADY

Owner of Brady C'est Bon Salon.

Chocolate Angelfood Cake

Cake:
¾ cup sifted cake flour
¼ cup sifted cocoa
1⅓ cups egg whites
¼ teaspoon salt

1 teaspoon cream of tartar
1½ cups sifted sugar
1¼ teaspoons vanilla

Sift flour, cocoa and ¾ cup sugar together 3 times. Separate egg whites, add salt and beat until foamy. Add cream of tartar and beat until egg whites cling to bowl. Fold in another ¾ cup sugar a little at a time. Add vanilla. Fold in dry ingredients. Pour into ungreased tube pan. Bake 45 minutes at 300 degrees and 5 additional minutes at 325 degrees. Invert and hang pan to cool for 1 hour.

Frosting:
⅓ cup margarine
⅓ cup butter

2 squares bitter chocolate
7-minute icing (any)

Wash butter and oleo in ice cubes. Beat butter and oleo and add melted chocolate; cool. Fold into 7-minute icing.

LAURIE BRADY

Astrologer.

Chocolate Mousse Cake

Crust:

½ package pie crust mix
1 square unsweetened chocolate, grated
  or ground
¼ cup brown sugar

¾ cup finely chopped pecans
1 teaspoon vanilla
1 tablespoon water

Mix the dry ingredients, then drizzle on the vanilla and water while stirring with a fork to make a crumbly mixture. Press it into a 9-inch pie plate and bake 15 minutes in a preheated 375 degree oven.

Filling:

1 square unsweetened chocolate
½ cup sweet butter
¾ cup brown sugar

2 teaspoons instant coffee (not freeze-
  dried)
2 large eggs

Melt chocolate over hot water. Set aside. Cream the butter, add the sugar. When fluffy beat in the chocolate, coffee and eggs. Pour the filling into the crust and refrigerate at least 5 hours.

Prepare the topping shortly before serving.

Topping:

2 cups heavy cream
2 tablespoons instant coffee (not freeze-
  dried)

½ cup confectioners sugar
grated unsweetened chocolate

Whip cream, coffee and sugar together until firm peaks form. Spread topping over the pie or pipe it on with a large star tube. Sprinkle with grated chocolate and refrigerate until ready to serve.

EDDIE BRAGNO

Wine merchant.

Chocolate Cream Grand Marnier

6 ounces semi-sweet chocolate, chopped
into coarse pieces
6 tablespoons strong coffee
¼ cup Grand Marnier or other orange-
flavored liqueur

¼ cup sugar
2 cups heavy cream
½ teaspoon vanilla extract
candied orange peel

Combine chocolate, coffee, and liqueur in top of a double boiler. Place over simmering water and stir until chocolate is melted and blended. Add sugar and continue to stir until very smooth and glossy. Remove from heat, and refrigerate until cool.

Whip cream with vanilla until thick but not buttery. Using a wire whisk, gradually blend in cooled chocolate mixture. Mix lightly and just long enough so that the mixture is of one color.

Spoon the mousse into six individual glasses, preferably wine goblets. Cover the tops with plastic wrap and refrigerate until ready to serve, several hours or overnight.

When ready to serve, top each serving with a few candied orange peels. Serves 6.

PERRY BRAND

Ad agency owner.

Chocolate Mousse

8 squares semi-sweet chocolate
8 egg yolks

8 egg whites
whipped cream

Melt chocolate over hot water. Beat egg yolks lightly and add to chocolate off the stove. Beat egg whites until stiff, fold into chocolate and yolks. Fill pot de creme cups or small bowls and chill one to two hours. Serve with whipped cream. Serves 6 to 10.

HOWARD AND JACKIE BRANDSTEIN

He's an attorney and both are patrons of the arts.

Frozen Brownies

2 sticks butter
4 squares unsweetened chocolate
4 eggs
2 cups sugar

1 cup flour
1 teaspoon vanilla
1 12-ounce package miniature chocolate
   chips

Melt butter with unsweetened chocolate. Set aside.

Beat eggs. Add sugar gradually, mix well. Add flour gradually, mix well. Add vanilla. Add cooled chocolate mixture. Mix well. Pour into 13 by 9 by 2-inch ungreased pan. Sprinkle top with miniature chocolate chips. Bake in preheated 325 degree oven for 30 to 35 minutes, until done. Cool completely. Cut and pat brownies into papers. Freeze. Thawing time is 10 minutes.

WILLIAM BRASHLER

Author and writer.

Mock Apple Pie (No Apples Needed)

36 Ritz (no substitutes, please) crackers
2 cups water
2 cups sugar
2 teaspoons cream of tartar
2 tablespoons lemon juice

grated rind of one lemon
butter or margarine
cinnamon
pastry for two-crust 9-inch pie

Roll out bottom crust of pastry and fit into 9-inch pie plate. Break Ritz (no substitutes, please) crackers coarsely into pastry-lined plate. Combine water, sugar, and cream of tartar in saucepan; boil gently for 15 minutes. Add lemon juice and rind. Cool. Pour syrup over crackers, dot generously with butter or margarine and sprinkle with cinnamon. Cover with top crust. Trim and flute edges together. Cut slits in top crust to let steam escape. Bake in hot oven, 425 degrees, 30 to 35 minutes, until crust is crisp and golden. Cut into 6 to 8 slices.

"Serve warm with great dollops of Reddi-Whip or similar non-genuine whip-like cream. The artificial topping will complement this recipe for something that is made out of nothing.

"Mock Apple Pie (No Apples Needed) has long been a fixture on the Ritz Cracker box and in my life. But no more—at least for the former. The Ritz people think it is old fashioned and soon will discard it, leaving millions of us Mock Apple Pie fans in the lurch."

MILTON BRAV

Artist

Kay's Double Chocolate Truffles

6 ounces semi-sweet chocolate chips
3 tablespoons corn syrup
½ cup white wine
1 8½ ounce package chocolate wafers, crushed
1 cup finely chopped nuts

½ cup confectioners sugar
¼ cup finely chopped candied red cherries
ground sweet chocolate or granulated sugar

In top of double boiler over hot (not boiling) water, melt chocolate. Remove from heat, stir in corn syrup and wine. In large bowl mix wafer crumbs, nuts, sugar and cherries. Add chocolate mixture, stir until blended. Let stand 30 minutes. Shape into 1-inch balls, roll in ground chocolate or granulated sugar. Makes about 52.

STUART BRENT

Bookseller, author.

Stuart's German Sweet Chocolate Cake

Cake:

1 4-oz. bar German sweet chocolate
½ cup boiling water
1 cup margarine
2 cups sugar
1 cup sour milk (milk plus 2 teaspoons
   vinegar)

5 egg yolks
1 teaspoon vanilla
2¼ cups sifted flour
1 teaspoon baking soda
½ teaspoon salt
5 egg whites

Melt chocolate in boiling water, cool. Beat egg whites until stiff, adding approximately ½ to ¾ cup sugar. Set whites aside. Cream sugar and margarine very fast. Don't overbeat. Add yolks one at a time. Blend vanilla into chocolate and add to creamed mixture. Then add sifted flour, baking soda and salt alternately with sour milk. Beat well. Fold in beaten whites. Pour into 2 9-inch round cake pans. Bake at 350 degrees for 35 minutes or until top springs back when pressed.

Frosting:

1 cup evaporated milk
1 cup sugar
3 beaten egg yolks
½ cup margarine

1 teaspoon vanilla
1½ cups coconut
1 cup chopped nuts

Combine first 5 ingredients; add coconut and chopped nuts. Divide between 2 cake layers and stack layers together.

JACK BRICKHOUSE

Sportscaster, Hall of Famer.

Pat's Favorite Wine Pie

1 pound raisins (prefer white)
¼ cup water
½ cup vermouth
16 ounces instant vanilla pudding
½ cup sweet vermouth

2½ cups milk
1 pint heavy cream
2 ½ ounces chopped nuts
prepared graham cracker crust

Soak raisins in water and ½ cup vermouth overnight. In the morning, prepare vanilla pudding, using sweet vermouth and milk. Whip cream and fold into pudding with drained raisins and chopped nuts. Pour this filling into graham cracker shell. Freeze until firm. To serve, thaw slightly and top with whipped cream. Yield: 2 pies.

RONALD BRISKMAN

Restaurateur, actor.

Ron's Revenge Cake

1 cup sugar
¼ pound butter or margarine
3 egg yolks
1 4-oz. bar German sweet chocolate
1 cup flour

1 teaspoon baking powder
½ cup heavy cream
3 egg whites
1 teaspoon vanilla

Cream the sugar and butter together, add egg yolks. Sift flour and baking powder together. Add flour mixture to sugar and butter, alternating with whipping cream. Melt chocolate and add vanilla. Beat egg whites until they form peaks and then fold gently into mixture. Bake in 6 by 9-inch greased pan 40 to 45 minutes at 350 degrees. Test with toothpick until pick is dry. When cool, sift confectioners sugar over cake.

EDWARD BROOKS

Food authority.

Bananas and Strawberries Mephisto

6 bananas, not too ripe
¼ cup lemon juice
6 tablespoons margarine or butter
1 cup brown sugar
½ cup frozen orange juice concentrate

grated rind of ½ lemon
¼ teaspoon cinnamon
1 ½ cups strawberry puree
⅓ cup rum, preferably dark

Peel bananas, slice lengthwise and then across to form quarters. Brush with lemon juice to prevent darkening. Melt margarine in chafing dish or skillet over medium heat. Add sugar and carmelize. Stir in orange juice concentrate, rind, cinnamon and puree. Simmer for 2-3 minutes, stirring. Add bananas and cook until tender, about 3-5 minutes. In a separate pan, heat rum until just warm. Ignite rum with a match and pour into chafing dish. Ladle sauce over bananas until flames expire. Serve banana quarters surrounding a scoop of ice cream and spoon sauce over each serving. Serves 6.

JOANNE BROOKS

Choreographer, producer.

Easy Chocolate Chip Brownies

1 package Duncan Hines white cake
   mix
½ cup cooking oil
2 tablespoons water

2 eggs
1 six-ounce package semi-sweet
   chocolate pieces

Pre-heat oven to 350 degrees. Blend cake mix, oil, water and eggs in one bowl. Stir in chips and put in 13 by 9-inch ungreased pan. Bake at 350 degrees for about 30 minutes. (They aren't too brown.)

BAIRD BROWN

Patron of the arts, civic leader.

Cornflake Ring

6 cups cornflakes
½ pound butter
1 cup brown sugar

1 ½ pints vanilla ice cream
1 package frozen strawberries, thawed

Blend brown sugar and butter in a frying pan until boiling and bubbling. Put the cornflakes in a bowl and pour the butter/sugar mixture over them, mixing well. Pack the mixture into a ring mold. Put the mold in the refrigerator for ten minutes, then take it out and unmold it on a serving platter and put it back in the refrigerator. Before serving, take the mold out at least 1 ½ hours in order to let it soften a bit. Fill the center with ice cream and pour the strawberries over the top. Serves 6 to 8.

RICHARD J. BRZECZEK

Lawyer and former police chief.

Applesauce Cake

17 whole graham crackers
1 stick butter, melted
1 14-ounce can sweetened condensed
   milk

¾ of a 25-ounce jar of applesauce
3 eggs, well beaten
½ cup lemon juice
1 ½ teaspoons vanilla

Combine graham cracker crumbs and melted butter. Grease a 9-inch pan and pat in crumbs on the bottom and sides, saving some to cover top of cake.

Combine in separate bowl milk, eggs, vanilla and applesauce. When above is well blended, slowly add lemon juice, making sure all is mixed well. Pour into graham cracker crust and cover with remaining graham cracker mixture. Bake at 350 to 375 degrees for one hour.

HENRY AND GILDA BUCHBINDER

Art collectors.

Charlotte Russe

3 packages ladyfingers
4 large fresh eggs
1 cup sugar
2 envelopes unflavored gelatin

1 quart fresh heavy cream
1 cup milk
2 tablespoons vanilla extract
½ teaspoon almond extract

Whip egg yolks with a pinch of salt, add sugar, then cream until mixture is light in color. Set aside. Heat milk almost to a boil, stirring to avoid scorching. Slowly add milk to gelatin which has been softened in ⅓ cup tap water. Pour this mixture over the creamed eggs and sugar, stir to mix, then set aside to cool.

Whip 4 eggs whites until stiff. In a separate bowl, whip the cream. Set aside enough to spread on the top. Gently fold egg whites into the remaining cream. Now fold in the mixture which had been set aside to cool, adding the vanilla and almond extract, and continue to fold just until the mixture is well mixed. Gently pour into a large spring form pan which has been lined with ladyfingers. Spread top with reserved whipped cream. Cover with waxed paper, refrigerate. It is best when made one or two days in advance. Fresh strawberries may be placed on top, or grated bittersweet chocolate.

DOUG BUFFONE

Chicago Bears all-time great; restaurateur.

Apple Crisp a La Mode from Sweetwater

6 slices stale bread
¼ cup melted butter
6 cups tart apples, cored, peeled and
    sliced vertically (about two pounds of
    apples)
¾ cup light brown sugar

½ teaspoon cinnamon
¼ teaspoon salt
1 cup raisins
½ cup crushed almonds
½ cup apple cider
vanilla ice cream

Grease a 9 by 9 by 2-inch baking pan with butter. Cut crusts off bread slices and cut the slices into one-half-inch cubes. Lightly toast the bread cubes in a shallow pan in the oven, then put them in a large bowl. Pour butter over the bread cubes and toss them with a fork. Put one-third of the cubes in the greased baking pan. Cover the bread cubes with half the sliced apples. Mix sugar, cinnamon and salt. Then add raisins and crushed almonds and mix thoroughly. Sprinkle half the sugar-cinnamon-raisin-almond mixture over the apples. Add another layer of bread cubes, another layer of apples and another layer of the sugar-cinnamon-raisin-almond mixture, and top with remaining bread cubes. Gently pour cider over the contents of the baking pan. Cover with aluminum foil and bake for 30 minutes in a pre-heated 400 degree oven. Then uncover the apple crisp and bake for about ten more minutes, until the top is brown and crusty. Serve warm with vanilla ice cream.

ALD. EDWARD AND ANNE BURKE

Both are lawyers; he is alderman of the 14th ward.

Plum Pie

Quick Pastry:
½ cup shortening
¼ cup cold water
1 ½ cups flour

½ teaspoon baking powder
½ teaspoon salt

Melt shortening, add water and mix with remainder of ingredients to a smooth dough. Chill before rolling on floured board. Shape dough into ungreased pie pan. Do not stretch the dough, ease into place to prevent shrinking. Trim edge ½ inch from pan. Then fold edge under, prick shell.

Plum Mixture:
3 pounds fresh small dark plums
1 cup sugar
juice from fresh lemon

¼ cup tapioca
1 teaspoon cinnamon
1 pat butter

Rinse plums and remove pits. Place plums in a saucepan with just enough water to cover the bottom of the pan. Cook plums in the water over low heat until they are soft, about 15 minutes. Add sugar and heat until dissolved. Add tapioca, cinnamon and mix, then cool. Pour plum/fruit mixture into pie shell. Squeeze fresh lemon juice over the mixture and top with butter. Carefully lay top crust over plum/fruit mixture. Fold edge of crust over bottom crust edge, pinching both together. Use fork to prick several holes in top of crust. Place in oven pre-heated to 425 degrees and bake for 45 minutes to 1 hour or until crust is golden brown. Serve warm with ice cream.

MARSHALL AND SUSAN BURMAN

He's an attorney. Both are patrons of the dance, active in local charities.

Carrot Cake

Cake:

2 cups sugar
1 cup oil
2 cups grated carrots
3 eggs (beaten)
1½ cups drained, canned crushed
   pineapple
4 ounces shredded coconut

1 cup chopped walnuts
2 teaspoons vanilla
2 cups flour, sifted
2 teaspoons baking soda
2 teaspoons cinnamon
1 teaspoon salt
9-inch springform pan

Stir sugar into beaten eggs, add oil. Mix all dry ingredients, then stir into liquid mixture. Add remaining ingredients and pour into springform pan (do not grease or flour pan) and bake at 350 degrees for 40 minutes.

Cream Cheese Frosting:

1 3-ounce package cream cheese,
   softened
1 tablespoon milk

1 teaspoon vanilla
dash salt
2 ½ cups confectioners sugar

Blend cheese, milk, vanilla, and salt gradually. Add confectioners sugar gradually, beating until smooth. Stir in more milk, if necessary.

MICHAEL BUTLER

Polo player, entrepreneur, social lion.

Moroccan Bananas Singapore

6 bananas peeled and sliced lengthwise
¼ cup butter
¼ cup honey

¼ cup lemon or lime juice
½ cup sliced roasted almonds

Melt butter in saute pan. Add honey and lemon juice. Add bananas and baste with sauce until soft. Serve sauce and bananas over ice cream. Top with roasted almonds. Serves 6.

BURNS CABOT

Multi-millionaire playboy.

Rhubarb Cream

1 ½ pounds rhubarb cut in 1-inch
  pieces *(I prefer rhubarb from France)*
1 cup sugar *(I prefer Hawaiian)*
1 cup water *(I prefer Evian water)*

1 tablespoon apricot jam *(I prefer
  Swedish)*
½ cup heavy cream *(I prefer cream from
  Devonshire, England)*

Simmer rhubarb, sugar and water in covered pan until tender, about 3 minutes. Strain and save the liquid. Set rhubarb aside. Reduce the liquid over medium heat to syrup. Mix in apricot jam and chill. Whip heavy cream. Fold half of the whipped cream into the syrup mixture. Add rhubarb pieces and pour into a glass serving bowl *(preferably Steuben)*. Decorate with rosettes of the remaining whipped cream.

ANTONIO CAGLIARINI

Gucci executive, sportsman.

Zuppa Englese

2 packages ladyfingers
1 cup cool black coffee
1 small package instant vanilla pudding,
   prepared according to package
   directions

cocoa
creme de cacao to taste
whipped cream
shaved chocolate

Line a 9 by 13 by 2-inch pan with ladyfingers cut in half lengthwise. Moisten ladyfingers to taste with cool black coffee. Spread with a layer of pudding and sift a little cocoa powder over it. Sprinkle white creme de cacao to taste over cocoa. Repeat layering, depending on depth of pan. To serve, add a layer of whipped cream topped with shaved chocolate.

LILLIAN CALHOUN

Publicist.

In Praise of Fresh Fruit

The good old days of chocolate cream and lemon meringue pies are gone. With a soul-wrenching effort, I have managed to transfer those sweet cravings to new desserts that are so much simpler anyway. What is more delectable than a dish of truly ripe, select fresh cherries in early summer? Or if one is lucky, or knows a good produce buyer, the delicious taste of a truly ripe (this is really the trick in all of these) honeydew melon with a wedge of lemon or lime, or a truly ripe, luscious cantaloupe or watermelon. If you are not watching the girth and can go mad with calories, nothing beats that half cantaloupe, with a scoop of good quality natural vanilla ice cream with perhaps a tablespoon or so of your favorite alcoholic topping—Grand Marnier, Cointreau or any old brandy around the house.

RAY CAPITANINI

Owner of the Italian Village restaurant.

Pere Al Vino (Pears Poached in Wine)

6 large, firm pears, preferably Bosc,
  with stems
4 cups good-quality dry red wine
1 cup tawny port

1 cup cold water
½ lemon
6 tablespoons granulated sugar

Peel the pears with a peeler rather than a knife, then flatten the bottoms by cutting off a thin slice. Stand the pears up in a large metal casserole. (The casserole should be large enough to fit pears closely together without crowding, but not large enough to allow them to fall over.)

Add wine, port, and water to the pears. Squeeze the half lemon and cut off a slice of peel. Add the juice and peel to the casserole, then sprinkle with 4 tablespoons of the sugar.

Cover the casserole tightly and let simmer slowly for about 25 minutes. Test with a toothpick to be sure the pears are well cooked before removing from flame, then leave the cooked pears in the casserole for 10 to 15 minutes to cool.

Stand cooled pears up on a serving dish. Cover the dish with aluminum foil, being careful not to bruise the pears. Place the dish in the refrigerator for an hour.

Remove lemon peel from casserole and transfer the sauce to a small saucepan. Add remaining sugar and simmer again until sauce is reduced to the consistency of a light syrup (30 to 40 minutes). Let the sauce cool for 20 to 30 minutes, then remove pears from the refrigerator and pour sauce over. Return pears to refrigerator for at least 3 hours more before serving.

"These whole pears make a fine presentation, simply accompanied by whipped cream. They should be cooked in a typically Italian wine; the finer the quality, the better. A good Chianti or Chianti Riserva will produce a really fine result."

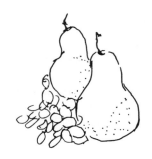

EVANGELINE GOULETAS-CAREY

Co-Founder of American Invsco real estate empire and wife of former New York Gov. Hugh Carey.

Baklava

2 cups blanched almonds
½ cup sugar
Ground cinnamon
Ground cloves
1 cup honey
2 cups sugar
2 cups water

A few lemon or orange rinds
1 cinnamon stick
1 cup melted butter
10-15 sheets fillo (strudel-like pastry sheets available at specialty groceries)
2-3 egg whites, beaten just until foamy

Grind almonds in food processor, blender or nut grinder. Add ½ cup sugar and ground cinnamon and cloves to taste. Set aside.

Boil honey, sugar, water, lemon or orange rind, and cinnamon stick together in heavy saucepan for 10 minutes. Allow this syrup to cool and reserve.

Brush a baking tray with a little of the melted butter. Cover it with one layer of fillo (2 or 3 sheets) and brush with butter. Combine ground almond mixture with the egg whites and spread a layer of this mixture over the butter-brushed fillo. Continue layering until ingredients are used up and baking tray is filled, ending with fillo. Baste with rest of melted butter and with a pointed knife score the top sheets into square or diamond shapes. Bake in a moderate oven (325 degrees) for 1 hour, increasing heat for last few minutes until top is golden brown. Let cool. Reheat syrup and pour hot syrup over cool Baklava.

Serve cold.

HELEN AND SAMUEL CASEY JR.

She is expert on women's networking, business potential. He is a veteran business executive.

Kadota Figs with Chocolate

1 7-ounce can fancy, whole Kadota figs, chilled
1 bar Swiss/Bavarian or rich American chocolate

cultured sour cream

Drain figs, arrange on sauce dish or small bowl. Add a dollop of sour cream and sprinkle with grated chocolate. One can serves 3.

SARA AND HAMMOND CHAFFETZ

Patrons of the arts, civic and social leaders. He is a prominent attorney.

Carrot Cake

Cake:

1½ cups corn oil
2 cups sugar
3 eggs
2 cups flour
2 teaspoons cinnamon
2 teaspoons baking soda

2 teaspoons vanilla
1 teaspoon salt
2 cups shredded carrots (easily done in food processor using steel blade)
1 cup chopped pecans
½ cup crushed pineapple

Use a 9 by 13-inch glass baking dish. Oil it before pouring batter in.

Combine all ingredients in a large bowl and mix until thoroughly blended. Pour batter into pan and bake 45 to 50 minutes in preheated 350 degree oven. Cool and frost with cream cheese icing.

Frosting:

1 3-ounce package Philadelphia cream cheese
1 ¼ cups confectioners sugar
1 stick butter (or margarine if preferred)

⅛ cup crushed pineapple
¼ cup chopped pecans

Cream butter, cream cheese and powdered sugar until just slightly fluffy. Stir in thoroughly pineapple and pecans. Makes 24 pieces.

ALSIE CHARNEY

Socialite and civic leader.

Apple Dream Cake

2 cups sugar
1 cup oil
3 eggs
1 teaspoon vanilla
1 20-ounce can apple pie filling

3 cups flour
½ teaspoon salt
2 teaspoons cinnamon (heaping)
2 teaspoons baking soda
1½ cups walnuts

Mix sugar, oil, eggs and vanilla together. Add apple pie filling. Mix flour, salt, baking soda, and cinnamon; add to oil and sugar mixture. Fold in 1½ cups walnuts. Bake at 350 degrees for 50 to 55 minutes, in buttered and floured 13 by 9-inch pan.

JONNA WOOD-PRINCE CHEWNING

Socialite, leader in charitable affairs.

Strawberry Pie

Filling:
4 cups strawberries
1 cup sugar
3 tablespoons cornstarch

1 teaspoon fresh lemon juice
confectioners sugar
prepared 9-inch pie crust

Crush 2 cups strawberries with sugar. Add cornstarch. Cook until thick and glossy looking (5 to 10 minutes). Add lemon juice and let cool. Sprinkle bottom of baked, cool pie crust with powdered sugar. Place the whole strawberries in pie crust. Pour berry mixture over. Chill.

Topping:
1 3-ounce package cream cheese
⅓ cup sugar
dash salt

½ cup heavy cream
thin slices lime, strawberries, etc.

Cream cream cheese with sugar, salt. Whip cream and fold in. Spread over filling and decorate with slices of fruit. Chill till serving.

MARY ANN CHILDERS

TV personality.

Mary Ann's Ultimate Pound Cake

1 cup butter
3 cups sugar
5 eggs, separated
2 teaspoons vanilla

½ teaspoon soda
1 cup buttermilk
3 cups all-purpose flour

Cream butter and sugar. Add egg yolks, one at a time. Beat well. Stir in vanilla. Dissolve soda in 1 teaspoon warm water. This step is important. Add soda water to buttermilk. Then add milk and flour alternately to sugar mixture, beginning and ending with flour. Fold in egg whites which have been beaten well. Pour into greased 10-inch tube pan, or a bundt pan. Bake at 350 degrees 1 hour and 10 minutes. Cool in pan. Do not invert. Great plain or serve under fresh fruit or ice cream.

This is Mary Ann's grandmother's recipe.

JUDGE WILLIAM AND ROSALEE CLARK

He is a veteran judge and she serves the City of Chicago as protocol chief.

Little Ears (Ausiukes krustai)

2 eggs
1¾ cups pastry flour

3 tablespoons heavy cream
1 tablespoon sugar

Beat eggs until light and fluffy. Add sugar and cream. Add enough flour to make a dough which can be rolled very thin. Cut into diamond shapes. Slash the center of each diamond, twist one end through the hole to form a knot. Fry in hot deep fat until lightly browned. Drain on absorbent paper. Dust with confectioners sugar.

MITCHELL COBEY

Caterer

Apple Tart

Crust:

1⅓ cups all-purpose flour
1 tablespoon sugar

½ cup unsalted butter
¼ cup water

Sift together the flour and the sugar. Cut in the butter. Sprinkle the water onto this mixture and form the dough into a ball. Roll it out on a floured surface and place in a greased 10-inch fluted tart pan. Put the shell in a refrigerator and chill for 1 hour. Line the shell with foil or parchment paper and sprinkle with a handful of beans to weight it. Bake the shell at 400 degrees until slightly browned, about 7 or 8 minutes. Remove the beans and allow to cool.

Filling:

6 Granny Smith or red Delicious apples, peeled, cored, and sliced
juice of 1 lemon
1 cup plus 1 tablespoon sugar
1 teaspoon ground cinnamon

½ cup raisins, marinated in ⅓ cup brandy for 2 or more hours
butter to taste
⅓ cup apricot preserves for glaze

Place 3 peeled, cored, sliced apples into a pan with the lemon juice and 1 cup sugar and cook over low heat until thick. Stir in cinnamon and raisins. Spread this mixture on the bottom of the tart shell. Top with remaining three apples. Sprinkle top with 1 tablespoon sugar and dot with butter. Bake in a preheated 450 degree oven until the apples begin to brown, between 20 and 30 minutes. Finally, melt the apricot preserves with a little water over low heat. Coat the top of the tart with this glaze. Serve warm or at room temperature.

COOKIE COHEN

Former model, socialite, charity leader.

Cookie's Bananas

1 medium-sized banana for each person
sour cream
brown sugar or cinnamon

shredded coconut
cognac (optional)

Peel bananas. Roll in sour cream, then sprinkle with brown sugar or cinnamon, whichever you prefer. Again roll in sour cream, then sprinkle with coconut. If you want to cut the sweetness a little, sprinkle with cognac before serving.

MERLE COHEN

Civic and charity leader.

Super Fabulous Chocolate Cake

Cake:
2½ cups flour, sifted
1½ sticks butter
2 cups brown sugar
1 teaspoon white vinegar
½ cup milk
½ cup sour cream

½ cup water
2 squares unsweetened chocolate
  (1 ounce each)
2 teaspoons baking soda, sifted
3 eggs
1 teaspoon vanilla

Mix vinegar into milk and sour cream and set aside. Cream well the butter and brown sugar. In saucepan bring water to a boil and add chocolate. When melted, set aside to cool. Sift flour and add sifted baking soda. Add eggs one at a time to sugar and butter mixture. Beat well. Add vanilla; then alternately add flour and milk mixture. Butter and then flour lightly large 12-inch round pan. Pour into pan and bake 40 to 45 minutes in 375 degree oven.

Super Frosting:

2 cups confectioners sugar
6 tablespoons butter
4 squares unsweetened chocolate
   (1 ounce each)
2 eggs

½ teaspoon salt
½ teaspoon vanilla
½ cup milk
½ to ¾ cup chopped pecans

Blend sugar, milk, eggs, salt and vanilla in bowl which has been set into larger bowl half full of ice cubes. Melt chocolate and butter together in double boiler. Add while warm to first mixture. Beat with electric hand mixer until fluffy, thick and light in color—about 15 minutes. Frost cake top and sides and sprinkle heavily with chopped pecans.

JOHN B. COLEMAN

Owner of Tremont, Whitehall Hotels.

Chocolate Mousse Cake

10-inch sponge cake:

4 or 5 eggs (8 ounces)
4 ounces granulated sugar
1½ ounces bread flour

1 ounce cocoa powder
2½ ounces cornstarch
2½ ounces hot butter

Combine eggs and sugar. Heat in double boiler until warm. Turn heat off and beat (take off double boiler). Add sifted flour, cornstarch and cocoa. Incorporate melted butter (warm). Bake in 10-inch springform pan 35 minutes at 350 degrees until cake feels firm.

Mousse:

1 cup heavy cream
⅓ ounce unflavored gelatin
3 ounces confectioners sugar (to taste)

3 ounces rum
2 ounces cocoa powder

Soften gelatin in double boiler with 2 teaspoons cold water. Whip together cream, cocoa powder and powdered sugar. Add gelatin and rum. Slice sponge cake in 3 layers. Use a 10-inch cake mold lined with waxed paper. Alternate layers of sponge cake and mousse. Refrigerate 1½ to 2 hours. Unmold cake and cover with thin layer of chocolate butter cream. Put back in refrigerator for about 15 minutes or until butter cream is hard.

CANDACE COLLINS
Model.

Mama Mary Johnson's Potato Pie

Filling:

4 medium-sized sweet potatoes
1 5-ounce can evaporated milk
3 cups sugar

½ teaspoon cinnamon
¼ teaspoon nutmeg
1 stick butter, melted

Wash and boil sweet potatoes until fork-tender (approximately 45 minutes). Remove from shell and mash. Add remainder of filling ingredients, mix well and pour into pie shell. Bake in oven at 400 degrees for approximately 2 ½ hours. Top with whipped cream if desired.

Crust:

2 cups flour
½ cup vegetable shortening

1 teaspoon baking powder
½ teaspoon salt

Mix above ingredients. Add water until mixture reaches doughy consistency. Roll out on board and press into pie pan.

MARVA COLLINS

Educator, founder of West Side Prep.

Divine Layers

graham crackers
1 stick margarine

½ cup sugar
½ to 1 cup chopped nuts (pecans best)

Line a jelly roll pan or cookie sheet with foil and place graham crackers over the surface. Place margarine and sugar in a pan and bring to a good boil. Pour this syrup over the graham crackers and cover with finely chopped nuts. Toast 8 minutes at 350 degrees in oven.

PATRICK COLLINS

Caterer.

Angel Torte with Raspberry Sauce

Torte:
10 egg whites
⅛ teaspoon salt
2 cups heavy cream

2 cups sugar
½ teaspoon baking powder

Beat egg whites with salt, gradually adding the sugar until stiff peaks are formed. Grease 2 10-inch pyrex pie plates and divide the mixture between them. In a preheated 275 degree oven bake for one hour. Let cool and then turn out on a flat surface. Whip cream until very thick, spread cream on one of the tortes, top with other one. Use the remaining whipped cream to frost the torte. Decorate with a few fresh raspberries.

Raspberry sauce:
2 pints fresh raspberries
juice of 1 lemon

½ cup sugar
2 ounces raspberry liqueur

Puree all of the ingredients in food processor, strain and serve with torte.

PUSHA COLTEA

Beauty expert, facialist.

Hazelnut (Filbert) Parfait

2⅓ ounces whole milk
1 egg, beaten
5½ ounces sugar

2 ounces hazelnuts (filberts)
12¼ ounces heavy cream
½ teaspoon vanilla

Boil milk and allow to cool. Add egg, vanilla and sugar to the cooled milk. Stir continuously over a medium flame until the mixture thickens and begins to boil. Remove from heat and cool the pan immediately in a bowl of ice cubes or cold water. Divide nuts into 2 equal batches. Roast the first batch lightly in the oven; the second batch must be browned more thoroughly. Grind all nuts between sheets of waxed paper with a rolling pin until of a fine texture. Whip the heavy cream and combine thoroughly with milk mixture and ground nuts. Pour into the pan of your choice and place in freezer to set. Serve with the topping of your choice. (Raspberries are divine.)

DONNA JO AND CHARLES COMISKEY II

He is business leader, sportsman. Both are active on social, charitable scene.

Fresh Strawberry Pie

1 9-inch baked pie shell
1 8-ounce package cream cheese

2 pints fresh strawberries
1 small jar currant jelly

Allow cream cheese to get soft and spreadable. Spread carefully over the bottom of the baked pie shell. Wash and hull strawberries. Be sure they are completely dry before using them. Choose the most perfect of the strawberries and place them point side up in your pie shell on top of the cream cheese. Place them in a pattern starting with the first one in the center. Heat currant jelly until melted, cool slightly and spoon over strawberries just enough to glaze them. Place in refrigerator and chill for at least two hours. Serve with whipped cream if desired.

SHELDON AND MARY COOPER

He's a WGN-TV executive and she's patron of the arts.

Date and Nut Family Cake

Cake:

12 ounces flour	12 ounces chopped dates and nuts
6 ounces butter or margarine	½ pint apple puree
6 ounces sugar	¾ teaspoon baking soda
1 teaspoon ground cinnamon	2 to 3 tablespoons milk

Topping:

1 tablespoon chopped dates and nuts	½ teaspoon ground cinnamon
1 tablespoon sugar	

Put flour into a bowl and rub in butter until mixture resembles fine breadcrumbs. Add sugar, cinnamon, dates and nuts. Make a well in center, add apple puree and last dissolve bicarbonate of soda in milk and add to mixture. Mix well and put in a prepared tin measuring about 8 by 5 inches.

Mix ingredients for the topping. Sprinkle over the surface of the batter, and bake in 350 degree oven for 1½ hours. Can be served topped with whipped cream cheese.

CHET COPPOCK

Sports announcer.

Anna Marie's Pistachio Cake

Cake:

1 box white cake mix
2 boxes instant pistachio pudding
½ cup oil

½ cup water
½ cup milk
5 eggs

Mix all together and fold into 2 8- or 9-inch greased cake pans. Bake at 350 degrees for 30 to 40 minutes.

Icing:

1 pint heavy cream
1 large carton Cool Whip

5 boxes pistachio pudding

Whip cream until fairly stiff. Add Cool Whip and pudding. Beat until stiff and frost.

PAT CROWLEY

Social activist, businesswoman, religious leader.

Lemon Squares

½ cup butter
¼ cup confectioners sugar

1 cup flour

Mix above and put in greased 9-inch square pan. Bake 20 minutes at 350 degrees. Cool slightly.

2 eggs, beaten
1 cup sugar
2 tablespoons flour

2 tablespoons lemon juice
½ teaspoon baking powder

Mix and put on top of crust. Bake for 20 minutes at 350 degrees. Sprinkle with confectioners sugar.

61

BARRY AND BEVERLY CROWN

He is a leader in business community, active in civic affairs. She is champion weight-lifter, business executive. Both support arts and charities.

Kiwi and Champagne Sorbet

2 cups syrup made of 1 cup sugar and 2 cups water boiled together for 5 minutes.

2 cups pureed kiwi
1 cup champagne

Have the simple syrup at room temperature or colder.

Mix the fruit puree with the champagne, then stir in the cool simple syrup. Place in an ice cream freezer and freeze according to the manufacturer's directions. If not serving immediately, keep in the freezer. Just before serving, beat the sorbet in a blender or food processor. Makes a generous 4 cups.

LESTER AND RENEE CROWN

Patrons of the arts, philanthropists, civic leaders.

Mile-Hi Strawberry Pie

1 baked pie shell
2 eggs (whites only)
1 cup sugar

1 teaspoon cream of tartar
1 8 ounce package frozen strawberries
1 cup heavy cream

In large electric mixer bowl, beat 2 egg whites until firm, gradually beating in one cup sugar and one teaspoon cream of tartar. Beat in partially thawed strawberries. Continue beating for 20 minutes, or until the meringue is a "mile-hi." Fold in 1 cup whipped heavy cream. Fill pie shell with mixture. Put in freezer for at least 6 hours. Better still, make it the day before—but always freeze.

SANDY CROWN

Patron of the arts, supports civic and charitable events.

Toffee

2 sticks butter (½ pound)
1 cup sugar

¾ cup chopped walnuts
8 milk chocolate bars, 1.45 ounce each

Melt butter and sugar in frying pan (preferably iron) on medium heat, stirring constantly until the color of toffee. Pour into cookie sheet with sides, ungreased. Place chocolate bars on top of sugar-butter (really the toffee) and after the bars melt, spread evenly. Sprinkle with nuts. After this hardens and cools, break into smaller chunks.

"A favorite to make with children, or to give in a pretty tin to friends and teachers."

MRS. ROBERT CRUIKSHANK

Party-planner, socialite.

Amaretto Chocolate Mousse

⅔ cup semi-sweet chocolate bits (4 ounces)
2 tablespoons strong coffee
2 tablespoons Amaretto liqueur

1 teaspoon vanilla
4 eggs, separated
1 tablespoon sugar
2 tablespoons toasted slivered almonds

Place the chocolate bits and coffee in a metal bowl and heat in a 300 degree oven for 10 minutes, or until melted. (Do not overheat). Remove from oven and stir in liqueur. Mix in the egg yolks, one at a time. Stir in the vanilla. Beat the egg whites until soft peaks form, then add the sugar, beating until stiff. Stir one-third of the whites into the chocolate mixture, then fold in the remaining whites. Turn into 6 dessert bowls, parfait glasses, or wine glasses. Cover until chilled and set, about 2 hours.

Sprinkle with toasted almonds at serving time. Serves 6.

ROBERT CUMMINS

Attorney, supporter of health research, charities, socialite.

Mousse Au (Blanco) Chocolate

4 ounces white chocolate
4 tablespoons unsalted butter

4 egg yolks
4 egg whites

Place chocolate and butter in saucepan and allow to melt over low heat. Remove pan from heat and stir in egg yolks until chocolate thickens. Pour into large mixing bowl. Beat egg whites until stiff. Fold half of stiff whites into chocolate with whisk. Add remaining whites and fold in with rubber spatula. Pour mousse into serving bowl or individual cups or glasses. Refrigerate for two hours to set. Serve cold. Serves 6.

HERTA AND JOHN CUNEO JR.

Philanthropists and socialites, wild animal protectors.

Gateau Moule Au Chocolate (Steamed Chocolate Cake)

3 ounces unsweetened chocolate*
6 tablespoons (¾ stick) unsalted butter
¼ cup water
3 eggs, separated
1 teaspoon vanilla

¾ cup sugar
¼ cup all-purpose flour
1 cup heavy cream
2 tablespoons sugar
1 teaspoon vanilla

Preheat oven to 375 degrees. Generously butter 4 cup mold (Savarin ring, heart-shaped, etc). Combine chocolate, butter and water in top of double boiler and heat until melted. Transfer to large bowl and beat in egg yolks one at a time, beating well after each addition. Add vanilla, then sugar and flour and beat about 3 minutes. Beat egg whites until stiff but not dry. Stir a few tablespoons egg whites into chocolate mixture to lighten. Fold remaining beaten egg whites into chocolate mixture. Pour into mold, set into large pan and add hot water to come half way up side of mold. Bake about 40 minutes. Remove from water bath and let cool in pan about 5 minutes. Unmold onto serving platter. Keep warm or let cool to room temperature. Just before serving, whip cream with sugar and vanilla (or prepare creme anglaise beforehand). Spoon into center of ring cake or pipe rosettes decoratively around top and sides of cake. Serves 8.

*Semi-sweet chocolate can be substituted, but reduce sugar to ½ cup.

"Almost like a steamed pudding, this dessert is light enough to serve after any meal. Serve warm or room temperature with vanilla flavored whipped cream, or a creme anglaise. From our cook, Leo Gonyea."

SUSANNA CUTTS

Model.

Huguenot Torte

4 eggs
3 cups sugar
8 tablespoons flour
5 teaspoons baking powder

½ teaspoons salt
2 cups chopped tart cooking apples
2 cups chopped pecans
2 teaspoons vanilla

Beat whole eggs in electric mixer or with rotary beater until very frothy and lemon-colored. Add other ingredients in above order. Pour into two well-buttered baking pans about 8 by 12 inches. Bake in 325 degree oven about 45 minutes or until crusty and brown. To serve, scoop up with pancake turner (keeping crusty part on top), pile on large plate and cover with whipped cream and a sprinkling of chopped nuts—or make 16 individual servings.

STEVE DALE

Writer and publicist.

Mandel Brot

3 eggs
¾ cup sugar
½ cup oil
1½ cups cake meal*
1 tablespoon potato starch*

½ teaspoon vanilla, cinnamon, and
   sugar for top
½ cup nuts, raisins, chocolate chips (or
   any combination)

Preheat oven at 350 degrees. Lightly grease cookie sheet. Beat eggs and sugar. Stir in oil and vanilla. Fold in cake meal and potato starch. Add nuts, raisins, chips or whatever. Spoon onto cookie sheet and form with floured hands or spatula into 2 long loaves about 2 inches wide by ¾ inch high. Bake for about thirty minutes. Cut into slices about ½ inch thick and put back in oven for about ten minutes.

*Cake meal and potato starch may be found in specialty food stores.

STATE'S ATTORNEY RICHARD DALEY

Son of the former mayor of Chicago, his prestige and political power are formidable.

Maggie's Chocolate Truffles

1 tablespoon instant expresso
3 tablespoons boiling water
8 ounces semi-sweet chocolate, cut into
   pieces

1 stick butter
3 tablespoons brandy or favorite liqueur
unsweetened cocoa

In top of double boiler combine expresso, water and chocolate until chocolate is dissolved. Remove from heat. Beat in butter, a little at a time, adding each piece just before the previous one is incorporated. Beat in brandy. Chill at least 4 hours until firm. Form into balls with a melon ball scooper and roll in cocoa. (Can be cut into squares and powdered with cocoa). Store in cool place in airtight container or it can be frozen. Makes 30 truffles.

AL AND TERRI D'ANCONA

He is in real estate. She models, owns sportswear shop.

Terri's Divine Rocky Road

8 ounces milk chocolate
8 ounces semi-sweet chocolate
1 tablespoon unsalted butter
pinch of salt

1 teaspoon vanilla
20 marshmallows snipped into quarters
¾ cup macadamia nuts or walnuts or
   peanuts

Butter 8-inch square pan. Melt chocolate with butter and salt in top of double boiler over very hot water. Add vanilla, marshmallows and nuts, stir. Spread in pan, chill. Cut into squares and put into paper candy cups.

DR. VICTOR AND TONI DEWEY DANILOV

He is president of the Museum of Science and Industry. She is director of public relations and advertising for Motorola.

Sunday Pie

vanilla wafers
1 cup evaporated milk
1 cup tiny marshmallows
6 ounces chocolate chips

½ cup chopped pecans
dash salt
2 pints softened vanilla ice cream

Line a 9-inch pie pan with wafers. Heat milk, marshmallows, chips, pecans. Mix thoroughly and cool. Smooth half of the ice cream over the bottom of the pie pan. Cover with half the sauce mixture. Smooth on the rest of the ice cream and cover with the sauce. Freeze at least four hours. Serves 8 to 10.

HERBERT DAVIDSON

Artist

Lee's Ring of Chocolate and Coconut Fudge Cake

Cake:

One 10-inch tube or bundt pan
2 cups sugar
1 cup cooking oil
2 eggs
3 cups all-purpose flour
¾ cup unsweetened cocoa
2 teaspoons baking soda

2 teaspoons baking powder
1½ teaspoons salt
1 cup hot coffee or water
1 cup buttermilk or sour milk
1 teaspoon vanilla
½ cup chopped nuts

In large mixer bowl combine sugar, oil and eggs; beat at high speed for 1 minute. Add remaining ingredients except nuts; beat 3 minutes at medium speed, scraping bowl occasionally. Stir in nuts by hand. Pour half of batter into generously greased and lightly floured 10-inch bundt pan. Carefully spoon filling over batter; top with remaining batter. Bake at 350 degrees for 70 to 75 minutes or until top springs back. Cool upright in pan for 15 minutes; remove from pan. Cool completely. Drizzle with glaze.

Filling:

¼ cup sugar
1 teaspoon vanilla
1 8-ounce package cream cheese, softened

1 egg
½ cup flaked coconut
1 6-ounce package semi-sweet chocolate pieces (1 cup)

In small mixer bowl combine sugar, vanilla, cream cheese and egg; beat until smooth. Stir in coconut and chocolate pieces and set aside.

Glaze:

1 cup confectioners sugar
3 tablespoons cocoa
2 tablespoons butter

2 teaspoons vanilla
1 to 2 tablespoons hot water

Combine and drizzle over cake.

IVAN DEE

Former editor and publisher, now director of public affairs
at Michael Reese Hospital and Medical Center.

Unassuming Apple Cake

2 medium tart apples
½ cup sugar
½ cup brown sugar, firmly packed
½ cup chopped filberts
⅓ cup melted butter
1 egg
1 teaspoon vanilla

1 cup sifted flour
1 teaspoon baking soda
1 teaspoon cinnamon
½ teaspoon nutmeg
½ teaspoon ground cardamom
¼ teaspoon salt

Preheat oven to 350 degrees. Peel, core, and dice apples. Combine with sugar and brown sugar in a bowl. Lightly toast filberts and rub skins off in a towel before chopping. Stir chopped nuts into apple mixture with melted butter. Add egg beaten with vanilla. Sift together flour, baking soda, cinnamon, nutmeg, cardamom, and salt, and stir into apple mixture. Turn batter into a buttered 8-inch round cake pan and bake 50 minutes, or until a cake tester comes out clean. Cool in pan on wire rack, then wrap cake tightly in plastic wrap and foil and let stand at room temperature for at least a day, preferably 2 or 3. Wrap cake in foil, reheat it, and cut it into wedges. Serve with unsweetened whipped cream. The modest appearance belies the flavor. It may also be served without reheating. Serves 6 to 8.

NORMAN DEHAAN

Interior designer.

Elysian Extravagance

at least one pint heavy cream
a splash of excellent brandy
a few cups of day-old German
   pumpernickel bread cut or crumbled
   into ¼ inch chunks

a jar of the best raspberry jam you can
   find, at a dribbly room temperature
one cup bittersweet chocolate shaved
   into curls

Whip up enough cream into a very stiff foam (flavored with brandy if you like) to indulge yourself and to satisfy your guests. Chill a crystal or glass bowl (a glass souffle dish is excellent) and cover the bottom with 1 inch of whipped cream. Sprinkle with the slightly dry pumpernickel crumbs and then dribble a thin webbing of raspberry jam over it all. Repeat with layers of whipped cream, pumpernickel, and raspberry jam until you have filled the bowl with several (at least three) layers. Top the bowl with a mounded layer of whipped cream and cover this with the bittersweet chocolate shavings. Refrigerate before serving. Serves 6 to 8.

OWEN AND BONNIE DEUTSCH

He's a photographer and both are socialites, supporting the arts, charities.

Chocolate Lovers' Mousse

1½ pounds semisweet chocolate chips
   (24 ounces)
½ cup strong coffee
4 egg yolks
2 cups chilled heavy cream

¼ cup granulated sugar
8 egg whites
pinch of salt
½ teaspoon vanilla extract

Melt chocolate chips in a heavy saucepan over low heat, stirring. Add coffee. Let cool to room temperature. Whip 1 cup cream until thickened, then gradually beat in sugar, beating until stiff. Beat egg whites with salt until stiff. Gently fold egg whites into cream. Set aside. To chocolate add egg yolks, one at a time, beating thoroughly after each addition. Stir approximately one-third of cream and egg mixture thoroughly into chocolate mixture. Scrape remaining cream and egg mixture over lightened chocolate base and fold together. Refrigerate for 2 hours or until set. Whip remaining cream, add vanilla (sugar optional) to taste and whip to peaks. Refrigerate. Top each portion of mousse with this cream. Serves 8.

BOB AND JOAN DJAHANGUIRI

Owners of Yvette's, Turbot restaurants.

Chocolate Velvet Cake

Chocolate Velvet:

1¼ pounds Baker's chocolate
2½ ounces butter
2 ounces kirsch
1½ ounces creme de cacao
2 ounces Meyer's dark rum
1 teaspoon instant coffee
2½ ounces filbert cream

3 eggs, separated
dash salt
1½ ounces sugar
1 pint heavy cream
1 10-inch round genoise or chiffon
    cake, sliced lengthwise into 2-¾-inch
    rounds

Melt chocolate and butter in a double boiler. Put to the side. Mix kirsch, creme de cacao and rum with instant coffee, in a large mixing bowl.

Blend the filbert cream with liqueur mixture. Mix until smooth. Add egg yolks and blend.

Whip cream until stiff, refrigerate.

Whip egg whites with dash of salt until peaks form. Add sugar and mix for one-half minute longer. Whip together filbert cream mix and chocolate. Fold in whipped cream. Fold in egg whites. Line bottom of cake pan with Saran wrap, overlapping edges enough to cover top of cake. Place one cake layer in the bottom of pan.

Fill pan with Chocolate Velvet. Top with cake layer. Chill for one hour or until set. Remove from pan and cover with chocolate topping.

Chocolate Topping:

3½ ounces semi-sweet Baker's chocolate
2½ tablespoons butter

2 tablespoons cold water
1 cup confectioners sugar

Sift sugar. Heat chocolate in double boiler until melted. Add sifted sugar and butter, cut in pieces. Stir until smooth, remove pan from heat, and add the water, one tablespoon at a time to cool the mixture. The icing must be luke-warm to ice the cake. If it is too hot it will run off cake. Serves 10.

DR. GEORGE DOHRMANN II AND DR. HELEN MORRISON

He is a surgeon and his wife is a psychologist.

Orange-Lemon Pudding

2 cups fresh orange juice
juice of two lemons
grated rind of one lemon
trace salt

½ pound sugar
3 tablespoons unflavored gelatin
3 cups whipped cream

Bring the juice to a boil and add sugar, salt, and rind. Dissolve the gelatin in a little additional juice separately. After the gelatin is cooled, put in the refrigerator until it just begins to thicken and add to sugar and juice. Fold in 3 cups of whipped cream. Serve at room or slightly cooler temperature.

KINGMAN AND BUNNY DOUGLASS

He is a banker and she is an author and fudge-topping maker.

Bunny's Baked Peaches

2 cans Freestone peaches, drained
1 cup brown sugar
1 stick butter

1 cup coconut flakes
whipped cream
rum to taste

Put peaches on baking sheet and top with mixture of brown sugar, butter, coconut flakes, rum. Bake in a slow oven, 250 degrees, for 2 to 3 hours. Serve hot with whipped cream.

RAYMOND DRYMALSKI

A lawyer, he is president of the Lincoln Park Zoological Society.

Sally's Snickerdoodles

1 cup confectioners sugar
2 cups flour
½ teaspoon baking soda
½ teaspoon cream of tartar
½ teaspoon salt

1 cup butter
1 egg
1 teaspoon vanilla
½ cup sugar mixed with 4 teaspoons
   cinnamon

Mix first eight ingredients and refrigerate several hours or overnight. Form into 1-inch balls and roll in sugar-cinnamon mixture. Flatten with bottom of a glass. Bake at 350 degrees about 10 minutes.

DANIEL DUBAY

Interior designer.

Cherry Clafoutis

4 eggs
6 tablespoons sugar
1 vanilla bean
⅛ teaspoon salt

1 tablespoon dark rum
1½ cups flour
1¾ cups milk
2 pints sweet, dark, ripe cherries, pitted

Beat the eggs and sugar to a frothy consistency. Add the seeds of the vanilla bean, salt and rum. Stir in the flour using a whisk and add the milk. Grease an oval baking dish with softened butter. Pour in one-third of the batter and then a layer of cherries. Fill the remainder of the dish with the batter. Bake 40 to 45 minutes in a preheated 350 degree oven.

"You should test this tart like any sponge cake by using a toothpick to see if the batter clings. When the tart is removed from the oven, the top should be covered with confectioners sugar immediately and it should be served hot. The proportions given above will serve eight people generously."

"This recipe has been handed down from one generation to the other in my family. It happens to be a simple French country or provincial dish, similar to a tart, from the Limousin region of France. It can be made from any fresh fruit and is especially good when accompanied by a liqueur made from the same fruit."

MARY MILLS DUNEA

Assistant to Secretary of State as Cultural Advisor.

Literate Chocolate

¾ cup milk, heated
1 cup chocolate chips
1 egg
2 tablespoons sugar

1 teaspoon rum extract or vanilla
   extract
pinch salt

Put all ingredients in blender and blend at low speed for one minute. Stir to remove bubbles and pour into serving dishes.

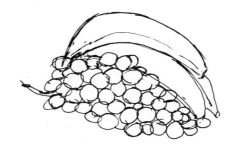

EVELYN ECHOLS

Travel and hotel authority, teacher, training school founder.

Athol Bros

1 cup heavy cream, whipped stiff
½ cup honey, folded into cream

¼ cup scotch, added very slowly

Whip cream until stiff. Add honey while you stir the cream and then add scotch—slowly. Pour into stemmed glasses or ramekins and freeze. Serves 6.

DANIEL AND RUTH EDELMAN

He is head of the Edelman Public Relations firm and both are active on the social scene, in political, literary, charitable affairs.

Chocolate Mousse

8 ounces semi-sweet, bittersweet or
  extra-bittersweet chocolate
1 tablespoon dry instant coffee
⅓ cup boiling water

5 eggs (graded large or extra large),
  separated
pinch salt

Coarsely chop or break up the chocolate and place it in a small, heavy saucepan. Dissolve the coffee in the boiling water and pour it over the chocolate. Place over low heat and stir occasionally with a small wire whisk until smooth. Remove from the heat and set aside to cool for about 5 minutes.

Meanwhile, in the small bowl of an electric mixer, beat the egg yolks at high speed for 3 to 4 minutes until they are pale lemon-colored. Reduce the speed to low, gradually add the slightly warm chocolate and beat, scraping the bowl with a rubber spatula. Beat only until smooth. Remove from the mixer.

Add the salt to the egg whites and beat with clean beaters only until they hold a definite shape but not until they are stiff or dry.

Without being too thorough, gently fold about one-quarter of the beaten whites into the chocolate mixture, then fold in a second quarter, and finally fold the chocolate into the remaining whites, folding only until no whites show.

Gently transfer the mousse to a wide pitcher and pour in into six large wine glasses, each with about a 9-ounce capacity. Do not fill glasses too full; leave generous headroom on each. (I always prepare this mousse in individual glasses and thought it had to be best that way. But it has been served to me many times at other peoples' homes from one large serving bowl and it was fine.)

Cover tightly with aluminum foil and refrigerate for 3 to 6 hours. (The mousse may stand longer, 12 to 24 hours, if you wish. The texture will become more spongy and less creamy. Delicious both ways.)

TARYN AND LARRY EDWARDS

Former owners of the Biograph Theater, both are movie buffs, active in real estate.

Biograph Theater Dillinger Cake

Cake:

1 cup butter
2 eggs
1 cup buttermilk
1 teaspoon white vinegar
1½ cups superfine sugar
2 ounces red food coloring
2 heaping teaspoons cocoa (powdered
    and unsweetened, such as Droste's)

2½ cups cake flour
1 teaspoon baking soda
2 teaspoons vanilla
white chocolate bar (optional)
3 9-inch aluminum cake pans

Preheat oven to moderate (350 degrees). Butter 3 nine-inch disposable cake pans. Combine butter with superfine sugar; cream until light in color and fluffy. Add eggs and mix well. Make a paste of red food coloring and powdered cocoa. Add to above and mix.

Sift cake flour, measure 2½ cups flour. Gradually add approximately ½ cup flour at a time alternating with a little buttermilk until all is added to creamed mixture.

Add vanilla. Mix in a glass cup white vinegar and baking soda. Add to mixture and continue to stir for 30 seconds longer.

Divide cake batter evenly into 3 cake pans. Bake at 350 degrees for 35 minutes. Test with a toothpick in center of one cake after 35 minutes; if it comes clean on inserting, cake is done. Remove from oven, let cool thoroughly. Turn out of pans and ice with frosting (shaved white chocolate over surface optional).

Frosting:

1½ cups sifted confectioners sugar
1½ cups butter
3 teaspoons unbleached flour

1 tablespoon butter
1 cup milk
1 teaspoon vanilla

Cream sugar and 1½ cups butter until very light and fluffy. Make a paste of flour and 1 tablespoon butter; add to milk and heat, stirring constantly until mixture thickens to the consistency of a light pudding. Let cool by immersing pan in cold water, still stirring. Add to butter-sugar mixture and mix well. Add vanilla and mix.

Keeps well in refrigerator; leave out before serving about 30 minutes.

SHERIFF RICHARD J. ELROD

Lawyer and Sheriff of Cook County.

Marilyn's Sour Cream Coffee Cake

Cake:
½ cup butter
1 cup sugar
2 eggs
1 teaspoon vanilla
1 cup sour cream

2 cups flour
1 teaspoon baking soda
1 teaspoon baking powder
pinch salt

Cream butter and sugar. Add eggs one at a time. Sift 4 dry ingredients together. Alternately add sour cream and dry ingredients to batter (start and end with dry ingredients). Add vanilla. Pour half of batter into greased angel food pan. Spread half of topping to cover. Add other half of batter, cover with rest of topping. Bake at 325 degrees for 40 minutes. Cool. Carefully lift off base.

Topping:
1 6-ounce package chocolate chips
1 package ground almonds

½ cup granulated sugar

Chop up chocolate chips. Mix all ingredients together.

JAMES ERRANT

Restaurateur, owner of Claim Co. eateries, Timber Char House.

Ice Cream Cake

12 ounces chocolate cream-filled
   cookies
¼ pound butter
½ teaspoon banana extract
½ gallon ice cream, any flavor, in a
   block

½ gallon ice cream, any other flavor, in
   a block
1 pound hot fudge sauce
whipped cream
maraschino cherries

Melt butter over a low flame, add banana extract. Roughly chop cookies between two mixing bowls or with a rolling pin. Pour the butter mixture over the chopped cookies, tossing as you pour to insure even distribution. Place mixture in the bottom of a 10-inch springform pan; press down firmly to form an even crust. Cover and freeze for three hours. Let two flavors of ice cream soften slightly. Cut each ice cream block into ¾ inch strips. Completely cover the cookie mixture with one flavor of ice cream strips. Take 4 to 6 ounces hot fudge sauce and spread it evenly over the ice cream. Completely cover the fudge with a layer of the second ice cream flavor. Cover and return to freezer for at least two more hours. To serve, remove from freezer and place a warm, wet towel around the outside of the pan to soften the outer ice cream; remove from pan. Slice and serve with hot fudge sauce, whipped cream and a maraschino cherry.

JOAN ESPOSITO

TV personality.

Hot Milk Chocolate Fudge Sauce

½ stick butter
½ pound rich milk chocolate, broken
   into pieces
½ ounce black coffee

1 ounce half-and-half
½ teaspoon arrowroot

Melt butter over gentle heat, add chocolate. When chocolate is melted, add coffee, stir constantly. Mixture will become grainy after coffee is added. Add cream, keep stirring! Add arrowroot, keep stirring. Mixture will quickly thicken, and when it's thick and shiny it's done. Pour it over ice cream.

JACKIE ETCHEBER

Chef-owner of Jackie's Restaurant.

Carrot Cake

Cake:

3 cups unbleached all-purpose flour
3 cups granulated sugar
1 teaspoon salt
1 tablespoon baking soda
1 tablespoon ground cinnamon
1½ cups corn oil
4 large eggs, lightly beaten

1 tablespoon vanilla extract
1½ cups shelled walnuts, chopped
1½ cups shredded coconut
1⅓ cups pureed cooked carrots
¾ cup drained crushed pineapple
cream cheese frosting (recipe follows)
confectioners sugar for dusting top

Preheat oven to 350 degrees. Grease two 9-inch layer cake pans lined with wax paper. Sift dry ingredients into a bowl. Add oil, eggs and vanilla. Beat well. Fold in walnuts, coconut, carrots and pineapple. Pour batter into the prepared pans. Set on the middle rack of the oven and bake for 30 to 50 minutes, until eggs have pulled away from sides and a cake tester inserted in center comes out clean. Cool on a cake rack for 3 hours. Fill cake and frost sides with cream cheese frosting. Dust top with confectioners sugar. 10 to 12 servings.

Cream Cheese Frosting:

8 ounces cream cheese at room
  temperature
6 tablespoons sweet butter at room
  temperature

3 cups confectioners sugar
1 teaspoon vanilla extract
juice of ½ lemon (optional)

Cream together cream cheese and butter in a mixing bowl. Slowly sift in confectioners sugar and continue beating until fluffy and incorporated. Mixture should be free of lumps. Stir in vanilla and lemon juice if you use it. Frosting is for a 2-layer cake.

RENA ETTLINGER

Exercise maven.

Chocolate Fondue

24 ounces milk chocolate
  (***I use Hershey bars***)

1 cup heavy cream
2 tablespoons cognac

Heat ingredients together while stirring over a low flame. When melted, put mixture in a fondue server or chafing dish with a candle below to keep it warm. Serve with maraschino cherries, mandarin orange sections, meringues, cubes of pound or angel food cake and sliced bananas, apples and peaches. Serves 10.

JUDITH BARNARD AND MICHAEL FAIN

Husband and wife authors (as Judith Michael) of *Possessions* and *Deceptions*.

Coffee Parfait

1 tablespoon unflavored gelatin
2 cups very strong cold coffee
⅓ cup sugar

¼ cup brandy or sherry
1 cup heavy cream
toasted, salted almonds (slivered)

Soften gelatin in ¼ cup cold coffee. Heat remaining coffee and add gelatin and sugar; stir to dissolve. Add brandy or sherry. Pour into shallow pan to a depth of about ½ inch; chill until firm. When ready to serve, cut jellied coffee into ½-inch cubes; whip cream and alternate coffee cubes, whipped cream and almonds in parfait glasses.

NOTE: If whipped cream is sweetened with two or three tablespoons of confectioners sugar, the dessert can be made an hour ahead of time and kept in the refrigerator until serving.

LARRY AND BEVERLY FALSTEIN

Community and religious leaders.

Florentines

½ cup heavy cream
3 tablespoons butter
½ cup sugar
1¼ cups chopped almonds
½ cup sifted all-purpose flour

¾ cup finely chopped candied orange
  peel
½ cup melted semi-sweet chocolate
  pieces

Combine cream, butter and sugar in saucepan; heat to boiling. Remove from heat and stir in almonds, flour and orange peel. Drop on foil-lined baking sheets, 2 inches apart. Bake at 350 degrees for about 10 minutes. Cool a few minutes and remove with spatula to cake rack to cool. If desired, frost back of each cookie with melted chocolate.

KAREN FIELD

Active in real estate sales, cultural activities.

Bananas Foster

6 tablespoons butter
1½ cups brown sugar
⅓ cups banana liqueur
¾ teaspoon cinnamon

6 bananas, peeled, cut in quarters (cut
  in half lengthwise and crosswise)
⅓ cup rum
6 scoops vanilla ice cream

Melt the butter over an alcohol burner in a chafing dish, flambe pan or on the stove in a large skillet. Add the sugar, banana liqueur, and cinnamon and stir well to mix. Heat for a few minutes. Place the bananas in the sauce and saute until soft and slightly browned. Pour the rum on top, but do not stir the rum into the sauce. Allow it to heat well and light it with a match. Tipping the pan in a circular motion will allow maximum flaming time. Allow the sauce to flame until it dies out.

Place a scoop of ice cream into each of six dessert dishes. Serve by carefully placing four pieces of banana over each ice cream portion. Then spoon the hot sauce from the pan over the top.

MILTON AND JOSIE FIELD

Bridalwear authorities and community leaders.

Lemon Sponge Cake

2 to 3 packages ladyfingers
8 eggs, separated
¾ cup sugar

juice of 3 lemons
1 envelope unflavored gelatin dissolved
  in ¼ cup cold water

Line bottom and sides of springform pan with ladyfingers. Beat yolks with sugar and add lemon juice and gelatin. Cook in double boiler, stirring, until thick.

Beat whites with ⅓ cup of sugar until stiff peaks form. Fold into yolk mixture. Put all into pan with ladyfingers and refrigerate at least 8 hours.

Before serving top with whipped cream beaten with 3 tablespoons confectioners sugar.

"Light, fluffy and tart."

MARSHALL FIELD V AND JAMEE FIELD

His business interests include restaurants, publishing. Both are active socially and support the arts.

Chocolate Kisses

2 egg whites
¼ teaspoon salt
⅔ cup sugar

1 teaspoon vanilla
1 teaspoon grated lemon rind
1 cup chocolate chips

Beat egg whites and salt at medium speed in mixer for 3 minutes. Add sugar gradually. Beat for 10 minutes. Fold in vanilla, lemon rind and chocolate chips. Drop from teaspoon onto ungreased cookie sheets covered with brown paper. Shape into mounds the size of a small walnut. Bake at 250 degrees for 45 minutes. Makes 3 dozen cookies.

NORMA FINLEY

Lawyer, socialite, patron of the arts.

Toffee Bars

1 cup butter	2 cups flour
1 cup brown sugar	¼ teaspoon salt
1 egg yolk	1 8-ounce "family size" Hershey bar
1 teaspoon vanilla	½ cup chopped pecans or almonds

Heat oven to 350 degrees. Mix firmly packed brown sugar, butter, egg yolk and vanilla. Stir in flour and salt. Press into lightly greased 13 by 9 by 2-inch pan.

Bake until very lightly browned, about 25 to 30 minutes. Crust should be soft. Remove from oven and immediately place separated pieces of chocolate candy on crust. Let stand on a wire rack until chocolate becomes soft. Spread chocolate evenly over crust and sprinkle with nuts. Cut into small bars while warm. Yield: about 3 dozen cookies.

COLIN FISHER

Advertising executive, supporter of the arts.

Watermelon—But Not Really!

1 watermelon	½ gallon raspberry sherbet
1 12-ounce bag chocolate chips	

Half or quarter a whole watermelon. Scoop out the inside so that the shell is remaining. Fill with semi-melted raspberry sherbet, sprinkle chocolate chips throughout (making sure they are blended through). Refreeze so that it is frozen solid.

To serve, cut and slice as you would watermelon. The seeds everyone sees aren't seeds at all, but little bits of chocolate among cool refreshing sherbet!

DR. LESTER FISHER

Director of the Lincoln Park Zoological Gardens.

Wendy's Zoogood Brownies

3 squares unsweetened chocolate
  (Baker's is best)
½ cup butter or margarine
1 cup unsifted all-purpose flour
¾ teaspoon baking powder
⅓ teaspoon salt

3 eggs
1½ cups sugar
1½ teaspoons vanilla
1 cup chopped walnuts
1 12-ounce package Toll House
  chocolate morsels (dark)

Preheat oven to 350 degrees and grease a 9 by 12-inch baking pan. Melt chocolate and butter. Mix flour with baking powder and salt. Beat eggs well; gradually beat in sugar. Blend in chocolate and vanilla. Mix in flour mixture. Add nuts and chocolate chips. Spread in greased baking pan. Bake at 350 degree for 25 minutes. Cool; cut into squares (makes about 30).

"Irresistible when served with fresh strawberries and pineapple compote or with lemon sherbet."

LEE FLAHERTY

President of Flair Communications Agency, founder of America's/Chicago's Marathon.

Kahlua Mousse

1 cup Kahlua
¾ cup strong, brewed coffee
¾ teaspoon instant decaffeinated coffee
  granules
1 cup confectioners sugar
¼ teaspoon almond extract

1 envelope unflavored gelatin
7 egg yolks, beaten
7 egg whites, beaten until stiff
1½ cups heavy cream, whipped stiff
½ cup heavy cream
2 tablespoons confectioners sugar

Fold waxed paper, 26 inches long, in thirds. With string, tie around 1-quart souffle dish, to form collar 2 inches high. In top of double boiler, combine Kahlua, brewed coffee, coffee granules, confectioners sugar, almond extract, gelatin and egg yolks: mix well. Cook over boiling water (water should not touch bottom of double boiler), stirring occasionally, until mixture thickens, 10 to 15 minutes. Remove from heat. Set top of double boiler in a bowl of ice cubes. Let stand, stirring occasionally, until mixture thickens and mounds when dropped from spoon. With wire whisk, using an under-and-over motion, fold egg whites and whipped cream into gelatin mixture. Turn mixture into prepared souffle dish, wine glasses or dessert dishes. Refrigerate until firm, several hours or overnight. Before serving: in chilled bowl, combine ½ cup heavy cream and 2 tablespoons confectioners sugar; beat together until stiff. Spoon into pastry bag with a number 6 star tip; decorate. Sprinkle lightly with coffee granules. If desired, press finely chopped pecans around edge. Makes 8 to 10 servings.

SHANNON FLAHERTY

Communications careerist, world traveler, socialite.

Secret Chocolate Cake

Cake:

2 cups flour
2 cups sugar
1 cup water
2 sticks butter or margarine
4 tablespoons cocoa

½ cup buttermilk
2 eggs
1 teaspoon baking soda
1 teaspoon vanilla

Combine flour and sugar in large bowl of electric mixer. Heat on stove water, butter and cocoa just to a boil. Pour over flour and sugar and beat well. Add with motor running: buttermilk, eggs, baking soda and vanilla. Beat well. Pour into greased and floured jelly roll pan (15½ by 10½ by 1 inch). Batter will be thin. Bake 25 minutes at 400 degrees.

Frosting:

6 tablespoons milk
1 stick butter or margarine
4 tablespoons cocoa

1 box confectioners sugar (4 cups)
1 cup chopped pecans

Bring milk, butter and cocoa to a boil on stove. Add confectioners sugar and pecans, stir with wooden spoon until sugar is thoroughly dissolved or use mixer. Mix while cake is baking and frost cake immediately after it comes out of the oven.

Serves 15 as cake or can be cut any size for a finger dessert, up to 64 one-inch pieces.

JANE FLANAGAN

Interior Decorator.

Pecan Torte

Cake:

2 tablespoons flour	1 cup sugar
½ teaspoon salt	1 tablespoon orange juice or rum
½ teaspoon baking powder	½ cup pecans, grated
4 egg yolks	4 egg whites, beaten stiff

Sift flour, salt and baking powder together. Beat egg yolks until thick and lemon colored; add to flour mixture. Beat in sugar, orange juice and pecans; blend well. Fold egg whites into batter and pour into two 8-inch greased layer cake pans. Bake in a preheated 350 degree oven for 25 minutes. No longer than 3 hours before serving, spread filling between layers and frost with Chocolate Cream.

Filling:

½ cup heavy cream, whipped	1½ teaspoons grated orange rind

Combine whipped cream and orange rind.

Chocolate Cream:

1 6-ounce package chocolate chips	dash salt
½ cup dairy sour cream	whole pecans

Melt chocolate chips over hot water. Stir in sour cream and salt. Spread on cake and garnish with whole pecans.

GRETA WILEY FLORY

Book reviewer, theatrical authority.

Quick Coffee Cake with Broiled Coconut Topping

Cake:

3 cups sifted flour	1 cup butter
1½ cups sugar	1 teaspoon vanilla
3 teaspoons baking powder	1 12-ounce can evaporated milk
½ teaspoon salt	3 eggs

Sift together all dry ingredients. Add butter—crumble in. Add 1 egg at a time and beat. Add vanilla, then evaporated milk. Beat well. Pour batter into a greased large loaf pan with inside measurement of 13 by 8½ by 2 inches. Place in a 375 degree oven 25 to 30 minutes (until cake springs away from sides of pan).

Topping:
2 tablespoons brown sugar   1 tablespoon heavy cream
2 tablespoons butter

Mix these 3 ingredients together and spread on cake within first few minutes after it comes out of oven. Sprinkle coconut (enough to cover the surface of cake) and place under broiler until toasted golden.

PAT AND PAULA FOLEY

He is president of Hyatt Hotels Corp. and she is the author of children's books. Both are active boosting charitable endeavors.

Chocolate Pound Cake

Cake:
3 cups all-purpose flour   2 sticks butter or maragrine
3 cups sugar   1¼ cups milk
½ cup cocoa   5 eggs
½ teaspoon baking powder   2 teaspoons vanilla
½ cup shortening   ¼ teaspoon salt

Cream butter and shortening with sugar. Add one egg at a time and blend well after each one. Sift all dry ingredients and add alternately with milk. Add vanilla and cook in greased tube pan at 325 degrees for one hour and 40 minutes.

Frosting:
½ cup shortening   2 teaspoons vanilla
2 cups sugar   2 tablespoons cocoa
¼ teaspoon salt   ⅔ cup milk

Mix above ingredients. Cook 2 minutes stirring constantly (begin timing when it starts boiling). Let cool; spread on cake. (If too thick add one tablespoon cream.)

DORSEY CONNORS FORBES

Syndicated household hints columnist, TV and radio commentator.

Rum Balls

1 4-oz. package Baker's German
   chocolate, finely grated
3½ cups finely ground walnuts

2½ cups confectioners sugar
2 egg whites
5 tablespoons rum

Mix ingredients. Roll into small balls. Dredge in granulated sugar. Place on plate and allow to dry out before serving.

GERALDINE FREUND

Founder and director of the highly acclaimed International Dance Festivals, authority on the arts.

Peaches in Champagne

2 medium-size ripe peaches
½ cup red raspberries

2 splits pink champagne, chilled

Peel peaches, halve and remove pits. Place 2 halves, cut side up, in each serving dish. Fill cavities with raspberries. Pour a little champagne over fruit. Serve the rest in champagne glasses. Serves 2.

MARY FREY

Socialite, active charity volunteer, on board of Chicago Tourism and Convention Bureau.

Souffle Glace Nobis

Amaretti Italian macaroons
⅓ cup coffee liqueur
5 egg yolks
⅔ cup sugar

4 teaspoons unsweetened cocoa
2 cups heavy cream
sweet almond oil (available at most
   pharmacies)

With a rolling pin crush coarsely enough Amaretti between two sheets of waxed paper to measure 1¼ cups crumbs. Transfer crumbs to a small bowl and stir in liqueur. In the bowl of an electric mixer beat egg yolks with sugar at high speed for 10 minutes, or until the mixture is thick and ivory-colored. Beat in cocoa and stir in the crumb mixture.

In a bowl beat cream until it holds stiff peaks, fold it into the yolk mixture and chill the mixture, covered, in the freezing compartment of the refrigerator for 25 minutes.

Fit a 1-quart souffle dish with a 4-inch wide band of waxed paper, doubled and oiled with sweet almond oil to form a standing collar extending 2 inches above the rim. Whisk the mixture lightly, pour into the dish and smooth the top with a spatula. Freeze the mixture in the freezing compartment of the refrigerator for at least 4 hours. Remove the collar, smooth the edges with a spatula and sift unsweetened cocoa over the top.

ALFRED FRIEDEN

Executive pastry chef, Drake Hotel.

Iced Sabayon Mousse

5 egg yolks
4 ounces granulated sugar
3 ounces Marsala wine

¾ pint whipped cream
nutmeg

Beat egg yolks, sugar and wine until thick, over a hot water bath. Cool in the refrigerator. Fold in the whipped cream. Fill champagne glasses and chill in the freezer for approximately 2 hours. Serve cold with a little ground nutmeg sprinkled on top. Serves 6.

JOHNNY FRIGO

Jazz violinist, composer, orchestra leader.

Danish Puff

1 cup flour
½ cup butter
2 tablespoons water
½ cup butter
1 cup flour
1 teaspoon almond extract
1 cup flour

3 eggs
1 cup confectioners sugar
2 tablespoons butter
2 3-ounce packages cream cheese
½ teaspoon almond extract
walnut pieces

Heat oven 350 degrees. Measure first cup of flour into bowl. Cut in butter. Sprinkle with water, mix with fork. Round in a ball and divide in half. Pat dough with hands into 2 long strips on a 9 by 12-inch cookie sheet (ungreased).

Mix second half cup butter and one cup water. Bring to a rolling boil. Add almond extract and remove from heat. Stir in flour immediately to keep from lumping. When smooth and thick add one egg at a time beating until smooth.

Divide in half and spread half over each strip of pastry. Bake 30 to 45 minutes until topping is crisp and nicely browned. Cool and frost with one cup confectioners sugar blended with cream cheese, butter and almond extract until smooth. Spread onto strips and sprinkle with walnuts.

EDITH GAINES

Authority on art; director, annual programs for the Art Institute.

Apricot Macaroon Cake

2½ dozen soft almond macaroons
4 cups dried apricots
2 envelopes unflavored gelatin
1½ cups unsalted butter
3 cups confectioners sugar

6 eggs, separated
rind and juice of 1 lemon
½ cup granulated sugar
whipped cream
chopped pistachio nuts

Crumble the macaroons and press enough on the bottom of a 9-inch spring form pan to make a crust about ½ inch thick. Cook the apricots in water to cover until they are very soft and water is absorbed. Soften the gelatin in ½ cup cold water, then stir into hot apricots until dissolved. Cool and puree in blender. Cream the butter and confectioners sugar until fluffy. Beat in egg yolks, one at a time. Beat in apricots, lemon rind and juice. Whip egg whites until foamy. Add granulated sugar and whip until soft peaks form. Fold into apricot mixture. Pour about ¼ apricot mixture into prepared pan. Add a layer of crumbled macaroons. Continue alternating layers until all are used. Chill 24 hours. Garnish with sweetened whipped cream put through a pastry tube. Sprinkle with chopped nuts. Serves 10 to 12.

SONDRA GAIR

Veteran WBEZ announcer and talk show host.

Wild Strawberry Shortcake

2 cups flour
2 teaspoons baking powder
1½ tablespoons sugar
½ teaspoon salt

4 tablespoons butter
1 egg, beaten
¾ to 1 cup milk
fresh strawberries, wild if possible

Combine the flour, baking powder, sugar and salt. Then cut the butter into that mixture until crumbly. Beat the egg and add the milk to it; then pour over the crumbly mixture. Stir together lightly only until it is all moistened. Bake at 400 degrees for 20 minutes in a cake or pie pan. Serve warm, covered with wild strawberries . . . or not so wild!

DUANE AND LISA GENGLER

He is an insurance tycoon. She is a sculptor and artist, heads National Society of Arts, Letters.

Watergate Cake

1 box white cake mix
1 box instant pistachio pudding mix
3 eggs
1 cup oil

1 cup 7-UP
½ cup chopped nuts (optional)
Dream Whip

Combine all ingredients. Bake in 9 by 13-inch greased pan at 350 degrees for 40 minutes. When cool, frost with 2 small packages Dream Whip blended with 1½ cups milk.

ANN GERBER

Lerner Newspapers columnist, editor of *Skyline* Newspaper, author of *Chicago's Classiest Cuisine* cookbook.

Chicago Fudge Pie

1 unbaked 9-inch pie shell
½ cup butter (1 stick)
3 squares (3 ounces) unsweetened
   chocolate
1½ cups sugar
4 eggs

3 tablespoons light corn syrup
¼ teaspoon salt
1 teaspoon vanilla
1 quart vanilla ice cream (optional) or
   whipped cream

Melt butter and chocolate together in a saucepan over very low heat. Beat in sugar, eggs, syrup, salt and vanilla with a rotary beater just until blended.

Pour into unbaked pie shell. Bake in a 350 degree oven for 40 to 45 minutes or until a knife inserted between center and edge comes out clean.

Do not overbake. Pie should shake a little. It will firm up in 15 minutes after being taken out of oven. Cool and serve with ice cream (or whipping cream) on top.

This pie won the Culinary Institute of America Regional Cuisine Award, 1984.

EMMA GETZ

Widow of Oscar Getz, founder of Barton Brands. She is a patron of the arts, active on cultural scene.

Boiled Custard

2 cups hot milk
yolks of 3 eggs

¼ cup sugar
½ teaspoon vanilla

Beat egg yolks slightly, add sugar and a few grains of salt. Stir the milk in gradually. Place in double boiler, stir constantly until the mixture thickens and coats the spoon. Cool and add vanilla. If custard separates or becomes lumpy, put kettle in cold water at once and beat with rotary beater until smooth again.

GERALD AND JANE GIDWITZ

Socialites, patrons of the arts, civic leaders.

Apple-Pecan Pie

Crust:
1 cup sifted all-purpose flour
2 tablespoons sugar
1 teaspoon double-acting baking powder
¼ teaspoon salt

1½ to 3 tablespoons butter
1 egg
½ teaspoon vanilla
milk

Resift flour with sugar, baking powder and salt. Add butter and work into flour mixture until crumbly. In a measuring cup beat egg and vanilla. Add enough milk to measure ½ cup. Combine egg-milk mixture with the flour mixture to form a stiff dough. Pat dough into a 9-inch pie pan with floured palm or a spoon.

English Custard:
3 eggs
¼ cup sugar

⅛ teaspoon salt
2 cups scalded milk

Beat eggs and add sugar, salt and milk. Cook over low heat, stirring constantly until custard coats a spoon. It takes about 8 minutes. Chill.

Filling:
1 cup English Custard
3 to 4 cups sliced, pared apples
1 cup chopped pecans

1 lemon, juice and grated rind
1 cup sugar
2 tablespoons butter

Combine apples, pecans, lemon juice and rind. Spread English Custard on crust, top with fruit mixture. Sprinkle with 1 cup sugar, dot with butter and bake 40 minutes at 425 degrees. Serve with a caramel sauce or whipped cream.

JENNIFER GIRARD

Award-winning photographer.

Puffed Chocolate Clusters

1 6-ounce package semi-sweet chocolate pieces

1½ cups puffed wheat or puffed rice cereal

Grease a platter. Place chocolate pieces in top of double boiler, with hot, not boiling, water in bottom. Heat until chocolate is melted. Add puffed wheat or puffed rice, mixing until kernels are well coated. Drop from teaspoon onto greased platter. Chill until chocolate hardens.

EDWIN AND BARBARA GLASS

Both are active in cultural, charitable endeavors. Art collectors.

Chocolate Icebox Cake Revillion

30 ladyfingers
1 cup heavy cream
5 eggs, separated
½ teaspoon vanilla

½ pound sweet chocolate
4 tablespoons water
4 tablespoons sugar
1 teaspoon cream of tartar

Melt chocolate in double boiler, add sugar and the water with the yolks of the eggs well beaten. Cool. Beat cream of tartar into the egg whites. Beat until stiff. When chocolate mixture is cool, add the stiff whites of the eggs and the vanilla. Line a springform cake pan with ladyfingers and layer the chocolate and ladyfingers alternately. The ladyfingers should line the top. Place in refrigerator overnight. Unmold cake, whip cream and place on top before serving.

This recipe comes from the Mayoress of Honfleur, France—Madame Revillion.

CARA GLATT

Writer, patron of the arts.

Cara's Chocolate Creation

¼ pound butter or margarine
1½ squares bitter cooking chocolate
1 cup sugar
2 eggs, beaten with a fork

1 teaspoon vanilla
¼ cup flour
2 tablespoons milk

Melt butter and chocolate together in a small saucepan; let cool. Add sugar, eggs, vanilla, flour and milk. Mix well and pour into buttered 8 or 9-inch pie pan. Place in 350 degree oven for 25 to 30 minutes. It should look moist. Serve with vanilla ice cream.

PAUL GLICK

Expert on hair design, makeup; writer, teacher.

Chocolate Cheesicles (Low Calorie Frozen Suckers)

1½ pounds ricotta cheese, drained
3 tablespoons Ghirardelli sweet all-
　purpose ground chocolate

2 tablespoons honey

In a food processor puree ricotta cheese until completely smooth. Blend chocolate into pureed cheese, then blend honey into chocolate and cheese mixture. Mix well to achieve a mousselike consistency. Spoon into popsicle molds and freeze.

NOTE: More chocolate and/or honey may be added to satisfy a sweeter tooth. Also, pureed fresh fruit (strawberries or bananas are excellent), preserves or carob powder may be substituted for the chocolate.

HERBERT GLIEBERMAN

Expert on divorce law, lecturer, teacher, author.

Evie's Sugar-Free Cookies

1 cup flour
1 glass red wine

¾ cup oil

Oil and wine should be warm. Put flour in bowl, and add oil and wine. Mix well. Roll out very thin, like a pencil, and make cookies into the shape of cheerios. Bake at 350 degrees for 5 to 10 minutes or until brown.

BERTRAM AND NANCY GOLDBERG

He is the famous architect. She formerly operated Maxim's in Chicago for 20 years.

Crepes Veuve Joyeuse

Crepes:
2 cups sifted flour
4 eggs
½ cup sugar

¼ cup melted butter
vanilla
salt

Mix the flour, sugar, and pinch of salt together in a bowl. Stir in the eggs one by one, a drop of vanilla, and the warmed milk, stirring constantly with a wooden spatula. The batter should be smooth and just thick enough to coat the spatula. If too thick, add a little more milk. Finally, add the melted butter and stir. Cover and chill for at least 1 hour before using.

Cook the crepes in a large, moderately heated, buttered pan, using just enough batter to coat the bottom of the pan. Brown lightly, shake to loosen, turn and brown the other side very lightly. Regrease the pan between each crepe. Keep warm in a moderate oven (350 degrees). (For extra light crepes, separate the eggs and stir in yolks into the dry ingredients. Beat the whites until stiff and add them at the end, after the melted butter.)

Souffle au Citron (Lemon Souffle Filling):
4 egg whites
3 egg yolks
1 lemon
½ cup milk

¾ cup granulated sugar
1 tablespoon flour
1½ tablespoons butter
½ teaspoon vanilla

Peel the rind of the lemon in tiny, surface strips. Blanch them in boiling water for 2 minutes and macerate in 1 cup of water and ½ cup of sugar which have been boiled together for 15 minutes. Make a thick white sauce by heating the butter, flour, milk, sugar and vanilla together. Remove from the fire and beat in the egg yolks and lemon rind. Finally, fold in the stiffly beaten egg whites.

Place a heaping tablespoon of the lemon filling on half of each crepe, fold over, and place in a hot oven (400 degrees). Cook about 15 minutes, at which time the crepes should swell and open. Remove from oven, sprinkle with sugar and brown rapidly under broiler. Serve at once.

LYNNE GOLDBLATT-DUROCHER

Socialite, active on the cultural, theatrical scene.

Mom Kelly's Apricot Up-Side-Down Cake

1 egg
1 cup granulated sugar
2 cups dark brown sugar
butter (the size of an egg)
1 12-ounce can apricot halves (drain and reserve juice)
½ cup milk

½ cup apricot juice (from canned fruit)
1 cup all-purpose white flour
1 pinch salt
1½ teaspoons baking powder
1 drop vanilla
½ pint heavy cream, whipped

In mixing bowl, mix white sugar, butter, salt and egg. When butter and sugar are mixed add one cup flour and ½ teaspoon baking soda. Add drop vanilla to ½ cup apricot juice and ½ cup milk. Add wet ingredients gradually to dry, beating by hand or electric mixer until batter is light and fluffy. Grease 12-inch cast iron frying pan with butter. Line pan with approximately 1 inch dark brown sugar. Place drained apricot halves round side down to completely cover bottom of pan and brown sugar. Pour cake batter over all and bake in pre-heated 350 degree oven for approximately half an hour. Test with toothpick for doneness. When done let cool and loosen edges with knife. Place cake plate over to flip over. Cover with whipped cream and serve.

MO AND DIANE GOLDIN

He is the Michigan Avenue jeweler. She is active on the theatrical scene, works for local charities.

Exotic Peaches

12 whole, pitted peaches or canned Alberta halves
½ cup orange marmalade

1 teaspoon ground ginger
½ teaspoon Chinese 5-spice powder
½ cup unsweetened coconut

Combine marmalade, ginger and 5-spice powder. If using whole peaches, cut small hole into peach and stuff cavity with mixture. For halves, spoon mixture onto center. Bake peaches till tender and sprinkle with plain or toasted coconut. Serve warm or chilled; also as a topping for French vanilla, coffee or peach ice cream.

"This is where the calories run amuck!"

LARRY GORE

Former Neiman-Marcus vice-president and manager of Michigan Avenue store, president and CED of RV. Limited Retailers.

Sandi's Harbor Chocolate Cheesecake

2 8½-ounce packages chocolate wafers
½ teaspoon cinnamon
½ cup melted butter
1¼ cups sugar
4 eggs
1 teaspoon vanilla

2 tablespoons cocoa
1½ pounds cream cheese
16 ounces semi-sweet chocolate
3 cups sour cream
¼ cup sweet butter, melted

In a blender or processor, crush chocolate wafers. You should have about 2 cups. Mix with cinnamon and ½ cup melted butter. Press crumbs firmly to the bottom and sides of a 10-inch springform pan. Chill.

Beat the sugar with the eggs until light and fluffy. Add the cream cheese gradually, beating well. Melt the chocolate and add to the egg mixture along with the vanilla, cocoa, sour cream, beating constantly. Add the melted sweet butter. Mix well. Pour the mixture into the chilled pan. Bake at 350 degrees for 45 minutes.

Chill overnight in the refrigerator.

To serve, remove pan sides. Decorate with chocolate shavings. Serve in small slices. 20 servings.

ZARADA AND THOMAS GOWENLOCK III

Socialites, both are active on the cultural scene. He is in options markets.

Cashew Nut and Chocolate Mousse

2 ounces unsweetened chocolate
½ cup sugar
5 egg yolks
1 cup unsalted, roasted cashew nuts,
   finely ground

1 cup heavy cream
5 egg whites

Melt chocolate with 2 or 3 tablespoons of water in a double boiler over hot water. Add sugar and stir until chocolate is melted and sugar dissolved. Remove pan from heat and beat in egg yolks on at at time, beating well after each addition. Stir in ground cashew nuts. Beat cream until it forms stiff peaks. Add to chocolate mixture, folding in carefully. Beat egg whites until stiff, fold into chocolate cream mixture. Pour into a 1-quart souffle dish and refrigerate for a few hours or overnight. Serve with whipped cream on the side. Serves 6.

RICHARD AND MARY GRAY

Art experts and owners of a Michigan Avenue gallery.

Lemon Fluff

Crust:
¾ pound vanilla wafers or graham
   crackers, crushed

¼ pound butter or as little as necessary,
   melted

Combine butter and wafers and line 9-inch springform pan. Set aside.

Filling:
4 lemons, juice and rind
½ to 1 cup sugar, according to taste
7 egg yolks, beaten
1 tablespoon unflavored gelatin

½ cup cold water
7 egg whites, stiffly beaten
½ to ¾ cup sugar
whipped cream

Place the lemon juice, rind, and ½ to 1 cup sugar in top of double boiler. Stir until dissolved. Add yolks slowly. Cook and stir until mixture coats spoon. Soak gelatin in cold water for 5 minutes. Add to egg yolk mixture and stir until dissolved. Remove top of double boiler from hot water and cool filling. Beat ¼ to ¾ cup sugar into stiffly beaten egg whites. Fold into the egg yolk-gelatin mixture and pour into lined springform pan. Refrigerate several hours or overnight. To serve, remove pan sides and top. Fluff with whipped cream.

DALLAS GREEN

President, General Manager of the Cubs.

Rice Pudding

2 12-ounce cans evaporated milk plus regular milk to make about a quart and a half of liquid
16 tablespoons uncooked long grain rice

20 tablespoons sugar
dash salt
1 tablespoon vanilla
1 tablespoon butter

Bring to simmer on top of stove in a heavy uncovered pot. Pudding must be watched and stirred now and then to prevent boiling over or scorching. Simmer 20 to 30 minutes until thick. Cool and serve to 8. (Raisins can be added, but Dallas doesn't like them in his pudding.)

JOEL AND MARSHA GREENBERG

He is a commodities trader, movie investor. Both support the arts, charitable endeavors.

Romancing Bananas Flambé

4 tablespoons butter
½ cup brown sugar
½ teaspoon cinnamon
4 slices fresh orange

6 ripe bananas peeled and sliced in half
½ cup your favorite 80-proof liqueur
6 servings vanilla ice cream

Melt butter in a silver chafing dish. Add brown sugar, cinnamon and orange slices, then heat. Place bananas in chafing dish until warm. Add liqueur (our favorite is Grand Marnier). Dim the chandelier over your dining table and carefully but romantically ignite the liqueur. Now serve over vanilla ice cream in your best china. Serves 6.

BURTON AND HELEN GREENFIELD

He is well known jeweler. She is authority on ivory, precious gems. Both are civic leaders.

Chocolate Souffle

2 tablespoons butter
4 tablespoons flour
1 cup milk
2 squares bitter chocolate

4 tablespoons water
6 tablespoon sugar
4 eggs
confectioners sugar

Melt butter and add flour. Then add milk. Cook until thick and smooth. Mix bitter chocolate, water and sugar in top of double boiler. Boil until thick and shiny; add to the milk mixture. Beat egg yolks well and add to the chocolate mixture. Then beat egg whites stiff and fold into the mixture. Bake in buttered 2-quart souffle dish 30 to 40 minutes in pan of hot water, in 325 degree oven. Serve hot and sprinkle confectioners sugar on the top before serving. Serves 6.

BENJAMIN GREEN-FIELD

Owner of the fabled Bes-Ben Hat Salon on Michigan Avenue which created chapeaux for movie stars and society's grande dames. World traveler, antiques expert.

Peach and Strawberry Pie

1 quart fresh strawberries
6 large ripe peaches
1 cup sugar
2 tablespoons cornstarch

1½ teaspoons lemon rind
2 drops vanilla extract
½ teaspoon cinnamon

Slice the fruit and mix all ingredients. Pour into a 9-inch unbaked pie shell. Cover top with pastry. Bake in a 350 degree oven for at least 20 minutes and until golden brown. Top with whipped cream if desired.

BRUCE GREGGA

Leading interior designer, socialite.

Fruites De Cointreau

1 honeydew melon
1 canteloupe melon
½ pound bunch seedless green grapes
1 pint raspberries
1 pint strawberries

4 kiwi fruit
1 pineapple
4 peaches
½ cup Cointreau

Peel, seed, hull, slice and/or cube the above fruits of the season. Combine together in large glass bowl. Make certain the fruit is drained before adding the liqueur. Chill one hour and serve.

"May be garnished with ¼ cup shredded coconut and ¼ cup slivered pecans. A wonderful accent for the lemon crisp and chocolate crisp cookies that I always keep on hand from the Moravian Sugar Crisp Co. in Clemmons, N.C."

PETER GRIGSBY

Lincolnshire Theater director.

Lucienne

Rumor has it, this recipe was originated by a 1920's New York chorus girl, Lucy Ann. Lucy Ann was being courted by a "stage-door Johnny" for several nights—the Stork Club, the Cotton Club, etc—but she was holding out for the jewelry!

In a valiant effort to impress her beau with her cooking, rather than her cooing, abilities, she invited him up to her 8th floor walk-up for a re-heated Automat dinner. For dessert, she mixed together everything on her windowsill and cupboard (she didn't know the cream was sour or that it would later catch on in Stroganoff).

Due to the lushness of the dessert, he did indeed propose that very night and returned to his wife in Rhode Island the next morning.

Lucy Ann quit the chorus; became a pastry chef at Woolworth's; eventually moved to Paris; was then discovered by Josephine Baker, who introduced her to an exiled Count from Czarist Russia. He made her a wonderful husband and, together, they re-amassed a fortune by selling Buicks to Italians.

Jeff Award-winning actress Alene Robertson swears this is a true story, and that the recipe has been handed down backstage in theaters throughout the free world.

1¼ cups sugar
¾ cup water
1¼ cups prepared unflavored gelatin
1½ cups heavy cream
2½ cups sour cream

½ teaspoon vanilla extract
1 teaspoon favorite liqueur
in-season fruit garnish to complement
    the liqueur.

Whip the clear gelatin following instructions on package; set aside. Slow boil sugar and ¾ cup water. At boiling point, lower heat and whip in gelatin mixture. Allow to cool. Mix remaining ingredients. Blend the two mixtures together and pour into fancy mold. Chill for 2 hours. Serve with fresh mint, raspberries or other in-season fruit garnish.

JAMES GUTH JR.

President, The Chicago Caterers.

Mangos with Raspberry Puree and Cointreau Creme Fraiche

Cointreau Creme Fraiche:
1 cup heavy cream
1 tablespoon buttermilk

⅓ cup Cointreau
1 teaspoon sugar

In a glass bowl combine the heavy cream and buttermilk and let sit overnight in a warm area.

In the morning whisk the creme fraiche and let it set in the refrigerator 3 hours. When creme fraiche has set, mix in the Cointreau and sugar. Let set again until ready to use.

Raspberry Puree:
1 pint raspberries

½ teaspoon lemon juice

Puree all the ingredients together in a food processor. Set aside.

2 Ripe Mangos

Slice the fruit off the seed from each mango and cut into 18 strips. Put 2 tablespoons of the raspberry puree on a dessert plate and, using the back of a spoon, smooth puree over the bottom to cover the plate.

Arrange 3 slices of mango per plate as a fan. Lightly sprinkle plate with chocolate shavings. Place a dollop of Cointreau creme fraiche at the core of the fan.

JACK AND SANDRA GUTHMAN

He is prominent attorney. She is IBM executive. Both support the arts.

Raspberry Mousse with Strawberry Sauce

1 envelope unflavored gelatin
⅓ cup orange juice
2 packages frozen raspberries, thawed
¼ cup sugar

2 tablespoons fruit liqueur
2 egg whites
1½ cups heavy cream, whipped

Sauce:
2 packages frozen strawberries, thawed

Soften the gelatin in the orange juice. Drain the raspberries well. Measure the juice and add water, if necessary, to make 1 cup liquid. Cook the juice and sugar in a saucepan over low heat until syrupy. Add the raspberries and cook 10 minutes. Add gelatin and mix until dissolved. Force through a sieve; cool. Stir in the liqueur.

Beat the egg whites until stiff but not dry and fold into the raspberry puree. Fold in the whipped cream. Pour into an oiled 1½-quart mold and chill until firm.

Puree the strawberries and their juice. Force through a sieve. Unmold the mousse and pour strawberry sauce over it. Serves 6 to 8.

THERESA GUTIERRIEZ

Producer, moderator for WLS-TV.

Zucchini Bread

2 cups zucchini, mashed
3 eggs
2 cups sugar
1 cup vegetable oil
3 teaspoons vanilla
3 cups flour

1 teaspoon salt
1 teaspoon baking soda
½ teaspoon baking powder
3 teaspoons cinnamon
½ cup nuts (*I use pecans*) if desired

Beat eggs until foamy. Add sugar and vanilla. Beat well. Add zucchini and stir well. Add flour, salt, baking soda, baking powder, cinnamon and stir. Add nuts if desired. Put into two greased bread pans. Preheat oven to 350 degrees. Bake for one hour.

PHIL AND BETTS HANDMACHER

He is well known retailer. Both are active socially and in charitable work.

Strudel

Dough:
3 cups flour
1 cup sour cream

2 sticks sweet butter
1 teaspoon vanilla

Blend and refrigerate overnight.

Filling:
6 ounces nuts, chopped (*I use walnuts*)
1 can Bakers coconut
1 box white raisins
½ cup sugar
cinnamon to taste

1 jar apricot-raspberry or peach
  preserves, or orange marmalade
1 small jar maraschino cherries without
  stems, drained

Combine filling ingredients exept preserves and cherries. Set aside. Cut dough into 4 quarters. Roll out one at a time on a floured board. Spread each with preserves, and then ¼ filling sprinkled over preserves. Place row of cherries across center and roll. Place on baking sheet and make slashes in each roll. Refrigerate for 4 hours before baking. Bake in 350 degree oven 30 to 35 minutes or until light brown. Slice when cool. Put each slice into miniature paper cups. Sprinkle with confectioners sugar. Freezes beautifully.

JOSEPH HANNON

President of the Chicago Tourism and Convention Bureau.

Denise's Strawberry Treat

2 pints fresh strawberries
½ cup sugar
⅓ cup Cointreau or Grand Marnier

½ pint vanilla ice cream
½ cup heavy cream
½ teaspoon almond extract

Wash berries in cold water, hull, slice. Turn into large bowl. Sprinkle with sugar, Cointreau, toss gently. Refrigerate 1 hour or more. Let ice cream soften in refrigerator. Beat heavy cream until just about stiff. Fold in almond extract. Gently fold whipped cream and softened ice cream into strawberry mixture. Serve at once. Garnish with whole berries.

MRS. ROBERT HANSON

Socialite, supporter of the arts, charities.

Meringue Torte

6 egg whites
2 cups sugar

1 teaspoon vanilla
1 teaspoon vinegar

Preheat oven to 275 degrees. Beat whites until stiff enough to hold up in peaks; beat in 2 tablespoons sugar at a time, 3 times, beating thoroughly each time. Add vanilla, vinegar, and the rest of the sugar, beating all the time. Grease and flour a 9-inch springform pan and fill with about ⅔ of the mixture. On a greased and floured tin, form a circle of small kisses with the rest of the mixture. Bake about 1 hour.

High Temperature Method:
Bake at 450 degrees for 7 minutes. Turn off heat and leave torte in oven for 3 hours. Before serving fill with whipped cream or ice cream and berries and decorate the top with the circle of kisses.

105

IRA AND NICKI HARRIS

He is a prominent financial figure. Both are active socially, support the arts, charities.

Hershey Cookies

1 cup butter
2 cups all-purpose flour
½ cup sugar
½ teaspoon salt

12 1.45-ounce Hershey bars
¾ cup slivered almonds, lightly toasted
under broiler

Blend first 4 ingredients together in a blender. Grease 16 by 11-inch jelly roll pan well. Spread dough evenly on bottom and bake 15 to 20 minutes at 350 degrees. Remove from oven and place Hershey bars side by side on top. Spread and cut into squares. Sprinkle top with toasted, slivered almonds. Cool and place in freezer, pan and all. Serve when you need a "fix".

"My mother's recipe called for 14 thin 5-cent Hershey bars. How times, and prices, have changed!"

ATTORNEY GENERAL NEIL AND MARGE HARTIGAN

His political star is rising. Both are popular in business, political and social circles.

Simple Cheesecake

1½ cups fine graham cracker crumbs
¼ cup sugar
¼ cup soft butter
6 eggs, separated
½ cup sugar

1½ pounds cream cheese
1 lemon
½ teaspoon salt
½ cup sugar

First line the bottom and sides of a well-greased 9-inch round springform pan with a crumb mixture made by blending graham cracker crumbs with ¼ cup each sugar and soft butter.

Separate 6 eggs. Beat yolks until thick, beat in ½ cup sugar, and continue beating until fluffy. Mash 1½ pounds softened cream cheese; add with the grated rind of a medium lemon to the egg yolks. Mix well. Beat 6 egg whites with ½ teaspoon salt until soft mounds begin to form. Then add ½ cup sugar 2 tablespoons at a time, and continue beating until egg whites are stiff. Fold into the egg yolk mixture, blending thoroughly. Turn into crumb-lined pan and bake in 350 degree oven for about 50 minutes.

NOTE: When in season you can use strawberries on top of cheesecake with a strawberry glaze.

JULIAN AND KATHERINE HARVEY

Civic, social leaders, active in supporting the arts, worthy endeavors.

Kiwi and Raspberry Tart

Ingredients:
Hat   **Wallet**
Coat

From the Gold Coast:
Grab your coat and get your hat, put your wallet in your pocket and ring for the elevator. Walk south on Lake Shore Drive to Walton Street. Turn right (west) on Walton and continue halfway down the block until you arrive at Cafe Croissant on the north side of the street. Open the door and go inside. Ask for the Kiwi and Raspberry Tart which you ordered the day before. When you arrive home, put box containing the tart in the refrigerator to keep it fresh. Remove from refrigerator at least one hour before serving. The tart should be presented on a silver tray and served tongue in chic.

"Cafe Crosissant can be reached from virtually anywhere, but then so can Paris. If you wish, pass Devonshire cream purchased at Treasure Island."

(There is a second Cafe Croissant in the Hotel Continental, 505 N. Michigan Ave.)

PAUL HARVEY

Radio personality and newscaster, socialite, MacArthur Foundation member.

Angel Lynne's Lemon Ice Box Cake

1 tablespoon unflavored gelatin
¼ cup cold water
½ cup sugar
½ cup lemon juice
½ teaspoon salt
4 egg yolks

1 teaspoon grated lemon rind
4 egg whites
½ cup sugar
1½ dozen ladyfingers
whipped cream (if desired)

Soak gelatin in cold water. Combine sugar, lemon juice, salt and egg yolks; stir and cook in double boiler until the consistency of custard. Stir in gelatin and grated lemon rind and cool. Whip four egg whites until stiff and slowly beat in ½ cup sugar.

When custard begins to thicken, beat it with spoon until it is fluffy. Fold in egg whites. Line a pan with waxed paper and line that with ladyfingers. Pour in mixture and cover with ladyfingers. Place in refrigerator 12 hours. Serve with whipped cream. Serves 8.

NOTE: Vanilla wafer crumbs can be used in place of ladyfingers.

JAMES AND CAMILLE HATZENBUEHLER

Prominent realtors, active supporting medical, literary, theatrical growth; socialities.

Saucepan Brownies

1 stick butter or margarine
2 squares unsweetened chocolate
1 cup sugar
2 eggs

½ teaspoon salt
¾ cup cake flour
1 teaspoon vanilla

Melt butter and chocolate over low heat. Beat in sugar and one egg at a time. Stir in remaining ingredients. Pour into greased 8-inch square pan. Bake at 325 degrees for 25 to 30 minutes, or until top springs back when touched. Cool and sprinkle with confectioners sugar.

EVE HEFFER

Socialite, supporter of the arts.

Egg Nog Pound Cake

2 tablespoons butter or margarine
¼ cup sliced almonds
2¾ cups sifted cake flour
1½ teaspoons salt
1½ teaspoons baking powder
1 cup shortening

1½ cups sugar
1 teaspoon rum extract
1 teaspoon vanilla
1 cup any commercial egg nog
4 eggs

Grease a 10-inch bundt or tube pan generously with the butter. Sprinkle with almonds. Sift flour, salt and baking powder together. Cream shortening. Gradually beat in sugar, creaming until light and fluffy. Add flavorings and egg nog, then flour mixture. Beat at a low speed on mixer until all flour is moistened, then beat for one minute. Add eggs, one at a time, beating one minute at low speed after each addition. Turn into prepared pan. Bake at 325 degrees on lowest oven rack, about 1 hour 5 minutes, until cake tester inserted in center comes out clean. Remove from oven and let stand 10 minutes, then turn onto wire rack to cool.

MARK HEISTER

Award-winning fashion designer.

Kahlua Cookies

½ pound butter
2 cups flour
2 cups dark brown sugar
2 eggs
1 teaspoon vanilla
¼ teaspoon soda

½ teaspoon salt
½ cup Kahlua
2 cups coconut
2 cups chocolate chips
2 cups pecans

Mix all ingredients together in a large bowl. Place teaspoonsful on a cookie sheet and bake at 375 degrees for 8 to 10 minutes.

JOYCE HEITLER

Professional comic, teacher, publicist.

Swedish Spice Cake

1 egg
1¼ cups sugar
2 cups flour
1 teaspoon baking soda
1 teaspoon cinnamon

1 teaspoon cloves
½ teaspoon cardamom
2 tablespoons melted butter
1 cup buttermilk

Combine and mix all ingredients. Grease round springform or bundt pan and bake for 50 minutes at 325 degrees.

BETTE CERF HILL

Civic leader, conservationist, authority on city planning.

Hangover Cake

This cake gets its name from being served in the wee hours of the new year. All those who tried the cake said that they had no hangover the next day.

One 9½-inch unfrosted angel food cake—from scratch, from package (most fun) or bought.

1 12-ounce package chocolate chips
6 teaspoons warm water
3 egg whites

3 tablespoons confectioners sugar
½ cup chopped walnuts
2½ cups heavy cream

Melt chocolate chips in top of double boiler. Add water and stir to mix. Remove from heat. Add chopped walnuts. (This is very stiff and sticky.) Beat egg whites until stiff and fold in chocolate. With all clean (bowl, mixer, etc.) whip cream until stiff, add confectioners sugar gradually. Fold chocolate mixture into whipped cream. Place covered chocolate mixture in refrigerator for 12 hours. After 12 hours, cut angel food cake horizontally into 3 layers. Cover each layer with frosting (chocolate mixture) and reassemble. Frost top and sides. Place frosted cake in refrigerator for another 12 hours. Add a few chocolate curls for decoration if you must. Serves 12.

STANLEY HILTON

Shubert Organization executive, active in theatrical circles.

Microwave 2-Minute Fudge

1 pound confectioner's sugar
½ cup Hershey cocoa
1 stick butter

¼ cup evaporated milk
½ teaspoon vanilla

Use butter wrapper to grease pie plate. In bowl put sugar, cocoa, butter, vanilla and milk. Do not stir. Put in microwave on full power for 2 minutes. Stir immediately until smooth. Put in buttered pie plate and refrigerate until firm.

111

DICK HIMMEL

Dean of Chicago's interior designers.

Ellie's Ice Cream Cornflake Ring

5 cups cornflakes
½ cup chopped pecans
¼ pound butter

1 cup brown sugar
¼ cup dark corn syrup
1 teaspoon vanilla

Combine cornflakes and pecans in bowl. In a saucepan melt butter, add sugar and corn syrup. Heat to soft ball stage (238). Remove from heat and add vanilla. Pour over cornflakes and toss lightly but thoroughly. Place in a buttered, 6-cup ring mold.* Do not refrigerate. Unmold after 20 minutes.

(*Butter ring mold and put in freezer for a while or put in refrigerator for a longer period so it becomes ice cold.)

Serve with your favorite flavors of ice cream. Serves 8.

LESLIE HINDMAN

Head of Hindman Auctioneers, socially active, patron of the arts.

Leslie's Luscious Truffles

¼ cup heavy cream
2 tablespoons Grand Marnier
6 ounces German sweet chocolate, broken up

4 tablespoons sweet butter, softened
powdered unsweetened cocoa, as required

Boil cream in a small heavy pan until reduced to two tablespoons. Remove from heat, stir in Grand Marnier and chocolate, and return to low heat. Stir until chocolate melts.

Whisk in softened butter. When mixture is smooth, pour into a shallow bowl and refrigerate until firm, about 40 minutes.

Scoop chocolate up with a teaspoon and shape into, roughly, one inch balls. Roll the truffle balls in the unsweetened cocoa.

Store truffles, covered, in refrigerator. Let truffles stand at room temperature for 30 minutes before serving. Makes 24 truffles.

(Variation: Substitute dark rum, Cognac or another liqueur for Grand Marnier. Try Kahlua, Drambuie, Creme de Menthe or Amaretto.)

STU HIRSH

Orchestra leader, composer.

Walnut Crunch Pudding Squares

1 cup sugar
1 cup chopped walnuts
1 beaten egg
1 small package instant vanilla pudding
  mix

1 cup dairy sour cream
1 cup milk
2 medium bananas, sliced

Combine sugar, walnuts and egg. Spread thinly on greased baking sheet. Bake in moderate oven (350 degree) for 20 minutes, or till golden brown; cool to room temperature.

Crush baked nut mixture; sprinkle half of the crumbs in the bottom of 8 by 8 by 2-inch baking pan. Combine pudding mix, sour cream and milk; beat on low speed of electric mixer or with rotary beater 1 to 2 minutes or till well blended. Fold in sliced bananas.

Spoon over crumbs in pan; top with remaining crumbs. Chill several hours before serving. Cut in squares; garnish each square with a dab of Cool Whip or to conserve calories, a walnut half.

SIDNEY AND SHIRLEY HOLAB

He is plumbing contractor. She imports Judaica. Both are community leaders.

Aunt Sue's Raspberry Cheese Cake

1½ cups zweiback crumbs   ¼ cup melted butter

Line 9-inch springform pan with crumb mixture and set aside.

Filling:
3 8-ounce packages cream cheese   2 teaspoons vanilla
4 eggs   1¼ cup sugar

Beat eggs until fluffy. Add sugar, cheese and vanilla. Beat for 20 minutes on low speed of mixer. Pour in crumb-lined pan. Bake for 1 hour, 20 minutes at 250 degrees. Cool.

Topping:
1 10-ounce package frozen raspberries   1 tablespoon cornstarch

Drain juice from frozen raspberries. Add 1 tablespoon cornstarch. Heat until thickened. Fold in berries. Pour over top of cake in pan. Cover with wax paper and refrigerate for 24 hours.

MARVIN AND JOAN HOLLAND

Suburban community leaders, socialites, health and exercise enthusiasts.

Lower Cholesterol Cheese Cake

Crust:
1¼ cups graham cracker crumbs   ¼ cup melted margarine
¼ cup granulated sugar

Combine all ingredients. If crumbs are not thoroughly dampened by margarine add another melted spoonful or two.

Grease a 9 or 10-inch springform pan with margarine. Pour crumbs into bottom of pan and press down with back of large spoon or heel of hand, bringing crumbs part way up side of pan. When crumbs are compacted and smooth, refrigerate while making filling.

114

Filling:

1 pound Neufchatel cream cheese (or
  any lower caloried "Lite" cream
  cheese)
½ cup granulated sugar

½ cup egg substitute such as Egg Beater
  or Scramblers (shake container first)
¾ teaspoon vanilla

Combine all ingredients in mixmaster or food processor until well blended. Pour into pan taking care not to break crumbs apart. Bake in preheated 375 degree oven 25 to 35 minutes or until batter starts to bubble at sides and looks set in center. Remove from oven, place on rack and let cool about 15 minutes. Raise oven to 475 degrees.

Topping:

1 pint sour cream substitute such as
  Sour Slim, Sour Delight or sour half
  and half

¼ cup granulated sugar
1 teaspoon vanilla

Mix gently until well blended. Do not overbeat. Spoon gently onto cool filling working from outside toward center. Bake in 475 degree oven about 15 to 20 minutes or longer until edges bubble and center sets. Remove from oven and cool. Do not remove from pan or cut until cake has been in refrigerator all night. Go around sides with spatula, loosen bottom carefully. Remove intact from pan onto serving platter.

WALTER HOLMES

Premiere fashion designer.

Grapes Divine

large bunch green seedless grapes
large container sour cream

2 tablespoons brown sugar
¼ cup creme de menthe

"Select one large bunch of plump green seedless grapes, wash them of course, and place in your favorite bowl (Amari, I'm sure). Now, in a large mixing bowl add one large container of sour cream and then pour in creme de menthe and mix slowly until the sour cream turns a rich green (but not too rich—we have to be careful with the Creme de Menthe—Hic)! Add two tablespoons of brown sugar and mix. Now pour this sinful mixture over the grapes and turn with a wooden spoon ever so gently. We do not want to bruise the babies! Cover the bowl and leave in the refrigerator over night to marinate. Serve chilled with a sprig of fresh mint."

STANLEY AND RUTH HORWICH

He is head of Weddings, Inc., power behind VIP parties. She is a publicist, fashion authority.

Apricot Noodle Pudding Souffle

½ pound noodles
⅔ cup butter
¾ cup milk
4 eggs

1 cup sour cream
12 ounces cottage cheese
cinnamon and sugar
1 jar Smuckers apricot preserves

Cook noodles and drain well. Melt butter and add half to noodles with half of the milk. Add sour cream and cottage cheese and mix well. Beat eggs and add to mixture. Add remainder of milk. Grease an oblong casserole and fold in noodle mixture. Put a little cinnamon and sugar on top, to taste, and add the rest of the butter. Bake 1 hour at 350 degrees. Remove from the oven and put the apricot preserves on the entire top of the noodle souffle. Return to oven until noodles become bubbly. Remove from oven and serve piping hot.

"It's easy and oh! so divine! My family requests this at every family gathering!"

MICKEY HOUSTON

Founder and owner of Houston Foods, gourmet gift company. Food industry pioneer.

Pineapple Icebox Cake

28 vanilla wafers
½ cup butter
1½ cups confectioners sugar

2 eggs
1 small can crushed pineapple, drained
½ pint heavy cream

Roll wafers into crumbs and put half of them in the bottom of a small square pan. Cream butter and sugar. Add eggs and beat until smooth and creamy. Pour mixture over crumbs. Whip cream and add the drained pineapple. Pour over mixture already in pan. Cover with remaining crumbs and put in refrigerator overnight. If cake is a little too soft, put in freezer a short time.

RICHARD HUNT

World-famous sculptor.

Lenora's Vanilla Wafer Cake

1 12-ounce box vanilla wafers, crushed
1½ cups chopped nuts
1 6-ounce package shredded coconut
2 sticks butter or margarine

2 cups sugar
6 eggs
½ cup milk

Cream butter and sugar and blend in eggs, one at a time. Add crushed wafers, nuts, coconut and milk. Mix well. Bake in greased tube pan one hour and 15 minutes. (Less time may be required due to your oven's temperature.

DAVID AND KAY HUSMAN

He is a banker. both are art collectors, support the arts, charitable causes.

Brownies

1 stick butter or margarine
2 squares baking chocolate
1 cup sugar
2 eggs, beaten
½ cup flour

1 teaspoon vanilla
pinch salt
pinch baking powder
½ cup chopped walnuts

Melt butter and chocolate together. Add sugar and eggs. Add flour, vanilla, salt and baking powder; stir in nuts. Bake in an 8 by 8-inch buttered pan at 350 degrees for 20 to 25 minutes. Cool, slice and sprinkle with confectioners sugar.

ARCHBISHOP IAKOVOS

Primate of the Greek Orthodox Archdiocese of North and South America.

Athenian Torte

Sponge Cake:

3 eggs

1 cup sugar

1 tablespoon grated lemon rind

6 tablespoons hot milk

¼ teaspoon salt

1 tablespoon lemon juice

1 cup sifted flour

1½ teaspoons baking powder

Beat eggs until thick and light. Add sugar and lemon rind gradually, then add lemon juice. Fold in sifted dry ingredients in small amounts. Add milk and mix quickly until smooth. Turn at once into 8-inch round pan which has been lined with waxed paper. Bake in oven at 350 degrees for 35 to 40 minutes. Cool the cake; remove from pan. Slice into 3 layers and fill as directed below.

Syrup:

⅔ cup sugar

½ cup water

2 tablespoons brandy or rum

Boil sugar and water together for 5 minutes. Add brandy or rum.

Cream Filling and Finishing:

½ cup sugar

2 cups scalded milk

3 eggs, well-beaten

½ cup sugar

5 tablespoons flour

1 square Baker's unsweetened chocolate, melted

½ cup toasted almonds

½ teaspoon almond extract

1 teaspoon vanilla extract

sponge cake layers

whipped cream

Place ½ cup sugar in small shallow pan with 1 tablespoon cognac (or water). Melt sugar over moderate heat until golden. Remove from heat and combine with scalded milk. In mixing bowl beat eggs well. Add ½ cup sugar and flour. Slowly add milk, blending thoroughly. Cook in double boiler over hot water stirring constantly until mixture thickens.

Divide cream filling in two parts. Add melted chocolate to one half, and to the other add flavorings and ¼ cup ground almonds (or cut almonds into small pieces and add ¼ cup to filling). Arrange layer of sponge cake in platter. Sprinkle with syrup. Cover with chocolate filling. Repeat with second layer of sponge cake, sprinkle with syrup and spread with almond filling. Finish with top layer of sponge cake (sprinkle with syrup).

Chill in refrigerator 3 to 4 hours. Spread top and sides with whipped cream. Decorate with remaining ¼ cup toasted almonds.

GINA ISRAEL

Dental hygienist, community leader.

Derby Pie

1 shallow frozen pie shell
1 cup sugar
½ cup flour
2 eggs, slightly beaten
1 stick margarine, melted and cooled
  (do not add margarine warm or chips
  will melt)

1 cup chopped pecans
1 6-ounce package chocolate chips
1 teaspoon vanilla

Mix above ingredients together and pour into pie crust. Bake 1 hour at 325 degrees. Yields 6 ample slices.

BRUCE IVAN

Authority on hair styling, advisor on beauty.

Date Walnut Cookies

Pastry Layer:
1¼ cups sifted all-purpose flour
⅓ cup granulated sugar

½ cup butter or margarine

Combine flour, sugar and butter and blend to fine crumbs. Pack into bottom of greased 9-inch square pan. Bake at 350 degrees about 20 minutes, until edges are lightly browned.

Top Layer:
⅓ cup light brown sugar, packed
⅓ cup granulated sugar
2 eggs
1 teaspoon vanilla extract
2 tablespoons all-purpose flour
1 teaspoon baking powder

½ teaspoon salt
¼ teaspoon ground nutmeg
1 cup chopped walnuts
1 8-ounce package pitted dates, snipped
  or chopped

Combine the sugars, eggs and vanilla and beat together. Sift flour with baking powder, salt and nutmeg and add to first mixture. Stir in walnuts and dates. Turn batter into pan over hot baked pastry. Bake at 350 degrees about 20 minutes longer. Cool in pan, sprinkle with confectioners sugar, then cut into bar cookies.

NENA IVON

Fashion director for Saks Fifth Avenue.

Pot De Creme

8 ounces semi-sweet chocolate, melted
2 egg yolks
¼ cup warm water

1 cup heavy cream
¼ cup confectioners sugar
½ teaspoon ground cinnamon

Stir chocolate in a double boiler over hot water until melted. Beat egg yolks with warm water, blend into chocolate, remove from heat and chill for about 10 minutes. Whip cream with powdered sugar and cinnamon. Fold cream into chocolate mixture and spoon into 6 individual pot de creme cups. Chill until ready to serve. Serve with stiffly beaten sweetened whipped cream and garnish with candied violets. Serves 6.

DAN AND ALINE JARKE

World travelers, socialites, supporters of the arts.

Hot Apple Strips

apricot jam
1 cup butter
1 cup creamed cottage cheese

1 cup flour
4 apples

Blend butter, cottage cheese, flour and chill in refrigerator. Spread dough on oiled 10½ by 15½-inch cookie sheet. Fill with paper-thin apple slices in rows crosswise. Bake 20 minutes in 475 degree oven or until edges start browning. Remove from oven, spread top with apricot jam. Cut in strips and serve hot with sour cream.

NADINE AND ALBERT JENNER JR.

He is the well known lawyer. Both are active in civic, cultural affairs.

Doctor's Favorite Squares

1 cup butter
1 cup brown sugar

1 cup chopped pecans
graham crackers

Melt butter and brown sugar together in a saucepan. Stir while gently boiling for just 2 minutes, then stir in nuts. Have ready: generously greased 11 by 14-inch shallow pan with rim to contain mixture, and whole graham crackers arranged in rows. Pour mixture over them. Bake 10 minutes in 350 degree oven. (They will bubble up). Remove from oven and mark (not cut) squares with a knife. Cool and remove from pan. They also freeze well.

ANN JILLIAN

Actress, singer, dancer, star of movies and TV. Left Chicago with "Sugar Babies." Married to former policeman Andy Murcia.

Jillian's Cheesecake

Bottom Crust:
1¼ cups graham cracker crumbs
3 tablespoons sugar

⅓ cup margarine or butter

Blend crumbs with melted butter and sugar. Pack mixture firmly into a 10-inch springform pan. Chill for one hour or bake for 8 minutes.

Filling:
1 cup milk
5 eggs, separated
3 8-ounce packages cream cheese
1 cup sugar

½ pint sour cream
1 teaspoon cream of tartar
2 teaspoons vanilla
2 tablespoons cornstarch

Beat together egg yolks and cheese. Add sour cream, sugar, vanilla, cream of tartar. Mix well. Mix together milk and cornstarch and add to cheese mixture until smooth. Beat egg whites until stiff but not dry and fold in. Bake for 1 hour and 30 minutes at 325 degrees in preheated oven. Let cool in open oven for 1 hour.

HENRY AND DARLENE JOHNSON

He is head of Spiegel Catalogue. Both are socialites active on the charitable and social scene.

Peanut Butter Stars

1 cup shortening (½ butter)	3 cups flour
1 cup brown sugar	2 teaspoons baking soda
1 teaspoon vanilla	½ teaspoon salt
1 cup peanut butter	1 cup granulated sugar
2 eggs	chocolate stars, one for each cookie

Cream shortening, butter, brown sugar, and vanilla. Beat in eggs thoroughly. Beat in peanut butter. Combine flour, baking soda, salt and granulated sugar. Slowly blend into butter mixture. Batter will be very thick. Form into small balls and arrange on ungreased cookie sheets. Bake 10 minutes at 350 degrees. Remove from oven and put on chocolate stars. Bake 2 minutes more.

JOHN AND EUNICE JOHNSON

He is the publisher of many magazines, books, and head of Fashion Fair cosmetics. She produces annual Ebony Fashion Show to benefit United Black College Fund.

Plum Crunch

Plums:

3 cups fresh pitted blue plums, cut in quarters	5 tablespoons sugar
3 tablespoons brown sugar	¼ teaspoon nutmeg

Topping:

1 egg, well-beaten	1 teaspoon baking powder
1 cup flour	¼ teaspoon salt
1 cup sugar	½ cup butter, melted

Place plums on bottom of pan 7 by 10 by 2 inches. Mix brown sugar, granulated sugar and nutmeg and sprinkle over fruit. Beat egg in a bowl and add sifted dry ingredients. Mix with pastry blender, or fingers, until crumbly. Sprinkle over plum mixture. Pour butter over all. Bake in a 375 degree oven for 45 minutes. Serves 6.

SUSANNE JOHNSON

Head of talent agency, former model.

Lemon Mousse

3 lemons
4 eggs, separated
1½ cups sugar
1 envelope unflavored gelatin
1 teaspoon cornstarch

¼ cup Grand Marnier
1½ cups heavy cream
3 tablespoons confectioners sugar
toasted slivered almonds

Grate the rind from the lemons and set aside. Squeeze juice and set aside. Beat the egg yolks with the sugar until the mixture is light colored and forms a ribbon when spooned back on itself. Soften the gelatin in ¼ cup cold water. Place over hot water and stir until gelatin is dissolved.

In a large bowl, combine the cornstarch with one third of the lemon juice and stir until smooth. Add remaining juice, lemon rind and gelatin to the mixture and stir well. Add to the beaten egg mixture. Turn mixture into a double boiler and cook over hot water until mixture thickens, stirring constantly. Add half the Grand Marnier and cook one minute longer. Do not allow to boil. Chill the mixture until it begins to set. Whip the cream with the remaining Grand Marnier and sugar until stiff but not dry.

Fold the cream and egg whites into the lemon mixture and spoon into a souffle dish, bowl or individual cups. Garnish with almonds. Serves 8 to 10.

LEIGH JONES

Hairdresser to the stars and to Chicago's leading ladies.

Dorothy's Banana Cake

Cake:

2 cups sugar
½ cup shortening
2 egg yolks
2½ cups flour
1 teaspoon soda

1 teaspoon salt
1 cup buttermilk or sour cream
1 teaspoon vanilla
1 cup mashed bananas

Bake at 350 degrees for 35 to 40 minutes.

Topping:

2 tablespoons butter
½ cup brown sugar
1 cup crushed nuts

2 egg whites
½ teaspoon vanilla

Beat egg whites until stiff, add sugar, nuts, flavoring and butter; then, spread on and bake for 10 minutes at 350 degrees.

PENNY LANE AND WAYNE JUHLIN

Comedy and commercial writers, creators of comedy records. Prize-winning talents.

Estelle's Chocolate Ecstasy Cake

1 6-ounce package semi-sweet chocolate
  morsels
¼ cup water
2¼ cups sifted cake flour
1 teaspoon soda
½ teaspoon salt

1½ sticks butter or margarine
1¾ cups sugar
1 teaspoon vanilla
3 eggs
1 cup buttermilk

Combine chocolate with water in saucepan and place over low heat. Stir until smoothly blended, then remove from the heat. Sift flour once, measure, add soda and salt, and sift again. Cream butter with sugar until light and fluffy. Add vanilla and blend. Add eggs one at time, beating well after each addition. Blend in chocolate mixture.

Add dry ingredients alternately with buttermilk, beating until smooth after each addition. Turn into 3 greased and floured 8-inch layer pans and bake in a 375 degree oven 22 to 25 minutes, or until done. Cool. Fill and frost layers with chocolate cream frosting as follows.

Chocolate Cream Frosting:

½ of a 6-ounce package semi-sweet chocolate morsels (or ½ cup)
2 tablespoons honey

1 tablespoon water
½ pint heavy cream
⅛ teaspoon instant coffee powder

Melt first 3 ingredients together and cool. Whip cream with instant coffee and gradually blend in honey-chocolate mixture. Spread between layers and on top and sides of cake.

MRS. STEPHEN JURCO

Civic leader, former owner of Ciao Restaurant.

Chocolate Torte

Crust:

1½ cups flour
1 scant teaspoon baking powder
½ stick butter, melted
½ cup shortening, melted

¾ cup sugar
2 eggs, beaten slightly
1 teaspoon vanilla or rum (either is good)

Mix flour and baking powder in large bowl. Make a well in center and add other ingredients. Mix. Form into ball and let stand for one hour. Roll out dough and place in pie dish that has been greased and floured.

Filling:

1 pound ricotta
1 pound milk chocolate
4 eggs

8 tablespoons sugar
2 cups milk

Combine chocolate and milk, place over heat and melt. Beat in sugar, ricotta and eggs one at a time. Bring to a boil. Fill pie crusts and bake at 375 degrees approximately 40 minutes.

This recipe has been handed down from generation to generation in Tuscany.

SANDY KAGAN

Fashion authority, I. Magnin fashion director, former model.

Bananas A La Creme

6 ripe bananas
2 tablespoons granulated sugar
1 tablespoon brown sugar
¼ pound butter

6 tablespoons brandy
6 mint leaves (if desired)
vanilla or coconut ice cream

Peel and cut bananas in half length-wise. In a large frying pan melt butter, bring to a sizzle. Add granulated sugar, stir for 30 seconds. Lay in bananas carefully and sautee for 2 minutes (they cook very fast). Sprinkle brown sugar on top and cook for 1 minute. Remove from stove. Place on plates. Top with a scoop of vanilla or coconut (my preference) ice cream. Pour remaining sauce from pan over ice cream. Top with mint leaves. Pour 1 tablespoon brandy over ice cream. Serves 6.

SHELDON AND PATTY KAPLAN

Theater buffs, patrons of the arts, active in charity work.

Solo Souffle

1 can Solo pastry filling (peach, apricot or blueberry)

5 egg whites at room temperature
sweetened whipped cream

Preheat oven to 375 degrees. Prepare 1 quart souffle dish by buttering bottom and sides and dusting with sugar. Shake excess sugar off. Put Solo in a large bowl. Beat egg whites until very stiff. Add a little bit of the egg whites to the Solo to thin out the mixture. Then fold in the rest of the egg whites. Pour into prepared dish. Bake for 15 minutes. Serve immediately with sweetened whipped cream. Serves 3 or 4.

SHERMAN KAPLAN

WBBM newscaster, restaurant critic. Author of restaurant guides.

Eileen's Praline Pumpkin Pie

Crust:
⅓ cup brown sugar
⅓ cup broken pecans

⅓ cup melted sweet butter

Press sugar, butter and pecans into the bottom of 9-inch graham cracker crust. Bake crust at 400 degrees for 10 minutes.

Filling:
2 eggs, beaten slightly
1¾ cups canned pumpkin
¾ cup sugar
½ teaspoon salt

1 teaspoon cinnamon
½ teaspoon ground ginger
¼ teaspoon ground cloves
1¾ cups evaporated milk

Mix well and fill the baked pie shell. Bake at 425 degrees for 15 minutes, then lower oven to 350 degrees and continue baking for 45 minutes.

THOMAS KAPSALIS

Commissioner, Department of Aviation, Chicago.

Pat's Coffee Cream

1 cup very strong black coffee
16 marshmallows
½ pint heavy cream, whipped

semi-sweet chocolate
creme de cacao
whipped cream for garnish

Heat coffee in heavy saucepan. Add marshmallows and bring to a boil. Simmer until foam disappears and mixture becomes clear. Cool about 1 hour. Fold in whipped cream. Put equal amounts in parfait glasses and refrigerate a few hours. Garnish with one jigger creme de cacao, whipped cream and semi-sweet chocolate shavings. Serves 4.

DR. MARC KARLAN

Prominent plastic surgeon.

Pears Poached in Cognac

8 medium, firm pears, peeled and left
   whole with the stems on
1 cup sugar
peel from 1 lemon

1 cinnamon stick
8 whole cloves
½ cup cognac

Put pears in a deep saucepan and add the sugar, lemon peel and enough water to just cover pears. Add the cinnamon stick and cloves. Bring to a boil, lower heat and simmer for 20 to 25 minutes or until pears are easily pierced with a fork but still hold their shape. When pears have cooled in the sauce, stir in the cognac and chill until ready to serve. Serve pears with poaching syrup spooned over them.

DR. ROBERT KARP

Heart transplant specialist.

Brownies A La Soni

2 sticks butter
4 squares Hershey unsweetened
   chocolate
4 eggs

1 cup flour
2 cups sugar
1 teaspoon vanilla
chopped nuts if you like

Melt butter with chocolate. Allow to cool. Add eggs, one at a time, Mix after each egg. Add sugar and vanilla, flour, and mix well. Pour into a 9-inch square pan and bake at 350 degrees for 30 minutes. Check with a toothpick in the middle. If you like them fudgy, take out sooner.

"The best thing about this recipe is that you only use one pan!"

BYRON AND DIANE KARZAS

Civic and cultural leaders. He is a financial advisor and she plans special events.

Lemon Tarts

4 egg yolks
½ cup sugar
½ stick butter

juice of two lemons, zest of one lemon
½ pint heavy cream
12 tart shells (you can buy them)

Mix together first 4 ingredients and cook them, stirring constantly, in a heavy pan over medium low heat until mixture coats a spoon. Transfer mixture to a bowl, add the lemon zest and cool thoroughly. Whip cream until stiff. Thoroughly fold ½ of the cream into lemon mixture, then lightly fold in the remainder. Divide the mixture equally among the tart shells. Trim as desired—a strawberry, mint leaf, dollop of whipping cream or crystallized ginger.

JOE AND LOU ANNE KELLMAN

He is founder of the Better Boys Foundation and active in charitable work. Both are supporters of worthy causes, the arts.

Rum Cake

Cake:
1 cup chopped pecans or walnuts
1 18½ ounce package yellow cake mix
1 3¾ ounce package instant vanilla
   pudding

4 eggs
½ cup cold water
½ cup Wesson oil
½ cup dark rum (80 proof)

Preheat oven to 325 degrees. Grease and flour a 10-inch tube or 12-cup bundt pan. Mix all cake ingredients together. Sprinkle nuts over bottom of pan. Pour batter over nuts. Bake one hour. Cool. Invert on serving plate.

Glaze:
¼ pound butter
¼ cup water

1 cup granulated sugar
½ cup dark rum

Melt butter in saucepan. Stir in water and sugar. Boil 5 minutes, stirring constantly. Remove from heat. (Secret: do not stir in rum until you have removed the glaze from the heat.) Pierce cake with long-tined fork and dribble glaze on top and sides of cake until all is absorbed.

"You don't even need to serve after-dinner drinks with this dessert!"

EDMUND KELLY

Chicago Park District General Superintendent, political power.

Marilyn's Double Chocolate Fudge Brownies

4 squares unsweetened chocolate
1 cup flour
¼ teaspoon baking powder
¼ teaspoon salt
1 cup (2 sticks) butter or margarine, softened
2 cups sugar

4 eggs
2 teaspoons vanilla
1½ cups coarsely chopped walnuts, divided
1 6-ounce package semi-sweet chocolate pieces

Preheat oven to 350 degrees. Lightly grease 13 by 9 by 2-inch baking pan. In small bowl set over simmering water, melt unsweetened chocolate. Remove from heat; cool. On waxed paper, sift flour, baking powder and salt; set aside. In large bowl, with electric mixer at medium speed, beat butter with sugar until light and fluffy; add eggs, 1 at a time, beating well after each addition. Beat in cooled chocolate and vanilla. Blend in flour mixture and 1 cup walnuts. Spread evenly into prepared pan. Sprinkle top of brownie batter with remaining ½ cup walnuts and chocolate pieces. Bake 35 minutes or until top is shiny and firm. Cool on wire rack. Cut into 24 squares.

BARBARA ANN SCOTT KING AND THOMAS KING

She is the famous ice skating star and he has credentials in real estate management. Both are active on the social and cultural scene.

Angel Pie

Meringue:
3 egg whites
¼ teaspoon cream of tartar

1 cup sugar

Beat egg whites and cream of tartar until frothy. Gradually beat in sugar. Beat until very stiff, spread on round waxed-paper-lined pan or shape individual meringue shells on cookie sheet lined with waxed paper. Bake one hour in 275 degree oven. Turn off oven and leave in oven until cool.

Lemon Filling:
4 egg yolks
½ cup sugar
4 tablespoons lemon juice

2 tablespoons grated lemon rind
½ pint heavy cream

Beat yolks until thick and pale yellow. Gradually beat in sugar. Blend in lemon juice and lemon rind. Cook over hot water, stirring constantly until thick (about 7 minutes). Let cool. Whip cream until very stiff. Put a layer of whipped cream on meringue, then a layer of lemon filling (thick), then top with layer of whipped cream. Chill in fridge about 12 hours before serving.

DR. JOSEPH KIRSNER

World-famous gastro-intestinal expert.

Minnie's Sweet Tooth Treat

sugar-free Dr. Pepper
rome beauty or any other good baking
    apples
lemon juice

seedless raisins
cinnamon
nutmeg
a drop of vanilla

Use one apple per serving. Cut in half and core. Fill centers with raisins and place in a deep baking dish. Cover apples with the Dr. Pepper and other seasonings. Bake 45 minutes at 350 degrees and baste often.

FRANCIS AND NANCY KLIMLEY

He is a rug and carpeting tycoon. She is guiding force behind city's most important charities and cultural events.

Strawberries "75"

4 cups strawberries
4 tablespoons sugar

2 tablespoons lemon juice
½ bottle chilled champagne

Heap hulled strawberries in a shallow glass bowl and sprinkle them with sugar and lemon juice. Allow to marinate for two hours. Then pour ½ bottle or more of chilled champagne over them. Serve immediately. Serves 8.

JUDGE THOMAS AND MELANIE KLUCZYNSKI

He is longtime judicial expert. Melanie is leader in Polish organizations, cultural events.

Creme Brulee a La Rive Gauche

3 cups heavy cream
6 egg yolks
⅓ cup brown sugar

1 tablespoon vanilla extract
⅓ cup brown sugar
½ ounce dark rum

Over medium heat, heat cream until tiny bubbles form. In a saucepan with wire whisk, blend yolks with sugar. Slowly stir in cream. Over medium-low heat cook mixture stirring constantly, until it just coats back of metal spoon, about 15 minutes (do not boil). Stir in vanilla. Pour mixture into 1½-quart broiler-safe casserole. Refrigerate until well chilled, about 6 hours. Pre-heat broiler. Sift brown sugar over chilled mixture. Broil 3 to 4 minutes until sugar melts. Serve immediately.

HELINA KONTOS

A real countess, she is head of Kontessa Originals fashion design house, and is active in social, cultural activities.

Bow-Knots (Diples)

5 eggs
2½ cups farina
juice of 2 oranges
juice of 1 lemon
1½ cups nuts

1½ cups honey
1 tablespoon cinnamon
½ cup water
1 teaspoon baking powder
olive oil

Break the eggs into a bowl. Add the juice of two oranges and a lemon and a cup of farina. Work with your hands to make a stiff bread-like dough. If the dough is too soft, add a little more farina. Roll dough out on a floured board like a pie crust. With a pastry wheel, cut in strips about three inches long and two inches wide. Fold the two ends to form a triangle and press with the fingers to stick. Make different shapes with the strips: ties, bows, triangles or pleats. In the meantime, have a deep frying pan ready with olive oil hot enough to smoke. Fry four to five strips at a time for 2 to 3 minutes, until they become golden. Drain while removing from the pan. Place on a dish until all the strips are fried. Then prepare the syrup. Boil the honey with half a cup of water. Arrange a layer of the diples in a platter, sprinkle with chopped nuts, cinnamon and the hot syrup. Arrange another layer on top and continue until all the diples are sprinkled with nuts and syrup. Most of the syrup will drip down in the platter, but it can be poured over the diples again when served in individual plates. Diples are usually eaten with the fingers as they break if pierced with a fork. Always serve diples cold.

MAXENE KOTIN

Public relations, promotion professional.

Banana-Split Pie

Crust:
2 cups graham cracker crumbs
½ cup sugar

1 stick butter or margarine

Filling:
½ pound butter or margarine
2 eggs
2 cups confectioners sugar
1 teaspoon vanilla
3 bananas (dip in lemon juice to prevent darkening) sliced horizontally

1 large can drained crushed pineapple
9 ounces Cool Whip or whipped cream
crushed nuts, melted chocolate or maraschino cherries for decoration

Melt butter and mix ingredients for crust together. Press and smooth out to form crust in 9 by 13-inch pyrex pan. Bake 8 minutes 350 degrees. Beat together margarine, eggs, sugar and vanilla for 5 minutes until consistency of whipped cream. Spread a layer of creamy mixture in bottom of crust and alternate with sliced bananas and pineapple until all is used up, ending with fruit layer. Spread Cool Whip or whipped cream on top of fruit and decorate with nuts, melted chocolate or cherries. Refrigerate several hours.

ARDIS KRAINIK

General manager of the Lyric Opera of Chicago.

Ardis' Chocolate Marshmallow Icebox Cake

Crust:
20 graham crackers, rolled   ½ cup soft butter

Mix and put half of mixture in bottom and sides of 8 by 8-inch pan. (Save the rest for top).

Filling:
30 marshmallows   1½ cups heavy cream
½ cup milk   2 squares bitter chocolate

Melt marshmallows and milk in top of double boiler. Cool and stir to make marshmallow sauce. Whip cream thoroughly and add bitter chocolate cut in small pieces. Then fold whipped cream mixture into marshmallow mixture. Put in pan and sprinkle rest of graham cracker mix on top and let stand in refrigerator till served. Put shaved nuts on top if desired.

SHIRLEY KRAVITT

Artist, expert in Far Eastern art, lecturer.

Chocolate Marshmallow Souffle

3 tablespoons margarine   32 marshmallows
3 tablespoons flour   3 egg yolks, beaten
¼ teaspoon salt   1 teaspoon vanilla
1 cup milk   3 egg whites, stiffly beaten
¼ cup sugar
3 1-ounce squares unsweetened
    chocolate, grated

Melt margarine in a saucepan, blend in flour and salt. Add milk and cook over low heat, stirring constantly, until thick and smooth. Add sugar, chocolate, and marshmallows, stir until chocolate and marshmallows are melted. Remove from heat. Slowly add egg yolks and vanilla to chocolate-marshmallow mixture and mix well. Cool. Fold egg whites into cooled chocolate mixture. Turn into a 1½-quart casserole and place in pan of hot water. Bake in a moderate oven, 350 degrees, for 1 hour or until set. Serve warm with cream.

CARL KROCH

Head of the chain of Kroch's and Brentano book stores, part owner of the Cincinnati Reds, supporter of the arts.

Jeanette's Blushing Maiden

1 10-ounce package frozen raspberries
granulated sugar (to taste)

1 tablespoon lemon juice
whites of 2 large eggs

Thaw raspberries and put through a fine sieve, keeping seeds out of the puree. Beat egg whites in a mixer (not a blender) until foamy and add raspberry juice, lemon and sugar to taste. Then once again beat in a mixer until very stiff. Serve with a soft vanilla sauce (recipe follows).

Vanilla Sauce:
2 cups milk
1 teaspoon vanilla extract
3 egg yolks

¼ cup sugar
2 teaspoons cornstarch

In the top of a double boiler scald milk and vanilla. Beat egg yolks with sugar and cornstarch until light and frothy. Pour vanilla flavored milk into egg yolk mixture slowly, stirring vigorously as you do so. Pour mixture back into top of a double boiler and set over hot, not boiling water that does not touch upper pan. Stir constantly until sauce becomes thick and custardy. Serve cold over Blushing Maiden.

NOTE: Since this dessert must be served stiffly made, prepare just before serving. The final mixing can be done during the meal. Any leftovers can be frozen. It becomes a wonderful frozen mousse.

PHIL KRONE

Political consultant, supporter of the arts.

Joan's Peppermint Frangos

1 cup butter
2 cups sifted confectioners sugar
4 squares unsweetened chocolate (melted)
4 eggs

2 teaspoons vanilla
2 teaspoons peppermint flavoring
1 cup vanilla wafer crumbs

Cream butter and sugar until light and fluffy. Add melted chocolate gradually. Add eggs, one at a time, beating thoroughly after each addition. Add vanilla and peppermint. Sprinkle half the crumbs in 24 small cupcake liners. Add filling; top with remaining crumbs. Freeze until firm. Serve frozen or cold. Serves 24.

ROBERT AND PAT KUBICEK

He is in banking public relations. Both are community, civic leaders.

Chocolate Torrone

½ pound semi-sweet chocolate
4 tablespoons dark rum
½ pound unsalted butter, softened
2 tablespoons sugar, superfine
2 egg yolks
1½ cups ground almonds

2 egg whites
pinch of salt
10-12 vanilla wafers cut into strips, all crumbs shaken free
1 teaspoon vegetable oil
½ cup heavy cream (optional)

Break chocolate into small pieces and combine with 4 tablespoons dark rum in a small heavy saucepan. Stir over moderate heat until chocolate melts. Do not let rum come to a boil. Let cool to room temperature.

Cream the softened butter with 2 tablespoons sugar in an electric mixer until butter is smooth and satiny. Add in 2 egg yolks one at a time, mixing until not a trace shows.

Add the almonds, pulverized dry in the electric blender, and the cooled chocolate. NOTE: chocolate must be completely cooled so it will not melt butter.

Beat 2 egg whites and pinch of salt until they cling to beater without dropping. Fold into chocolate mixture until no white streaks show.

Sprinkle wafer pieces over top of mixture and gently fold into chocolate, distributing evenly.

Coat inside of a 1½-quart loaf pan with vegetable oil. Drain any excess by turning upside down over towel. Turn the torrone into the pan; rap pan 2 or 3 times on table to release air bubbles. Cover tightly with clear plastic wrap and refrigerate overnight.

To unmold, run a knife around sides of pan, then dip in hot water. Turn onto a chilled platter; smooth surface and return to refrigerator.

Serve cut into thin slices—it is sinfully rich—accompanied by a bowl of whipped cream. Serves 8.

BARBARA KUCK

Award-winning chef at the Bakery Restaurant, teacher.

Blueberries and Banana Fluff

2 fresh bananas, mashed
2 tablespoons sugar
2 to 3 tablespoons good quality orange
  liqueur
2 egg whites beaten stiff with 1
  tablespoon sugar

1 pint blueberries, washed and picked
  over
4 orange slices, to decorate
orange zest, to decorate

Mash bananas with a fork, add sugar and orange liqueur. In an electric mixer beat egg whites and sugar until fluffy. Fold into the mashed banana mixture, then add blueberries. Spoon into four individual serving dishes, decorate the top of each with a thick slice of peeled orange and sprinkle with orange zest. Serves 4.

NOTE: For sugar restricted diets, you may omit the sugar.

Carl's Stohns

Cream Puffs:

1 cup water
½ cup butter

1 cup sifted flour
4 eggs

Pre-heat oven to 400 degrees. Heat water and butter to a rolling boil in saucepan. Stir in all the flour at once. Stir vigorously over low heat until mixture leaves the pan and forms a ball (about one minute). Remove from heat. Beat in eggs thoroughly, one at a time. Beat mixture until smooth and velvety. Drop from spoon onto ungreased baking sheet forming 18 tiny puffs the size of small stones. Three to 4 inches apart is best. Bake 30 minutes or until puffed, golden brown and dry. Allow to cool slowly, away from drafts. Cut off tops with sharp knife. Scoop out any filaments of soft dough. Fill with any ice cream (or just vanilla). Build them into a pyramid and serve with hot chocolate fudge sauce dribbled all over and pass more chocolate sauce.

Hot Chocolate Fudge Sauce:

4 squares Baker's unsweetened
   chocolate
2 cups sugar
½ teaspoon salt

1 teaspoon vanilla
½ cup butter
1 cup milk or cream

Over low heat, stir all ingredients until smooth and thick. Cook for 45 minutes on low heat.

French Raspberry Tart

Tart Shell:

1⅔ cups flour
¼ cup fine granulated sugar
½ teaspoon salt
10 tablespoons sweet butter (1¼ sticks),
   chilled

2 egg yolks
1 teaspoon vanilla
2 teaspoons cold water

Sift flour, sugar, salt in bowl. Cut chilled butter into pieces in bowl until mixture resembles coarse meal. Stir egg yolks, vanilla and water together and add to flour mixture with a fork. Shape into a ball.

Place dough on pastry board. With heel of hand, smear ¼ cup of dough away from you into a 6 to 8 inch smear; repeat until all dough has been dealt with. Scrape dough together, reform into a ball, wrap in wax paper and chill 2-3 hours.

Roll out dough between 2 sheets of wax paper into a 10-inch round. Work quickly; dough can become sticky.

Line a 9-inch tart pan with removable bottom with the dough, fitting it loosely into pan and pressing to fit sides. Chill.

Line dough in tart pan with foil and weight with beans. Bake in a preheated 425 degree oven for 8 minutes. Remove foil and beans. Prick bottom of dough with fork. Return to oven for 8 minutes or until edges are light brown.

Pastry Cream:

2 cups milk	**2 egg yolks**
½ cup granulated sugar	**1 tablespoon sweet butter**
4 tablespoons unbleached flour	**2 teaspoons vanilla**

Scald milk in saucepan. While milk is heating, whisk sugar and flour together in bowl. Remove skin from milk and slowly pour milk into flour and sugar, whisking constantly. Place bowl over a saucepan of simmering water and cook, stirring until mixture lightly coats back of spoon, about 10 minutes.

Add egg yolks and cook, stirring constantly, until mixture heavily coated back of spoon, about 10 minutes more. Remove from heat. Add butter and vanilla and mix well. Cool slightly. Cover top of pastry cream with plastic wrap to prevent skin from forming and chill.

To assemble tart:
Fill the cooled pastry shell with pastry cream. Arrange fresh raspberries (or other fruits) on top. Brush with raspberry glaze or dust with a shaker of confectioners or granulated sugar.

MICHAEL J. KUTZA JR.

Founder and director of the Chicago International Film Festival and movie critic.

Technicolor Nightmare Cake

Cake:

9 cups sifted all-purpose flour
6 teaspoons double-acting baking
  powder
1 ½ teaspoons salt
1 cup oil or butter
6 cups sugar

9 whites of eggs (save the yellows for
  something fun, like an omelette)
3 cups water
1 cup white Bacardi Rum
liquid food coloring: large bottles of
  red, yellow, blue

Preheat oven to 350 degrees. Grease 3 rectangular cake pans (15" x 8" x 2") and dust with flour. Sift the flour, baking powder, and salt into a large bowl. Add the butter/oil and begin using the electric mixer. Add the sugar and beat 3 minutes, add the water, eggs and rum, scraping the bowl as necessary and continue beating until smooth. Separate the batter into 3 separate bowls. In each bowl add a different color. Bowl one gets the red, bowl two gets the yellow and the third gets the blue. Beat the batter of each bowl separately and completely. The colors should be quite vivid. Clean the beaters after each bowl, so no mix of color occurs. Pour the red in one pan, yellow in the next, and blue in the last. Place all three in the oven for 25 minutes. Each is done when a toothpick placed in the cake comes out clean. Place each layer on a rack to cool for about 30 minutes. Sprinkle each layer with more rum and let absorb before frosting.

Frosting:

1 cup butter
6 cups confectioners sugar, sifted

8 tablespoons heavy cream
1 teaspoon vanilla

Cream butter, add remaining ingredients and continue creaming until mixture is well blended and fluffy. This should cover all sides and tops of all layers. Refrigerate the entire thing for a night.

"Beware! Lifting the cake can hurt you! At this point it may weigh close to 8 pounds. The real thrill of this project is cutting it. The colors will knock your socks off. Actually, the rum may do that anyway. This cake is worthy of an Academy Award for special effects or at least color cinematography. You see, Technicolor was originally a 3-strip color process."

JEWEL LAFONTANT

Lawyer, Deputy Solicitor General for the U.S. 1972–75, civic leader.

Custard Cream Pies

3 prepared pie shells
1½ sticks butter
6 eggs
2 cups sugar
1 cup cream

2 cups milk
1 tablespoon flour
2 teaspoons lemon extract
pinch baking soda

Melt butter. Add flour, sugar and eggs. Add cream, lemon, soda and milk. Pour into pie shells. Bake 45 minutes at 375 degrees. Makes 3 pies.

DOUGLAS LAMONT

International business authority, professor at Kellogg School of Management, NU.

Blackberry Cake

Cake:
⅔ cup butter
2 cups white sugar
3 eggs
½ teaspoon salt
1 teaspoon soda
1 teaspoon cinnamon
1 teaspoon allspice
1 teaspoon nutmeg

3 cups sifted all-purpose flour
1 cup buttermilk or SACO buttermilk
   powder (3–4 tablespoons powder and
   one cup water)
1 cup lightly drained canned
   blackberries, save the juice
1 teaspoon vanilla

Cream butter and sugar until light and fluffy. Add eggs one at a time and beat into creamed mixture. Add soda, salt, spices to flour. Then alternate the flour mixture with the buttermilk. Blend in well. Add vanilla to cake mixture. Beat in the berries (do not fold in as they will sink to bottom). Add 2 to 3 tablespoons of the berries' juice. Pour batter into greased and floured angel food or bundt pan and bake at 350 degrees for slightly over one hour or until done.

Frosting:
2 tablespoons melted butter
2 tablespoons cream

½ teaspoon vanilla
1½ cups confectioners sugar

Beat all of the above. Frost just the top of the cake or make frosting thinner in order to dribble over cake.

Doug prefers the cake without the frosting. It is moist and spicy. This cake has been in his family for generations.

LESTER AND MAUREEN LAMPERT

He is Michigan Avenue jeweler, designer. Both are active in social, charitable endeavors.

Bananas Foster

1 cup firmly packed brown sugar
½ cup butter
8 bananas, peeled and quartered
½ teaspoon cinnamon

2 tablespoons lemon juice
1 cup light rum
½ cup banana liqueur
vanilla ice cream

Melt brown sugar and butter in chafing dish or skillet, stirring often. Add the bananas and saute for 2 to 3 minutes. Sprinkle with cinnamon and lemon juice. Heat rum and banana liqueur in separate saucepan. Pour over bananas but do not stir in sauce. Light the liqueur and continue to spoon the sauce over the bananas until the flame dies.

Spoon bananas and sauce over scoops of ice cream and serve immediately. Serves 8.

BRIAN LASSER

Brilliant song-writer, arranger, pianist.

Sour Cream Cake

1 cup sugar
2 eggs
1 cup sour cream
½ teaspoon soda

1 teaspoon baking powder
½ teaspoon salt
1 teaspoon lemon extract
1¾ cups flour

Beat sugar and eggs until very light. Add the flavoring. Stir soda into sour cream and add alternately to the egg mixture, with the flour mixed and sifted with salt and baking powder. Bake in layers or loaf in moderate oven, 350 degrees, 45 minutes.

LEONARD AND BERNICE LAVIN

Alberto-Culver executives, horse-breeders, socialites, philanthropists.

Chocolate Carrot Cake

Cake:

1½ cups all-purpose flour
¾ cup sugar
½ cup light brown sugar
1¼ teaspoons baking powder
1 teaspoon cinnamon
½ teaspoon salt
3 eggs

¾ cup vegetable oil
2 teaspoons vanilla
2 cups grated carrots
2 cups semi-sweet chocolate chips (use smallest size)
½ cup chopped walnuts

Combine all dry ingredients in large mixing bowl. Beat eggs, oil and vanilla in small bowl; add to dry ingredients. Blend together. Stir in carrots, chocolate and walnuts. Pour into well greased and floured 13 by 9-inch pan. Bake at 350 degrees for 40 minutes. Cool, frost. Serves 10 to 12.

Cream Cheese Frosting:

3 ounces softened cream cheese
¼ cup softened butter or margarine

2 cups confectioners sugar
1½ teaspoons vanilla

Beat together cream cheese and butter or margarine until blended. Add confectioners sugar slowly; stir in vanilla. Beat until smooth.

EPPIE LEDERER (ANN LANDERS)

Syndicated advice columnist.

French Silk Chocolate Pie

½ cup butter, room temperature
¾ cup sugar
1 square (1 ounce) bitter chocolate, melted and cooled

1 teaspoon vanilla
2 eggs

Electric mixer is a must. Cream butter. Add sugar a little at a time until smooth (use a small mixing bowl). Add cooled chocolate and vanilla. Add eggs one at a time and beat 5 minutes after each egg. Turn into a 8-inch graham cracker pie shell. Top with whipped cream and shaved bitter chocolate.

SHERRY LEHR

Civic and social leader, supporter of the arts.

Tippler's Fancy

Cake:

1 package white cake mix
1 small package instant chocolate
   pudding
4 eggs

1 cup oil
⅔ cup vodka
⅓ cup coffee liqueur
¼ cup water

Combine white cake mix, instant chocolate pudding, eggs, oil, vodka, coffee liqueur and water in large bowl and beat thoroughly. Pour into greased and floured bundt pan. Bake at 350 degrees for approximately 30 minutes. Let cool in pan 5 minutes. Invert onto rack.

Topping:

¼ cup coffee liqueur

¼ cup confectioners sugar

Blend coffee liqueur and confectioners sugar in bowl until smooth. Drizzle evenly over warm cake. This cake should be made the day before serving. Serve with vanilla ice cream. Serves 12 to 15.

MORRIS AND MARY LEIBMAN

He is the prominent attorney and she is active in charitable work, social events.

Apple Crumb Pie

4-5 large tart apples, peeled and sliced
1 Pet-Ritz deep dish pie crust
1 teaspoon cinnamon

1 cup sugar
¾ cup flour
⅓ cup butter

Sprinkle ½ cup sugar and cinnamon over apples; mix and turn into pie shell. Sift another ½ cup sugar with flour; cut in butter till crumbly. Sprinkle over apples.

Bake at 400 degrees for 40 to 50 minutes.

ROY LEONARD

Veteran WGN radio personality.

Lemon Fluff

1 12-ounce can evaporated milk
½ cup sugar
1 package lemon Jello

1 box Nabisco vanilla wafers
⅓ cup lemon juice
1 cup lukewarm water

Chill milk in ice cube container until crystally. Dissolve Jello in 1 cup lukewarm water. Add lemon juice and cool until quite thick, then beat Jello mixture until frothy. Put milk in large mixer bowl and beat until thick and light. Add sugar and Jello mixture to milk and beat together until stiff. Crush wafers with rolling pin and line bottom and sides of bowl. Pour in mixture and top with more crushed wafers. Chill until served. Looks pretty in sherbet glasses with cherry on top.

MICHAEL LERICH

Orchestra leader, composer, multi-talented musician.

Crepes Marnier

Crepes:
1 large egg
½ cup milk
¼ cup flour
2 teaspoons sugar

1 pinch salt
1 tablespoon melted butter
2 teaspoons brandy
butter for crepe pan

Beat egg and milk until they are blended. Combine flour, sugar, and salt, and gradually beat the liquid into them, making a smooth batter. Add melted butter and brandy. The batter should have the consistency of heavy cream. Let the mixture stand ½ hour.

Brush a hot 8-inch crepe pan with some butter. Pour 2 tablespoons of premeasured batter into the pan, and quickly tip the pan to coat the bottom evenly with the batter. When the crepe is lightly browned on the bottom, turn it and brown the other side. Prepare 6 crepes this way.

145

Filling and Topping:

5 tablespoons butter
½ cup brown sugar
½ cup fresh orange juice
3 small bananas

¼ cup Grand Marnier
½ cup coarsely chopped pecans
¼ cup brandy

In a large frying pan melt 5 tablespoons butter and blend in brown sugar. Stir the mixture over low heat until sugar is dissolved. Add Grand Marnier.

Slice bananas in half lengthwise. Roll each half in a crepe. Place all 6 crepes in frying pan with sauce and sprinkle them with pecans. Simmer the crepes gently for 8 minutes, turning once. Pour brandy into the pan and flame. Remove crepes from heat and serve immediately.

From Chef Richard Hesson of Ravinia Green Country Club.

ROBERT AND FLORENCE LEROY

He is expert in hotel management. Both are socialites, support charities and the arts.

Sour Cream Chocolate Mousse

2 cups sour cream
½ cup sugar
½ cup crumbled macaroons

6 tablespoons melted sweet chocolate
1 tablespoon brandy
1 teaspoon vanilla

Mix thoroughly sour cream, sugar and macaroons, melted chocolate, brandy and vanilla. Pour into refrigerator tray and freeze about three hours or until solid. Pile mousse in sherbet glasses and garnish each with shaved sweet chocolate.

DONALD AND ELAINE LEVINSON

He is owner of Trabert-Hoeffer Jewelers. Both are active in charity work.

Paradise Pecan Pie

1 cup white corn syrup
1 cup firmly packed dark brown sugar
3 eggs
⅓ cup sweet butter, melted
dash vanilla

pinch salt
1½ cups coarsely chopped pecans
1 unbaked 9-inch pie shell
16 pecan halves for garnish

Preheat oven to 375 degrees. Combine first six ingredients in medium bowl and mix well. Stir in chopped pecans. Pour batter into pie shell. Arrange pecan halves decoratively around top of pie. Bake until center is set and crust is golden brown, about 50 to 60 minutes, depending on your oven. Serve at room temperature with whipped cream or ice cream if desired. Serves 6 to 8.

HARRY AND MARILYN LEVINSON

He is dean of Chicago jewelers. Both are supporters of charities, civic projects.

Original Bacardi Rum Cake

Cake:

1 package yellow cake mix	**½ cup vegetable oil**
1 small package vanilla instant pudding	**½ cup dark rum**
4 eggs	**1 cup chopped pecans (optional)**

Pre-heat oven to 325 degrees. Heavily butter and flour bundt pan. Sprinkle pecans over bottom of pan. Mix all ingredients in large bowl and beat with electric mixer at high speed full 4 minutes. Pour batter over pecans. Bake 60 minutes. Set out on rack to cool 20 minutes. Invert on serving plate. Let cook another 30 minutes. Prick cake all over with toothpick. Drizzle and brush cake with glaze.

Glaze:

¼ pound margarine	**1 cup granulated sugar**
¼ cup water	**½ cup dark rum**

Melt butter in saucepan. Stir in water and sugar. Boil 5 minutes stirring constantly. Remove from heat and stir in rum.

You may dust finished cake with confectioners sugar for added decoration.

EADIE, LARRY AND MARK LEVY

Real estate developers, restaurateurs (Spiaggia, Chestnut Street Grill and a dozen others), One Magnificent Mile entrepreneurs.

Chocolate Chocolate Chip Cake

1 package Pillsbury fudge cake mix
1 small package Royal instant chocolate
 pudding
¾ cup water

¾ cup sour cream
4 eggs
6 ounces chocolate chips

Beat first five ingredients for eight minutes and then add chips. Mix. Place batter in a well greased bundt pan and bake at 350 degrees for 50 minutes.

ILA LEWIS

Vice-president of Gerber Plumbing Co., Supporter of the arts, charities.

Gottlieb's Savannah Bakery Chocolate Chewies

3 cups firmly packed confectioners
 sugar
7 tablespoons leveled and packed cocoa
 (½ cup minus 1 tablespoon)

2 tablespoons all-purpose flour
3 egg whites
2 cups (8 ounces) finely chopped pecans

Preheat the oven to 350 degrees. Line two baking sheets with parchment paper. In a medium mixing bowl, combine sugar, cocoa and flour. Add egg whites and beat at high speed for 1 minute. Stir in pecans.

Using 1½ tablespoons of batter for each, drop cookies 2 inches apart onto baking sheets. Press tops of cookies to lightly flatten.

Bake for 15 minutes. Cool cookies on the parchment paper before removing them. Store in an airtight container. Yield: 2 dozen cookies.

MARILYN LEWIS

Founder of Hamburger Hamlets Restaurants, former model, fashion designer.

Cinnamon Creme De Cassis Syrup over Lemon Ice and Blueberries

4½ cups water
3 cups sugar
24 whole allspice berries
24 whole cloves

4 cinnamon sticks
juice of 4 lemons
3 cups creme de cassis

Place into a non-metallic pot water, sugar, allspice berries, cinnamon and cloves. Cover and place over medium heat to dissolve sugar completely. Shake the pan in slow circular swirls only, now and then. Do not stir with a spoon. When all the sugar dissolves, uncover and bring to a boil over medium heat. Boil 4 minutes. Add lemon juice and boil 2 minutes.

Finally, add the creme de cassis. Boil 2 more minutes. Pour the syrup into a mason jar and cool to room temperature. Place in the refrigerator. After it's cool and you're ready to use it, strain.

Serve lemon ice and fresh blueberries covered with this syrup. (You can also use this syrup warm, on pancakes, french toast or crepes.)

MAURY AND HARRIET LEWIS

Gerber Plumbing Co. executives, major supporters of JUF, housing for aged; civic leaders.

Bourbon Pound Cake

1 pound butter or margarine
3 cups sugar
8 eggs, separated
3 cups sifted all-purpose flour

2 teaspoons vanilla
2 teaspoons almond extract
⅓ cup bourbon
½ cup chopped pecans

Cream butter and two cups sugar until light and fluffy. Add egg yolks one at a time. Beat thoroughly after each addition. Add alternately the flour with flavoring and bourbon in thirds, beating until smooth after each addition.

149

Beat egg whites until stiff but not dry. Beat remaining sugar into egg whites gradually. Fold egg yolk mixture into meringue gently.

Sprinkle pecans in bottom of a well buttered 10-inch tube pan, or blend into the batter.

Carefully turn batter into the pan. Bake at 350 degrees for 1½ hours. Bake full time. Let cool in pan.

S. BARRY LIPIN

Head of U.S. Auto Leasing, supporter of projects to aid the deaf.

Rachel's Strawberries Zabaglione

Per Serving:
5 large strawberries
½ shot glass Grand Marnier

½ shot glass Triple Sec
½ tablespoon sugar

Remove stems, wash strawberries. Marinate in Grand Marnier, Triple Sec, sugar. Toss and let stand 20 minutes. Put a little vanilla ice cream in large goblet and place strawberries on top of ice cream.

Sauce:
3 egg yolks
1 shot glass Marsala wine

1 teaspoon sugar

Put all in top of double boiler, beat with electric beater until stiff. Do not let get too hot or eggs will scramble. Pour cream over strawberries and serve immediately.

SHIRLEY SAGE LITT

Stockbroker, patron of the arts.

Brownie Alaska Pie

Pie shell:

½ cup butter
3 ounces chocolate
2 eggs, well beaten

1 teaspoon vanilla
1 cup sugar
½ cup all-purpose flour

Place butter and chocolate in top of double boiler and heat until melted. Cream eggs and sugar and add to the cooled chocolate mixture. Add sifted flour and vanilla. Blend well and pour into two 9-inch pie pans (use one and freeze one). Bake in a 350 degree oven for 25 minutes.

Filling and topping:

1 quart softened vanilla ice cream
¼ cup sugar
1 10-ounce package frozen raspberries,
   thawed

2 teaspoons cornstarch

Fill pie shell with vanilla ice cream. Blend sugar and cornstarch and stir into raspberries. Cook over moderate heat stirring constantly until mixture thickens and is clear. Cool before serving.

DIANE LEGGIE LOHAN

Architect, supporter of the arts.

Great-Grandma Hudson's Molasses Cookies

1 cup molasses
2 rounded teaspoons soda in 6
   tablespoons boiling water
4½ cups flour

1 cup light brown sugar
1 cup vegetable shortening
2 eggs

Mix molasses, water and flour. Add remaining ingredients. Chill, then cut or roll into balls. Put raisin in center. Bake at 350 degrees until golden.

DIRK LOHAN

Prominent architect, art collector.

Great-Grandma Roney's Fruit Salad Dressing

whipped cream
4 tablespoons vinegar
2 tablespoons sugar
2 tablespoons butter

1 beaten egg
kirsch to taste
fresh grapes, dates, oranges, bananas,
   apples

Boil the vinegar, sugar, butter and egg until thick. Refrigerate. Add to beaten, lightly sweetened whipped cream. Blend into cut-up grapes, dates, oranges, bananas, apples. Add kirsch to taste.

DR. JOHN AND ENID LONG

Prominent obstetrician, chef, UNICEF leader. Enid is active in CRIS radio for the blind, myriad charities.

Apple Macaroon

4 or 5 apples
1 cup sugar
½ cup flour
1 teaspoon baking powder
pinch salt

1 egg
1 heaping tablespoon butter
1 teaspoon vanilla
cinnamon

Butter bottom and sides of large shallow cake pan. Line with apples peeled, cored, and sliced thick. Cover apples with ½ cup sugar and plenty of cinnamon. Sift together remaining sugar, flour, baking powder and salt. Add egg, butter and vanilla, mix well. Spread this mixture over apples. Bake at 275 degrees for 45 minutes. Serve with ice cream or cheese.

GEORGE AND LISA LOVE

He was an executive at Marshall Field's. Both are socialites, support the arts.

Orange Pecan Pie

1 cup white corn syrup
1 cup brown sugar
3 eggs
3 tablespoons flour
¼ teaspoon salt
1 teaspoon vanilla

½ stick butter
1 cup pecan pieces
orange rind and pulp of whole orange
   finely chopped in blender
2 tablespoons Grand Marnier or
   Triple Sec

Combine all ingredients and bake in unbaked pie shell at 360 degrees on bottom shelf of oven for 40 to 45 minutes, or until knife blade comes out clean. Serve warm or room temperature.

JAMES LOWRY

Management consultant, socialite, patron of the arts.

Carrot Cake Lowry

Cake:
1½ cups corn oil
2 cups sugar
3 eggs
2 cups flour
½ cup drained crushed pineapple
1 cup chopped walnuts

2 teaspoons cinnamon
2 cups shredded or grated carrots
2 teaspoons vanilla
1 teaspoon salt
2 teaspoons baking soda

Combine all ingredients in a large bowl and mix well. Pour batter into 9 by 13-inch buttered pan. Bake at 350 degrees for 45 minutes to 1 hour.

Cream Cheese Icing:
3 ounces cream cheese
1 stick butter or margarine
1¼ cups confectioners sugar

⅛ cup canned crushed pineapple
¼ cup chopped walnuts

Cream butter, cream cheese and sugar until slightly fluffy. Add pineapple and walnuts. Spread on cake when cool.

153

JORIE LUELOFF

TV personality, writer.

Richard Friedman's Trifle

1 pint half and half
4 egg yolks, beaten
3 teaspoons cornstarch
3 or more tablespoons cream sherry
6 tablespoons sugar
2 tablespoons vanilla

5 small packages frozen strawberries
   and raspberries, thawed
2 Sara Lee pound cakes, cut into 1-inch
   cubes
sweetened whipped cream

Place half and half in top of double boiler. Bring to boil slowly. Remove from fire. Combine with egg yolks, stir until well blended.

Dissolve cornstarch in sherry and add to milk mixture. Add sugar and vanilla. Return to double boiler and stir constantly until mixture thickens. Add sugar and sherry to taste and allow to cool.

Place thawed fruit in bowl, reserving several whole pieces for garnish. Line a deep serving dish with ⅓ of the cake cubes, sprinkle with a little fruit juice and ⅓ of fruit. Pour ⅓ of cool cream sauce over this layer; repeat twice, using all cake, cream and fruit, but leaving most of the juice. Cover and place in refrigerator for at least 24 hours, to allow flavors to blend. To serve, pile whipped cream on top and garnish with fruit.

JEAN PIERRE LUTZ

Maitre d' of Cricket's Restaurant.

White Chocolate Mousse

1 quart heavy cream
3 ounces confectioners sugar
1 cup (8 ounces) egg yolks

1 ounce cocoa butter
5 ounces white chocolate

Melt cocoa butter and chocolate together in double boiler, stirring until liquid. Remove from heat. Whip yolks and 1 ounce sugar together until fluffy; add chocolate mixture and whip until smooth. Whip cream, gradually adding remaining sugar, until soft peaks form. Add ¼ whipped cream to chocolate mixture, stirring until smooth. Then fold chocolate mixture into rest of whipped cream. Chill for 3 hours before serving. To serve, put a few spoonfuls of pureed raspberries or strawberries on each of 12 dessert plates. Mound mousse to top. Serves 12.

JOHN AND MARY MADIGAN

He is the WBBM radio political editor. Both are active in charitable endeavors.

Pralines

24 graham crackers
1 cup butter

1 cup brown sugar
1 cup chopped pecans

Generously grease a jelly-roll pan. Spread graham crackers in jelly roll pan. Melt butter, add brown sugar and bring to a boil. Continue to boil for three minutes. Remove from heat and add pecans. Spread mixture over crackers. Bake in 350 degree oven for about 12 or 13 minutes. Remove, cool, and cut into squares.

JAMES AND MITZI MAGIN

Business and social leaders, both support civic and charitable events.

California Cheesecake

Crust:
9 ounces vanilla wafers, crushed
¼ pound melted butter

¼ cup sugar and 1 teaspoon cinnamon

Mix together and pack in springform pan, keeping out ½ cup mixture for topping.

Filling:
3 eggs, separated
1 cup sugar
½ pint heavy cream

juice and rind of 1 lemon
2 teaspoons vanilla
1 pound cream cheese

Beat yolks and sugar till light and fluffy. Add softened cream cheese, lemon juice and rind and vanilla. Stir till very smooth. Add stiffly beaten cream and mix well. Fold in stiffly beaten egg whites, pour in mold and top with crumbs. Refrigerate, garnish with thin slices of lemon. Serves 8 to 10.

COLLEEN MOORE MAGINOT

Former actress, donor of famous doll house to the Museum of Science and Industry.

Cream Cheese Pie

Crust:

16 zwieback crushed
2 tablespoons sugar

¼ cup melted butter
sprinkle of cinnamon

Mix above together well and press into a pie pan.

Filling:

1½ pounds Philadelphia cream cheese
¾ cup sugar

3 eggs
1 tablespoon vanilla

Mix well. Fill prepared crust not quite to top. Bake 20 minutes in 375 degree oven. Remove from oven and cover with topping.

Topping:

¾ pint sour cream
2 tablespoons sugar

¼ teaspoon vanilla

Mix and spread over top of pie, bake 5 minutes longer in 400 degree oven.

ROBERT AND MARY LOU MAHER

Active Gold Coasters, both support community and cultural needs.

Chocolate Mousse

5 ounces chocolate liqueur
6 ounces semi-sweet chocolate bits
¾ stick butter
4 eggs, separated

1 teaspoon confectioners sugar
3 packages ladyfingers
4 ounces chocolate liqueur

Heat 5 ounces of chocolate liqueur, combine in a blender with semi-sweet chocolate bits. Blend well and add small pieces of softened butter. The mixture becomes quite thick but continue blending well, adding the beaten yolks of the eggs.

Beat whites of eggs in copper bowl until very stiff. A bit of confectioners sugar may be added at this point. Fold chocolate mixture into egg whites very carefully. Sprinkle ladyfingers with 4 ounces chocolate liqueur and stand up around edge of a one-quart souffle bowl. Pour in mixture and chill well.

156

MARC MALNATI

Operator of Malnati Pizza restaurants.

Aunt Gregie's Hot Fudge Sauce

3 1-ounce squares unsweetened
   chocolate
½ cup butter, cut up
1¼ cup confectioners sugar

½ cup cocoa
½ cup sugar
1 cup heavy cream
1 teaspoon vanilla

Mix chocolate and butter in top of double boiler. Add confectioners sugar, sugar and cocoa, stirring occasionally until butter and chocolate are melted and mixture is well mixed. Continue beating with an electric mixer. Beat until chocolate begins to clump and sticks to beaters. Slowly beat in whipping cream until fudge is smooth and creamy. Beat in vanilla.

"Serve warm over anything. Guaranteed to make even lousy ice cream taste good."

LAUREL MANENTI

World-class publicist, head of Communications Group, Inc., socialite.

Mango Bran Mousse

1½ cups lowfat milk
¼ cup water
1 envelope unflavored gelatin
1 large ripe mango, peeled and chopped

2 tablespoons unprocessed bran
1 tablespoon chopped dates
½ teaspoon vanilla extract

Put water in a small saucepan and sprinkle gelatin on top. Allow gelatin to soften. Put on low heat, stirring constantly until gelatin is dissolved. Do not boil. Slowly pour milk in, stirring constantly. Place mixture in refrigerator until jelled. When jelled, combine this jelled mixture and all other ingredients in a blender. Blend on high speed until frothy. Divide into 6 champagne glasses. Chill in refrigerator until set.

STEVEN MANENTI

Top manufacturer's rep of health and beauty aids.

Wheat Germ Waffles

1 cup non-fat milk
2 tablespoons ground dates
4 eggs, separated
1 cup water

2 tablespoons sesame oil
2 cups wholewheat flour
1 cup wheat germ

Combine milk and dates; set aside for 10 minutes. Beat egg whites until dry, set aside. While beating egg yolks with a fork, add milk mixture, water, oil; mix in flour and wheat germ. Fold in egg whites gently. Cook in preheated waffle iron until well browned and crisp. Serve topped with low-cal ice milk. Serves 6.

DEANNA MANNIX

Leader in providing at-home nursing care; active in charitable work.

Deanna's Bananas

2 ripe bananas
1 package low-calorie sweetener

dash cinnamon

Cut bananas into slices and freeze in plastic bag. Put frozen bananas in blender a few at a time, add sweetener and cinnamon and blend until smooth. Serve in attractive sherbet glasses with several slices of fresh bananas on top. Makes 4 servings at approximately 44 calories each.

JERRY AND HELEN MARCO

Importers of fine wines and liquors, community leaders.

Buttercrunch a La Mode

12 tablespoons butter
3 cups brown sugar, firmly packed
6 tablespoons flour
¾ cup water

15 cups crisp cornflakes
ice cream, your favorite choice or
   choices
3 pints red raspberries or other fruit

Melt the butter and stir in the combined sugar and flour. Add water, stirring until blended. Cook over low heat until mixture forms a soft ball when tested in cold water, or to 236 degrees. Pour at once over the cornflakes, mixing well. Spread on large buttered pan and partially cool. Pack at once into a well-oiled one-quart ring mold. Chill in refrigerator. Loosen edges with a knife and turn out onto a chilled serving platter. Fill center with ice cream. Sprinkle fresh berries over the top. Serves 12.

STATE SEN. WILLIAM MAROVITZ

Dynamic 3rd district lawmaker.

Quick Chocolate Mousse

6 ounces semi-sweet chocolate chips
⅓ cup strong, hot coffee
2 eggs

1 tablespoon rum
1 cup heavy cream, whipped

In a food processor fitted with steel blade or in a blender, blend the chocolate chips and hot coffee until chocolate is melted. Add the eggs and the rum and blend until mixture is smooth. In chilled bowl whip the cream until it holds stiff peaks and fold in the chocolate mixture. Put in dessert glasses, chill for at least 30 minutes and garnish with additional whipped cream or grated chocolate if desired. Serves 4 to 6.

KAREN MASON

Dynamite singer with star quality.

Fat Man's Misery

8 ounces Hershey's almond chocolate
8 large marshmallows
¼ cup milk
½ pint heavy cream, whipped

vanilla to taste
16 graham crackers, rolled
¼ cup butter
¼ cup sugar

Put chocolate, marshmallows and milk into double boiler. Melt. Cool (not too cold). Fold in whipped cream and a little vanilla. Mix together by hand the graham crackers, butter and sugar. Put half of the crumb mixture in the bottom of refrigerator tray and pat out. Add filling, then remaining cracker mixture on top. Freeze. Serves 6 to 8.

DIANE MAYNE

Lawyer, civic leader, socialite.

One Pot Cheesecake

1 pound small curd creamed cottage
    cheese
4 eggs
1 pound Philadelphia cream cheese
1½ cups sugar
3 tablespoons corn starch

dash salt
juice of ½ lemon (or concentrate)
1 teaspoon vanilla
¼ pound melted butter
1 pint sour cream

Blend well with electric mixer or food processor all ingredients except sour cream. When well blended, fold in sour cream by hand. Pour mixture into a greased springform or lasagna pan. Bake at 325 degrees until nicely brown on top. Minimum time 1 hour. May take much longer. Turn oven off and let stand 2 hours with oven door closed. Serve chilled or warm, with or without fruit topping.

"I prefer it chilled with a fruit topping."

BROOKS AND HOPE MC CORMICK

Society leaders, supporter of the arts, the Lincoln Park Zoo, the Historical Society, etc., etc.

Pumpkin Pie Josephine Woolridge

Filling:

1 16-ounce can pumpkin
1 cup sugar
1 teaspoon each ginger, cinnamon,
   nutmeg

¼ teaspoon salt
1 tablespoon unflavored gelatin
¼ cup cold water
4 eggs, separated

In top of double boiler, pour in can of pumpkin. Add sugar, ginger, cinnamon, nutmeg and salt. Mix together well and heat at medium temperature.

In the meantime, dissolve gelatin in cold water. Set aside. Separate eggs, putting the whites in a large mixing bowl and the egg yolks in a small mixing bowl. Beat yolks until well dissolved. Set aside. When pumpkin mixture is hot, add gelatin. Mix well in double boiler. Stir until heated. Pour some pumpkin into beaten egg yolks and beat until well mixed, then return to remaining pumpkin mixture still in double boiler. Mix together and remove from heat. Pour into bowl and refrigerate until it begins to jell.

Crust:

2 cups gingersnap crumbs   ½ cup melted butter

Finely crush gingersnap crumbs, add melted butter. Mix well. Press into 10-inch pie plate. Bake until crust is set, about 5 minutes in 350 degree oven. Remove and cool. When pumpkin has jelled, beat egg whites until stiff peaks have formed. Beat into pumpkin mixture at medium speed. Turn into crust and chill.

Topping:

½ pint heavy cream   ½ cup toasted pecans

Whip cream and spread on top of pie. Refrigerate. Optional: before serving, top with toasted pecans.

Mincemeat sauce:

2 cups mincemeat   2 tablespoons brandy

Mix mincemeat in heavy saucepan with brandy. Heat slowly. Serve hot with pie if desired.

161

DOLPHY AND NORA MC LAUGHLIN

Consulate of Jamaica representatives in Chicago. Dolphy is also an attorney.

Jamaican Corn Pudding

3 cups water
1 cup yellow corn meal
1 cup brown sugar
1 teaspoon vanilla
½ teaspoon grated nutmeg

½ teaspoon salt
¾ cup seedless raisins
1 cup unsweetened coconut milk or 1
    12-ounce can evaporated milk
2 tablespoons butter or margarine

Heat water in saucepan. Add corn meal, sugar, vanilla, nutmeg, and salt. Boil over medium heat, stirring constantly until a thick syrupy consistency is reached. Pour mixture into greased 9 inch by 3 inch baking pan and stir in raisins, coconut milk or evaporated milk and butter or margarine. Bake in moderate oven, 350 degrees, for 45 minutes. Test for doneness as you would a cake.

DAVID MEITUS

Manufacturer, patron of the arts, philanthropist.

Linzertorte Gerry Westphal

1½ cups all-purpose flour
⅛ teaspoon ground cloves
¼ teaspoon cinnamon
1 cup finely ground unblanched
    almonds
½ cup sugar
1 teaspoon grated lemon peel
2 hard-cooked egg yolks, mashed

1 cup unsalted butter (2 quarter-pound
    sticks), softened
2 raw egg yolks, lightly beaten
1 teaspoon vanilla extract
1½ cups thick raspberry jam
1 whole egg, lightly beaten
2 tablespoons light cream
confectioners sugar

Sift the flour, cloves and cinnamon together into a deep mixing bowl, then add the almonds, sugar, lemon peel and mashed egg yolks. With a wooden spoon, beat in the butter, raw egg yolks and vanilla extract. Continue to beat until the mixture is smooth and doughy. Form the dough into a ball, wrap it in waxed paper or plastic wrap, and refrigerate it for at least 1 hour, or until it is firm. Remove about ¾ of the dough from the wrapping and return the rest to the refrigerator.

With a paper towel or pastry brush, lightly butter a round 9 by 1- or 9 by 1½-inch false-bottomed cake pan. Add the dough (if it is too firm, let it soften a bit) and, with your fingers, press and push it out so that it covers the bottom and sides of the pan, making a shell about ¼ inch thick. Spoon in the raspberry jam and spread it evenly over the bottom of the shell with a spatula. On a floured surface with a floured rolling pin, roll out the rest of the dough into a 6 by 9-inch rectangle ¼ inch thick.

With a pastry cutter or sharp knife, cut the dough into strips ½ inch wide, 2 of them 9 inches long and the rest 8 inches long. Lay one of the 9-inch strips across the center of the jam and flank that strip on each side with one of the 8-inch strips placed halfway between the center and sides of the pan. Rotate the pan about ¼ of the way to your left and repeat the pattern with the other 3 strips, so that they create X's with the first 3 in a latticelike effect.

Run a sharp knife around the top of the pan to loosen the part of the bottom dough that extends above the strips. Press this down with your fingers into a border about ¼ inch thick. Lightly beat the whole egg with the cream and, with a pastry brush, coat all the exposed pastry. Refrigerate for ½ hour.

Meanwhile, preheat the oven to 350 degrees.

Bake the torte in the middle of the oven for 45 to 50 minutes, or until is is lightly browned. Set the pan on a large jar or coffee can and slip down the outside rim. Let the torte cool for 5 minutes on the bottom of the pan, then sprinkle it with confectioners sugar. Linzertorte should cool to room temperature before being served.

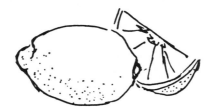

RICHARD MELMAN

President and founder of Lettuce Entertain You Enterprises, he has created a dozen theme eateries plus Ambria, a world-class fine-dining experience.

Martha's Carrot Pudding

10 medium carrots (about 1¼ pounds),
  peeled
1¼ cups sugar
¾ cup unsalted butter
1¼ cups flour
1 teaspoon baking powder
1 teaspoon baking soda
2 teaspoons cinnamon

1 teaspoon ground ginger
1 large pinch grated nutmeg
2 large eggs
1½ cups milk
1 cup heavy cream
½ cup dark raisins, if desired
1 teaspoon vanilla

Preheat oven to 350 degrees. Shred carrots with shredding disc of a food processor. Combine shredded carrots with ½ cup of the sugar and 4 tablespoons of the butter in a heavy 2-quart saucepan. Place over low heat and simmer, tightly covered, 30 to 40 minutes or until the carrot shreds are very soft. If all the moisture evaporates, add 1 or 2 tablespoons water to prevent scorching. Measure and set aside 2 cups of the cooked carrot mixture.

Melt the remaining ½ cup butter and set aside. In a 3-quart bowl, sift together the dry ingredients, including the remaining sugar. In a medium bowl beat the eggs slightly; beat in the milk and cream; stir into the dry ingredients. Add the melted butter, raisins, vanilla and 2 cups of cooked carrots. Mix well.

Pour into a buttered 2-quart oven-proof bundt pan and bake 1 hour and 15 minutes or until pudding feels slightly springy to the touch. Serve warm or at room temperature with whipped cream.

DAVID AND SHARON MELTZER

Head of Evans, the country's largest furrier, David is a business genius. Sharon, a former model, shares his sporting, cultural pursuits.

Individual Pear Souffles

3 very ripe pears
½ teaspoon pear liqueur
4 tablespoons sugar or equivalent in
   sugar substitute

2 egg yolks
7 egg whites
2 tablespoons softened butter

For the syrup:
2½ cups water
5 tablespoons sugar or equivalent in
   sugar substitute

1 vanilla bean, cut in half lengthwise

Put the ingredients for the syrup in a saucepan and bring to a boil. Peel the pears with a potato-peeler, quarter and core them, then poach them in the syrup for fifteen minutes.

Drain pears and blend them in a food processor with sweetener and pear liqueur.

Pour the mixture into a bowl and add the egg yolks. Mix. Brush insides of 8 small souffle dishes (3½" × 1½") with softened butter. Preheat oven to 425 degrees.

Beat the egg whites to soft peaks. Mix one quarter into the pear puree. Gradually add the rest of the egg whites, folding them in carefully with a spatula.

Fill souffle dishes right up to the top with the mixture. Level the surface with the back of a knife. Push the mixture away from the edges of each dish with your thumb to help the souffles to rise. Cook for about eight minutes in the oven. Serve the minute they are removed from the oven. Serves 8.

HERBERT AND AUDRE MENDEL

He is in metal processing. She is a former ballerina, active in the arts.

Sorbet by Herbert

(Best results are obtained in a Simac Gelataio Ice Cream Maker, large model.)

6 ounces frozen orange juice
   concentrate
6 ounce can any fruit juice, not
   concentrated
1 lemon, juice and rind
2 bananas, cut-up

6 ounces Cointreau, Grand Marnier
   or cognac
½ cup currants
½ cup white grapes
2 peaches, cut-up
2 plums, cut-up

Mix a six-ounce can of frozen orange juice according to instructions. Add a six-ounce can of any fruit juice, add liqueur and the juice of one lemon. Place this blend in the machine. Add bananas and cut-up lemon rind, chopped to ⅛ inch pieces. Add cut-up peaches, plums; whole grapes and currants. Ingredients should fill Gelataio within ½ inch of top. Turn on machine, and your dessert will be ready to serve in 35 to 40 minutes.

RAY MEYER

Legendary coach of the De Paul basketball team.

Blueberry Fluff

1 pint fresh blueberries
3 cups miniature marshmallows
1 cup granulated sugar
2 cups diced apples

½ cup green grapes
½ cup chopped walnuts
2½ pints heavy cream

Mix blueberries, marshmallows and sugar in large bowl. Cover with foil. Refrigerate overnight. Next day add apples, grapes and walnuts. Whip cream. Fold into mixture. Serve in parfait glasses. Serves 10 to 12.

HOWDEE AND LUCIA PERRIGO MEYERS

Creators of movie travelogues. Lucia was publicist for the Pump Room in its heyday.

Kahlua Mousse

1 dozen custard cups
½ cup sugar
½ cup water
1 small package chocolate chips
pinch salt

2 eggs
2 tablespoons Kahlua
2 tablespoons cold coffee
1½ cups heavy cream, whipped

Combine sugar with water in a saucepan and heat until the sugar dissolves. Put chocolate chips, eggs, and salt in blender, then pour sugar and water mixture in while blending until smooth. Add Kahlua and coffee. Fold in whipped cream, and pour into custard cups and chill several hours.

WILLIAM AND DOROTHY MEYERS

Civic leaders, patrons of the arts.

Hot Fudge Sauce Rose Butchness

1 8-ounce package bittersweet chocolate
1 pound marshmallows
½ stick butter
½ cup brown sugar

¼ cup perked coffee
½ cup milk
¼ cup brandy, if desired

Melt chocolate and butter in top of double boiler. Add sugar, coffee, milk. Stir. When all melted, add marshmallows. Stir to combine as marshmallows melt. Add brandy if desired. Serve over cake or ice cream. The Meyers love it over Haagen Dazs Boysenberry. (If sauce gets too thick upon standing, add more coffee to thin.)

MARILYN MIGLIN

Head of a national cosmetics empire that stars Pheromone perfume.

Sugar-Coated Nuts

3½ cups pecan halves
1 cup sugar
pinch salt

2 beaten egg whites
1 stick margarine

Beat egg whites stiff. Fold in sugar and salt. Melt margarine in pan in oven. Fold nuts in egg whites and put in pan with margarine. Cook 30 minutes in 325 degree oven. Stir every 10 minutes to see that nuts are completely coated.

(For spiced nuts, add 1 to 2 teaspoons allspice. For brandied nuts, add 2 tablespoons brandy or whiskey into either margarine or egg whites).

PHILLIP MILLER

Chairman and CEO of Marshall Field and Co.

Strawberries Romanoff

1 quart fresh strawberries
¼ cup Cointreau or Triple Sec
¼ cup orange juice

½ pint heavy cream
2 tablespoons confectioners sugar
grated orange peel for garnish

Hull, clean and marinate strawberries for two hours in mixture of liqueur and orange juice, stirring occasionally. Whip cream, adding confectioners sugar. Serve in sherbet glasses. Spoon whipped cream on strawberries and garnish with grated orange peel. Serves 6.

HELEN AND RALPH MILLS JR.

Both are socialites, active in cultural circles.

Orange Jello with Whipped Cream and Bits of Chocolate

2 tablespoons unflavored gelatin
    softened in one fourth cup cold water
    for five minutes
1 cup cold water
1 cup boiling water
¾ cup sugar
dash salt

¼ cup lemon juice
1½ cups orange juice
1 tablespoon grated orange peel
1 tablespoon Cointreau
whipped cream for garnish
Bitter chocolate curls for garnish

Soften gelatin in cold water. Add boiling water after gelatin is dissolved. Stir until melted. Add salt, sugar, lemon juice, orange juice, grated orange, Cointreau, and cup of cold water. Mix all together. When cool pour in mold and put in refrigerator. Serve topped with whipped cream and curls of bitter chocolate.

THOMAS MINER

Lawyer, international business consultant, founder and head of Mid-America Committee.

Lucyna's Chocolate Decadence

1 8-inch springform pan or cake pan
    lined with parchment or buttered and
    floured
1 pound chocolate (sweet dark, semi-
    sweet or bittersweet)
5 ounces sweet butter

4 eggs
1 tablespoon sugar
1 tablespoon flour
raspberry puree
½ cup heavy cream, whipped softly

In top of double boiler over simmering water melt chocolate with butter; remove from heat. Place eggs in heat-proof mixing bowl with sugar over (not in) simmering water; with wire whip whisk till mixture begins to thicken. When lukewarm, mixture is done. Remove from heat. (If it begins to curdle, whisk vigorously and lower heat.) Whip egg mixture with mixer till light and fluffy, like foamy, softly whipped cream. Fold in flour. Fold ¼ egg mixture into chocolate, then fold all chocolate into egg mixture. Pour into pan and bake not more than 25 minutes at 425 degrees. (415 degrees if electric oven). Cool. Cover

169

with plastic wrap. Freeze. To unmold, dip bottom of pan in warm water 20 to 30 seconds; invert, tap on bottom.

To serve, spoon 2 to 3 tablespoons raspberry puree onto plates; top with 1½-inch sliver of chocolate. Top with whipped cream.

HARRY MINTZ

World-famous artist.

Rosabelle's Apple Cake

½ stick butter
1 cup sugar
1 cup flour
1 teaspoon baking powder

2 eggs
4-5 apples, cored and quartered. Don't forget to peel apples.

In a small bowl, cream butter and sugar. Add eggs, one at a time. Beat until nice and foamy. Mix flour and baking powder and fold in.

Grease springform pan with butter. Spoon batter into pan. Place apples thickly on top. Apples are higher when baked, as dough rises to height of apples. Bake at 350 degrees for 1½ hours. Cool and serve with cream or ice cream.

MARJORIE MITCHELL

Founder of Mary Lawrence JCB, longtime charity leader, philanthropist, civic leader.

Marjorie's Angel Cookies

2 sticks margarine or butter
⅓ cup sugar
1 teaspoon cold water

2 cups all-purpose flour
2 teaspoons vanilla

Cream together the butter and sugar in a large bowl. Add water. Add flour and vanilla and mix well. Make balls the size of large walnuts. Place on buttered cookie sheet and bake in a 300 degree oven until lightly browned; about 40 minutes. Remove from oven and sprinkle with powdered sugar.

DR. MARY ANN AND JOHN MOLLOY

She's a prominent doctor; he is in the liquor business. Both support the arts, charitable, health causes.

Molloys' Favorite Fudge

4½ cups sugar (2 pound box)
½ pound butter
1 12-ounce can evaporated milk
1 jar marshmallow fluff

3 6-ounce packages Nestle's chocolate chips
1 teaspoon vanilla
1 cup walnuts if desired

In a large saucepan, bring sugar, butter and milk to a rolling boil over medium heat, stirring continually for 10 minutes. Remove from heat and add marshmallow, chocolate chips. Beat until smooth. Add vanilla, add walnuts if desired. Pour into a buttered 9 by 13-inch pan. Cool at least 4 hours before cutting.

"This recipe makes about 5 pounds of candy and is fool-proof!"

PETER MORGAN

Owner-chef of Colombo's Restaurant.

Caramel Custard

Custard:
1 quart milk
6 eggs

9 ounces white sugar
1 tablespoon pure vanilla extract

Caramel:
8 ounces white sugar

4 ounces water

Place 8 ounces sugar and 4 ounces water in saucepan. Cook until amber brown for about 20 minutes. Pour into oven-proof custard cups, making sure to distribute evenly. Let cool. Heat milk. Add to eggs. Add remaining sugar and vanilla. Beat with a wire whisk to blend well. Pour into cooled mixture in custard cups. Place cups into a shallow pan with water coming up to ¾ along side of cups. Bake 45 minutes at 400 degrees. When done, remove from oven, take out of water bath. Let cool for 10 minutes. Refrigerate overnight. To remove from cup gently but firmly press the top of caramel around edges. Put plate on top, invert and gently shake onto individual serving plate. Serves 8.

ARNIE MORTON

Veteran restaurateur, owner of Arnie's, Zorine's, Morton's. Innovator, expert on tourism, marketing.

Zorine's Walnut Pie

3 eggs
½ cup firmly packed brown sugar
1 cup light corn syrup
¼ cup butter, melted
1 teaspoon cinnamon

¼ teaspoon salt
1 teaspoon vanilla
1 cup walnuts (chips or halves)
9-inch unbaked pastry shell

Beat eggs, stir in brown sugar, corn syrup, melted butter, cinnamon, salt and vanilla. Gently stir in nuts and pour mixture into an unbaked pastry shell. Bake on lowest oven shelf at 375 degrees for 50 minutes, or until filling jiggles only lightly when dish is shaken. Cool on a wire rack at least 2 hours before cutting. Pie is best when made one day ahead. Keep refrigerated.

MOLLY MULLADY

Socialite, lady farmer, horse-breeder. Active in cultural, charitable endeavors.

Powdered Lemon Squares

Crust:
½ cup butter
¼ cup confectioners sugar

1 cup sifted flour
2 to 3 tablespoons water

Mix well and press into 9-inch square pan. Bake at 350 degrees for 15 minutes. Cool.

Filling:
1 cup granulated sugar
2 eggs, slightly beaten
2 tablespoons flour

3 tablespoons lemon juice
½ teaspoon baking powder

Combine and pour over above mixture. Bake at 350 degrees for 25 minutes. While still warm sprinkle with confectioners sugar. Yields 3 dozen squares.

JOSEPH AND "BOOTSIE" NATHAN

He is premium advertising expert. She is active with arts and charitable groups.

Chocolate Macaroon Icebox Cake

½ pound semi-sweet chocolate
4 tablespoons water
4 eggs, separated
1 cup confectioners sugar

1 teaspoon vanilla
pinch salt
macaroons (½ to ¾ pound)

Melt chocolate with water in double boiler. Add well-beaten egg yolks and sugar and cook slowly until smooth, stirring constantly. Cool, add vanilla, and fold in lightly the stiffly beaten whites.

Line a springform pan with macaroons; fill with chocolate mixture and cover top with macaroons. Let stand several hours in refrigerator. Serve, garnished with whipped cream.

DANNY NEWMAN

Lyric Opera publicist and author of *Subscribe Now.*

Exotic Flambed Fruits

½ cup orange marmalade
½ cup apricot preserves
2 tablespoons grated lemon rind
1½ cups brown sugar
½ cup brandy
¼ cup lemon juice

1 can peaches
1 can pears
1 can pineapple chunks
2 bananas
1½ teaspoons cinnamon

Combine marmalade, preserves, lemon rind and lemon juice. Simmer for 10 minutes, cool. Combine sugar and cinnamon. Drain and dry canned fruits. Dip in marmalade mixture and coat with sugar mixture. Arrange in shallow casserole, bake at 400 degrees for 15 minutes. Before serving, warm brandy, ignite, pour over fruit and bring flaming dish to table.

MURIEL NEWMAN

Art collector, patron of the arts.

Mangoes for Reflective Moments

**4 large very ripe mangoes, peeled and
sliced**
2 tablespoons lime juice
¼ cup rose-petal syrup

¾ cup heavy cream, whipped, or
1 cup creme fraiche
¼ cup fresh rose petals
edible silver leaf

Gently mix mango slices with lime juice in a bowl and then arrange them on a beautiful serving plate. Gently fold 1 tablespoon of rose-petal syrup into whipped cream or creme fraiche and drizzle remainder over mangoes. Spoon cream over mangoes. Decorate with the rose petals and, if desired, bits of the edible silver leaf. Serves 4.

Rose-petal syrup is available in shops specializing in Near Eastern delicacies. Edible silver leaf may be found in shops specializing in Indian delicacies.

This recipe comes from California artist Penelope Fried.

RALPH AND PAT NEWMAN

He is an expert on Lincolniana, historical memorabilia, Civil War, etc. Both are active on the cultural scene here, in Washington and Springfield.

Shaker Lemon Pie

2 large lemons, seeds removed
4 eggs, well beaten

2 cups sugar
dough for 2-crust pie

Slice lemons as thin as paper, rind and all. Combine with sugar; mix well. Let stand 2 hours or longer, preferably blending occasionally. Add beaten eggs to lemon mixture; mix well. Turn into nine-inch pie shell, arranging lemon slices evenly. Cover with top crust. Cut several slits near center. Bake at 450 degrees for 15 minutes. Reduce heat to 375 degrees and bake for about 20 minutes or until silver knife inserted near edge of pie comes out clean. Cool before serving.

NICK NICKOLAS

Veteran restaurateur, owner of Nick's Fishmarket.

Creme Anglaise over Papaya and Strawberries

1 cup half and half
2 tablespoons sugar
⅛ teaspoon vanilla extract

2 egg yolks
3 ripe papayas, halved and seeded
fresh strawberries, washed and hulled

Combine half and half, 1 tablespoon sugar and the vanilla in a saucepan. Bring just to a boil over medium heat. In a mixing bowl, whisk together yolks and remaining sugar until they are pale yellow in color. Add ¼ cup of the half and half mixture to the yolk/vanilla mixture and blend well. Then add this combination to the saucepan mixture. Cook, stirring vigorously, until the mixture thickens slightly. Be careful not to boil or yolks will set and create lumps. Refrigerate well before serving.

To serve, fill hollow of each papaya half with 1 tablespoon of creme Anglaise, add strawberries, then dribble 2 more tablespoons of sauce over the top. Serves 6.

ALD. MARTIN OBERMAN

Lawyer and veteran member of the City Council.

Bonnie's Raspberry Crisp

1 quart fresh raspberries
1 tablespoon lemon juice
¼ teaspoon cinnamon
1 cup flour

1 cup sugar
½ cup butter
1 quart ice cream, or
1 cup whipped cream

Place washed fresh berries in a 1½-quart casserole. Add lemon juice and sprinkle with cinnamon. Sift flour and sugar together; chop butter until crumbly. Spread over the berries. Bake at 375 degrees for 45 minutes. Serve with ice cream or whipped cream. Serves 6.

JAMES AND ELLEN O'CONNOR

Head of Commonwealth Edison, James and his wife are active in charitable and cultural endeavors.

Ellen's Snow Cap Chocolate

3 egg whites, beaten to soft peaks
1 teaspoon vanilla
1 teaspoon baking powder
¾ cup sugar
1 4-ounce bar sweet chocolate

1 cup Ritz cracker crumbs
½ cup chopped pecans
1 cup heavy cream
2 tablespoons sugar
1 teaspoon vanilla

Combine ¾ cup sugar and baking powder and add to beaten egg whites. Beat until stiff. Add chocolate, vanilla, cracker crumbs and pecans, reserving 2 tablespoons chocolate for garnish. Blend thoroughly. Put in 9-inch greased pie pan. Bake at 350 degrees for 25 minutes. Cool. Whip cream with sugar and vanilla. Spread over meringue. Sprinkle chopped chocolate on top. Chill before serving.

DAVID AND SUE OFNER

He is president of Foote, Cone & Belding Advertising Midwest and both are active in theatrical development.

Chocolate Marshmallow Souffle

Souffle:
2 tablespoons butter or margarine
3 tablespoons all-purpose flour
¼ teaspoon salt
1 cup milk
¼ cup sugar
3 1-ounce squares unsweetened
   chocolate, grated

32 marshmallows
3 egg yolks, beaten
1 teaspoon vanilla
3 egg whites, stiffly beaten

176

Melt butter or margarine in a saucepan; blend in flour and salt. Add milk and cook over low heat, stirring constantly, until thickened and smooth. Add sugar, chocolate, and marshmallows; stir until chocolate and marshmallows are melted. Remove from heat. Slowly add egg yolks and vanilla to chocolate-marshmallow mixture and mix well; cool. Fold egg whites into cooled chocolate mixture. Turn into 1½-quart casserole and place in pan of hot water. Bake in moderate oven (350 degrees) for 1 hour or until set. Serve warm or chilled, with cream or custard sauce.

Sauce:

1 3¼-ounce package instant vanilla
  pudding mix
1 cup milk

½ teaspoon vanilla
1 cup heavy cream, whipped
dash salt

Make instant pudding according to package directions, using only one cup of milk. Add vanilla and salt to beaten cream and fold into the custard just as it begins to thicken.

MRS. CHRISTOPHER OGDEN

Socialite, civic leader.

Cheesecake with Cherries Ogden

Fill a 9-inch pie dish with graham cracker crust. Cook in oven 7 minutes at 350 degrees and allow to cool.

Raise oven temperature to 375 degrees.

Filling:

2 eggs
¾ pound cream cheese
½ cup sugar
1 teaspoon lemon juice

1½ cups sour cream
2 tablespoons sugar
½ teaspoon vanilla
⅛ teaspoon salt

Beat well the eggs, cream cheese, sugar, and lemon juice. Pour into pie shell and bake at 350 degrees about 20 minutes. Remove from oven and cool.

Mix sour cream, sugar, vanilla, salt and pour over the cooled pie.

Bake in the oven for about 5 minutes. Let cool somewhat before adding cherry topping.

Cherry Topping:

1 can pitted cherries
1 tablespoon cornstarch

1 tablespoon cherry juice
1 teaspoon lemon juice

Take can of pitted cherries and drain juice into a saucepan. Mix cornstarch with 1 tablespoon juice and add to saucepan. Over medium heat begin to stir. Also add a teaspoon of lemon juice. Arrange the cherries on the top of the pie and pour the thickened juice over the cherries. Allow to cool in the refrigerator at least two hours before serving.

177

CYNTHIA AND CHARLES OLSON III

She is a former actress, he is an insurance executive. Both are socially prominent.

Magic Macaroons

1 14-ounce package shredded coconut
1 13-ounce can sweetened condensed
  milk

1 teaspoon vanilla

Mix ingredients. Place on greased cookie sheet. Bake until browned, 10 to 12 minutes. Remove quickly, place on waxed paper. Cool.

PATRICK AND HELEN O'MALLEY

He is Canteen Corp. chairman emeritus with a long list of civic, educational and charitable works. Both are active socially.

Devil's Food Cake

Cake:
butter size of walnut
1 cup sugar
1 egg
1 cup sour cream

1 teaspoon baking soda
1¼ cups flour
1 teaspoon vanilla
2 squares chocolate, melted

Cream butter and sugar, add beaten egg and melted chocolate. Then add flour, which has been sifted with baking soda, alternately with cream. Add vanilla. Bake in layer cake pans to 350 degrees for 20-25 minutes.

Chocolate Frosting:
3 squares chocolate
1 14-ounce can sweetened condensed
  milk

2 tablespoons cold water

Melt chocolate in double boiler, add milk, and cool until thick. Remove from fire, add 2 tablespoons cold water and beat. Spread when cool.

THOMAS AND VERONICA O'NEILL

He is head of Lester B. Knight and both are active socially and in local charities.

Creme Brulee

3 cups heavy cream
6 tablespoons sugar
6 egg yolks

2 teaspoons vanilla extract
½ cup light brown sugar

Preheat oven to slow 300 degrees. Heat cream over boiling water in top of double boiler. When cream is hot but not boiling stir in sugar. Beat egg yolks until very light in color and pour hot cream mixture into them gradually, stirring vigorously. Stir in vanilla and strain mixture into a baking dish.

Place dish in a pan containing 1 inch of hot water and bake until a knife inserted in the center comes out clean, or 35 minutes. Do not overbake; custard will continue to cook from retained heat when it is removed from the oven. Chill thoroughly. Before serving, cover surface with brown sugar. Set dish on a bed of cracked ice and put creme under the broiler until sugar is melted. (Be very careful not to let it burn). Watch it constantly. It only takes 2 or 3 minutes. Serve immediately or chill again and serve cold. Serves 6 to 8.

MARY OPPENHEIM

Lawyer, active in charities, civic leader.

Sour Cream Apple Pie

Filling:

4-5 cups peeled, sliced apples
1 tablespoon lemon juice
2 tablespoons flour
¾ cup sugar
2 eggs, slightly beaten

1 cup sour cream, skinny sour cream or
    yogurt
½ teaspoon vanilla
¼ teaspoon salt
1 9-inch unbaked pie shell

Pre-heat oven to 350 degrees. Toss sliced apples with lemon juice, set aside. Mix flour and sugar in bowl. Add eggs, sour cream, vanilla and salt and stir until smooth. Add apples and pour in prepared (store bought) pie shell. Bake 30 minutes.

Topping:

⅓ cup sugar
⅓ cup chopped almonds

¼ cup butter

In interim, mix sugar, almonds and cut in butter to resemble coarse crumbs. Take pie out of oven, spoon topping over pie and bake another 15-18 minutes until golden brown on top. Serve hot or cold.

Blueberries, cherries, rhubarb, strawberries, etc., can be substituted for apples. You can modify sugar to taste and cut calories.

RUTH PAGE

Legendary ballerina, creator of ballets, teacher, author.

Ruth's Favorite Cookies

1 cup butter or margarine
1½ cups confectioners sugar
1½ cups flour

1 teaspoon vanilla
½ cup nuts
raspberry jam

Whip all but raspberry jam together. Roll dough into small balls. Flatten. Bake in oven at 375 degrees until golden, about 8 to 10 minutes. Put two together with raspberry jam in between.

MARIA TALLCHIEF PASCHEN

Legendary ballerina, founder and artistic director, Chicago City Ballet.

Date Loaf Cake

2 sticks butter
2 cups sugar
1 teaspoon cinnamon
1 teaspoon nutmeg
1 teaspoon cloves
2 cups sifted flour

1 teaspoon soda
1 teaspoon salt
2 cups water
1 cup cut-up dates
1 cup chopped pecans

Sift soda and salt with flour. Boil water and dates 3 minutes. Add sugar and butter, let cool. When lukewarm add rest gradually. Pour into buttered and floured 9 by 13-inch pyrex dish. Bake ½ hour in preheated 350 degree oven.

ROSLYN CHING PASTOR

Authority on jade, precious gems, pearls; world traveler.

Almond Float

2 envelopes unflavored gelatin
½ cup cold water
1½ cups boiling water
8 tablespoons sugar

1 pinch salt
2 cups milk
1 teaspoon almond extract

Melt gelatin in cold water. Add salt, sugar, boiling water. Add milk and almond extract. Put in ice cube tray in refrigerator. After it is firm, cut in small cubes. Serve with canned fruit salad or orange segments if desired.

BEVERLY AND DOROTHY PATTISHALL

He is a lawyer, both are active in charitable and social endeavors.

Schaum Torte

1 cup sugar
4 egg whites, at room temperature
1 teaspoon vinegar

1 teaspoon vanilla
½ pint heavy cream, whipped
1 quart strawberries

Using an 8-inch round layer pan as a pattern, cut 2 8-inch circles from smooth brown paper and place on baking sheet. Preheat oven for 10 minutes at 300 degrees. Sift sugar, beat egg whites and add sugar in five portions, beating well each time. Beat in vinegar and vanilla. Spoon meringue on circles, keeping mixture ¼ inch from edge. Spread to uniform thickness. Keep oven door open slightly and bake 30 minutes.

Turn off oven and let meringue dry out in oven for 30 minutes. Remove from oven and carefully remove from paper. Place one layer on serving plate, spread with whipped cream, then with strawberries. Top with second torte and spread with remaining cream. Serve at once. Serves 8.

(Although meringues may be made day ahead, strawberries and cream should not be added until shortly before serving.)

STANLEY PAUL

Orchestra leader, composer.

Frozen Peach Mousse

2 packages frozen peaches, partially thawed
1 tablespoon peach brandy
4 eggs

½ cup granulated sugar
1 envelope unflavored gelatin, dissolved
1 cup heavy cream. whipped

Puree the peaches and brandy in a blender and put aside. Whip the eggs and sugar in an electric mixer bowl until they are light and fluffy and tripled in bulk. Then add the dissolved gelatin to eggs and combine well. Gently fold in the peach puree and whipped cream. Put into an oiled 2-quart mold or bowl and put in freezer for 2 hours. Serves 6.

BOB PAYTON

Chicagoan who owns Chicago Pizza Pie Factory restaurants in London, Paris, Barcelona, and the Chicago Rib Shack in London.

Banana Cheesecake

1 pound bananas, sliced thin (they should weigh one pound with the skins on, when you buy them)
¾ to 1 ounce cornstarch
juice of ½ lemon
1 drop vanilla
pinch salt

¾ ounce gelatin powder
4 ounces butter
2 pounds, 2 ounces cream cheese
8 ounces granulated sugar
4 eggs, whisked
2 pounds, 2 ounces sour cream
6 ounces graham cracker crumbs

Put the sliced bananas, cornstarch, lemon juice, vanilla and salt into a blender and mix to a rich, creamy consistency. Put the gelatin powder in a little cold water, and melt it by heating it in a double boiler over hot water. Melt the butter over hot water in another double boiler. Add cheese and sugar to the banana mixture. Cream the mixture and add the whisked eggs. Add the gelatin to the butter. Then add the butter and gelatin to the banana mixture. Add sour cream to the banana mixture and mix together. Line a cake pan with the graham cracker crumbs. Pour in the cheese cake mixture. Bake the cake in an oven preheated to 350 degrees for 45 minutes to one hour.

This recipe is a specialty of the Chicago Rib Shack, London.

ROBERT PEITSCHER

Advertising and promotional expert.

Gilotti A La Blue

2 quarts fresh heavy cream
3 pints fresh blueberries

1 cup clover honey

Mash and juice blueberries. Add all ingredients into sorbet machine and produce Gilotti. Serve in chilled crystal bowl and top with whole berries. Serves 10 to 16.

VERNON AND FRAN PELLOUCHOUD

He is an insurance tycoon. Both are active with charitable and social affairs.

Creme De Cacao Souffle

3 tablespoons butter
4 tablespoons flour
1 cup milk
4 eggs, separated

¼ cup sugar
1 extra egg white
¼ cup creme de cacao

Butter a 1-quart souffle dish on the bottom only. Melt the butter, stir in the flour, and cook for a minute or two. Add the milk and stir over low heat until the sauce is thick and smooth. Beat the egg yolks until thick and lemon-colored. Beat in the sugar. Stir in the hot mixture slowly, beating as you add. Beat the egg whites until stiff but not dry. Fold into the egg-yolk mixture. Add the creme de cacao and pour into the souffle dish. Bake in a 375 degree oven for 45 to 55 minutes, or until it is done. Test with a knife. Serve immediately with chocolate sauce if desired.

FRANK PENNING

Comedian and Gold Coast Court Jester.

Chocolate Mousse

1 12-ounce package semi-sweet
   chocolate pieces
½ cup sugar
3 eggs

1 cup hot milk
2 to 4 tablespoons brandy
whipped cream

In blender, combine chocolate pieces, sugar and eggs. Pour in hot milk and brandy; blend on medium speed until mixture is smooth. Pour into demitasse cups and chill in refrigerator for 1 hour. Garnish with whipped cream. Keep under refrigeration until ready to serve.

NORMAN AND KATHY PERLMUTTER

He is chairman of the board of Heitman Financial Services. Kathy is an actress and Options Exchange trader.

Creme Brulee

7 egg yolks
8 ounces granulated sugar
3 cups heavy cream

1 cup milk
1 vanilla bean
brown sugar

Beat eggs slightly with a fork and mix with granulated sugar. In a pan, bring the heavy cream, the milk and the vanilla bean (which you have cut open), to a boil. Take off heat and remove vanilla bean as soon as it comes to a boil. Next, add the yolk and sugar mixture. Fill small porcelain oval molds or round shallow molds (approximately 1 inch deep and 6 inches in diameter) with the mixture. Place them in a baking pan in water up to one-half the level of the porcelain molds. Place in the oven at 350 degrees and bake for one-half hour. Cool. Sprinkle brown sugar on top and put in broiler very close to flame in order to melt the sugar quickly. Serve at room temperature.

JAMES AND PAT PETERSON

He is a management consultant. Both are active in cultural and civic events.

Grasshopper Pie

Crust:

1½ cups chocolate wafer crumbs   ¼ cup butter, melted

Reserve 2 tablespoons crumbs. Mix remaining crumbs with butter, press evenly on bottom and sides of a 9-inch pie plate. Then chill while making filling.

Filling:

25 large marshmallows   3-4 tablespoons white creme de menthe
⅔ cup light cream   1 cup heavy cream, whipped
3-4 tablespoons green creme de menthe

Put marshmallows and light cream over low heat and beat constantly with spoon until marshmallows have melted. Cool thoroughly. Fold in liqueurs and whipped cream. Pour into chilled crust. Sprinkle top with remaining crumbs. Freeze until firm. (You can make it weeks ahead of time.) Remove from freezer just 15 minutes before serving. Serves 8.

ARTURO PETTERINO

Former maitre d' of the Pump Room.

Chocolate Walnut Pie

3 eggs   1 cup walnut pieces
⅔ cup sugar   8 ounces semi-sweet chocolate, melted
1 cup dark corn syrup   1 9½-inch pie shell
⅓ cup butter, melted

Blend the eggs and sugar and beat them together for one minute. Add the remaining ingredients, except the pie shell, and blend thoroughly. Pour the mixture into the shell. Bake on a cookie sheet in a 350 degree oven for one hour. Cool before serving. Serve with lightly whipped, unsweetened heavy cream.

WALLY PHILLIPS

Top radio personality, WGN's ace. Charitable on the air and off.

Praline Nuggets

1 cup firmly packed light brown sugar,
  sieved
2 tablespoons ground pecans
1 tablespoon cornstarch

1 tablespoon bourbon or dark rum
1 large egg white, room temperature
pinch cream of tartar
2 cups pecan halves

In a bowl whisk together brown sugar, ground pecans and cornstarch. Add bourbon and whisk until well blended. In another bowl beat egg white with cream of tartar and pinch of salt until holds stiff peaks. Stir ⅓ into sugar mixture and fold in remaining white. Mix will become more liquid. Add pecan halves, stirring to coat well. Arrange individually, rounded side up, 2 inches apart on buttered baking sheets. Bake in 300 degree preheated oven for 12 minutes or until puffed and gold. Cool on sheet for 1 minute. Transfer to racks and cool completely. Will keep in airtight containers for 5 days. (Makes about 100 nuggets).

WILLIAM A. PHILLIPS

Interior designer, active socially, charitably.

Russian Cream with Strawberries Romanoff

Russian Cream:
1 cup plus 3 tablespoons heavy cream
½ cup sugar
1 envelope unflavored gelatin

½ pint sour cream
1½ teaspoons vanilla

Mix together the cream, sugar and gelatin in a saucepan and heat gently until the gelatin is thoroughly dissolved. Cool until slightly thickened. Fold in the sour cream and flavor with vanilla. Whisk until the mixture is quite smooth.

Pour the mixture into a serving bowl or 3-cup metal mold. If you want to make individual servings, pour the cream into 6 small half-cup individual molds. Cover and chill until set, at least 4 hours.

To unmold, dip the container in hot water until the edges just begin to liquefy. Invert the mold onto a serving dish and surround liberally with Strawberries Romanoff.

Strawberries Romanoff:

4 cups fresh strawberries (or equal amount of frozen, thawed)
½ cup confectioners sugar

1½ ounces vodka
1½ ounces Triple Sec
1½ ounces rum

Wash and hull the strawberries and toss them with the sugar. Put them in a bowl and pour over the vodka, Triple Sec and rum. Chill. When ready to serve, surround the Russian Cream mold with the marinated chilled strawberries.

JAN PHILIPSBORN

Career-woman, patron of the arts.

Lemon Slices

2 cups sifted flour
½ cup confectioners sugar
1 cup butter or margarine
4 eggs
2 cups sugar

½ cup lemon juice
¼ cup flour
1 teaspoon baking powder
grated rind of 1 lemon

Mix flour with confectioners sugar, cut in butter as for pie crust. Press into bottom of a 15 by 10-inch jelly roll pan. Bake at 350 degrees for 15 minutes. In small bowl of electric mixer, beat eggs until light. Gradually beat in sugar. Add lemon juice. Sift ¼ cup flour with baking powder; add to batter with rind. Beat until blended. (Mixture is liquid in consistency.) Pour into hot crust. Return to oven, bake 25 minutes longer. Cool; sprinkle lightly with confectioners sugar. Makes 48.

SILVIO PINTO

Chef-owner of Sogni Dorati restaurant.

Sweet Ricotta Blueberry Cheese Cake

2 pounds ricotta cheese
4 eggs
¼ cup flour
⅓ cup sugar

1 pinch salt
drop almond oil
2 cups blueberries

Combine all ingredients except blueberries in food processor or blender. Blend well. Wash blueberries and lightly roll in flour. Fold blueberries into batter.

Line 2 molds 4 by 8 by 2½ inches deep with Saran wrap, torn large enough to envelope entire outer surface of mold. Pour batter in and fold Saran over. Place in a Baine-Marie, or a shallow pan that will hold both molds, and fill pan half-full of water. Cover entire pan and molds with tin foil. Place in oven at 350 degrees for 40 minutes or until cake is spongy when touched lightly. Remove from oven and take molds out of water, but do not remove cakes from molds. When cooled refrigerate; unmold just before serving. Slice and serve with raspberry or strawberry sauce. Makes 2 cakes.

COLLETTE POLLACK

Catholic women's leader, charity volunteer, civic leader.

Chicago's Whitehall Chocolate Roll

Cake:
5 eggs
½ cup sugar
½ teaspoon vanilla extract

3 tablespoons cocoa
¾ cup flour

Preheat oven to moderate 350 degrees for 15 minutes. Butter a baking sheet, line with waxed paper, and butter the waxed paper. Separate 5 medium eggs at room temperature. Beat the egg yolks with sugar and vanilla extract (using an electric mixer for 5 to 10 minutes) until thick and very pale in color. Put in double boiler over simmering water and whip until light and fluffy. Remove from heat. Fold into double boiler cocoa and flour after sifting them together. Spread the batter on the prepared baking sheet approximately ½ inch deep. Bake in the oven 8 to 10 minutes. Remove from oven and roll cake immediately, lengthwise, leaving cake on waxed paper.

189

Filling:
2 tablespoons butter
⅔ cup cream

10 ounces dark sweet chocolate
2 ounces coffee liqueur

Bring cream and butter to a rapid boil. Remove from heat. Add dark sweet chocolate, which has been cut into pieces, and stir until chocolate is melted and mixture is smooth. Refrigerate until chilled but still workable. Beat vigorously using an electric mixer. Add coffee liqueur and continue to beat until filling is thick. Refrigerate until proper consistency for spreading.

Topping:
3 ounces dark sweet chocolate
1 ounce coffee liqueur

1 cup heavy cream

Melt chocolate with coffee liqueur. Whip heavy cream and fold cream into chocolate mixture thoroughly but gently, using a hand-whip or spatula.

Unroll cake, removing waxed paper, spread with filling and roll again. Place on a long serving board. Swirl the topping over top and sides of the roll and sprinkle generously with shaved chocolate. Serves 8.

A.N. AND LORRAINE PRITZKER

Brilliant lawyer, business tycoon, A.N. is a philanthropist, civic leader. Lorraine is active in charities, social work.

Pumpkin Cake

Cake:
2 cups pumpkin
1¼ cups oil
2 cups sugar
4 eggs, well beaten
3 cups flour

1 teaspoon salt
2 teaspoons baking soda
3 teaspoons cinnamon
chopped or ground nuts

Sift dry ingredients. Beat eggs well and add sugar. Add pumpkin, mix; add oil and mix well. Bake in a greased and floured tube pan 40 to 50 minutes in a 350 degree oven.

Frosting:
1 package cream cheese
2 cups confectioners sugar

3 teaspoons milk
1 teaspoon vanilla

Cream together and frost cake.

JAY AND CINDY PRITZKER

He is Pritzker and Pritzker business genius. Both he and Cindy are active in cultural, charitable, civic affairs.

Chocolate Cherry Cake

Cake:
1½ cups cake flour
1 teaspoon baking soda
1 cup sugar
¼ pound butter
2 whole eggs

1 cup sour cream
2 ounces melted chocolate
1 4-ounce bottle maraschino cherries
  cut fine with juice

Mix butter, eggs, sugar, add soda, cherries, juice, sour cream, flour, chocolate. Bake in 350 degree oven for 25 minutes. Cake is better if not overdone.

Frosting:
2 squares chocolate
2 tablespoons butter
1 cup sugar

1 tablespoon cornstarch
1 cup warm milk
1 egg yolk

Melt chocolate and butter in double boiler. Blend in sugar, cornstarch, milk, yolk. Boil till thick, stir constantly. When cool, frost cake.

MARCIA PROFFITT

Fitness expert, photographer's model, exercise teacher.

Orange Chiffon Pie

1 envelope unflavored gelatin
½ cup water
3 eggs, separated
1 tablespoon finely shredded orange
   peel

1 cup orange juice
2 tablespoons lemon juice
⅓ cup sugar
1 baked 9-inch pie shell
¼ cup flaked coconut, toasted

In small saucepan combine gelatin, water and egg yolks. Cook and stir over low heat until gelatin dissolves and mixture thickens slightly. Remove from heat and beat in peel and juices. Chill over ice water, stirring frequently until thickened. Meanwhile, beat egg whites until stiff but not dry. Gradually beat in sugar until stiff, shiny peaks form. Fold into thickened gelatin and pour into baked pie shell. Top with toasted coconut. Chill several hours before serving.

ALLIN AND RUTH ANN PROUDFOOT

He is vice-president, development, for Northwestern University. Both active socially, in civic affairs.

Choc-O-Date Dessert

12 packaged cream-filled chocolate
   cookies, crushed
1 8-ounce package pitted dates, cut up
¾ cup water
¼ teaspoon salt

2 cups tiny marshmallows or 16 large
½ cup chopped California walnuts
1 cup heavy cream
½ teaspoon vanilla

Reserve ¼ cup cookie crumbs; spread remainder in 10 by 6 by 1½-inch baking dish. In saucepan, combine dates, water and salt; bring to boil, reduce heat and simmer 3 minutes. Remove from heat, add marshmallows and stir until melted. Cool to room temperature. Stir in chopped nuts. Spread date mixture over crumbs in dish. Combine cream and vanilla; whip, swirl over dates. Sprinkle with reserved cookie crumbs. Top with nuts or cherries and cut in squares. Serves 8.

LAWRENCE PUCCI

Founder of Wedgwood Society, designer of men's and women's tailored garments.

Lorenzo's Fantasia Spice Cake

1½ cups brown sugar
3 cups sifted flour
1½ teaspoons baking powder
1½ teaspoons cinnamon
¾ teaspoon allspice
¾ teaspoon nutmeg
¾ teaspoon cloves
½ cup orange juice

1½ cups assorted raisins
1 cup chopped nuts
¾ cup pure vegetable oil
2 eggs, beaten
1½ teaspoons baking soda
¾ teaspoon salt
1 8-ounce can tomato sauce

Place flour, brown sugar, baking powder, spice and salt in large mixing bowl. Mix tomato sauce and soda in small bowl. Add to flour mixture. Stir in eggs, oil, nuts, raisins and fruit juice; mix well.

Pour mixture into greased 10-inch pan. Bake at 350 degrees for about 50 minutes. Cool in pan for about 15 minutes before turning out on serving plate.

MADELINE MURPHY RABB

Executive director, Chicago Council on Fine Arts.

Utterly Self-Indulgent Hot Fudge Sauce

1 12-ounce can evaporated milk
1¾ to 2 cups granulated sugar
   (depending on your sweet tooth)
4 squares unsweetened chocolate

1 thin pat butter
1 pinch salt
1 teaspoon vanilla

Heat together evaporated milk and sugar, stirring constantly. Boil and stir one minute. Add chocolate squares and salt; continue heating and stirring until chocolate is melted and smooth (about 2-3 minutes). Remove from heat, stir in butter and vanilla.

Serve immediately over ice cream. Top with a huge dollop of whipped cream.

NOTE: This sauce gets very thick once refrigerated. Store sauce in a heat-proof Mason jar and you can place it uncovered in a pan of water to heat fudge.

NEIL RAMO

President, department stores division, Carson Pirie Scott & Co.

Famous Chocolate Refrigerator Roll

1 teaspoon vanilla extract
2 cups heavy cream, whipped, or
1 8-ounce container frozen whipping
    topping, thawed

1 package Nabisco chocolate wafers
chocolate curls, optional

Stir vanilla extract into whipped cream or frozen whipped topping; spread 1½ to 2 cups on wafers; put wafers together in stacks of 4 or 5. On serving platter, stand stacks on edge to make one roll; frost with remaining whipped cream or topping. Chill 4 to 6 hours. If desired, garnish with chocolate curls. To serve, slice diagonally at 45 degree angle. Serves 12.

MICHAEL RAUTBORD

Student.

Sugar Rautbord's Fabulous Fudge

4 cups sugar
1 12-ounce can evaporated milk
1 12-ounce package chocolate chips
1 7-ounce jar marshmallow creme

1 teaspoon vanilla
1 cup broken nuts
2 sticks butter

Combine sugar, milk and butter, mixing thoroughly. Cook slowly over low heat until a soft ball forms when dropped in cold water. Remove from heat. Add chocolate chips, marshmallow, vanilla and nuts, stirring until smooth and creamy. Pour into buttered pan. Chill. Cut into squares when firm.

This fudge is derived from Eleanor Roosevelt's personal recipe.

194

DEBBIE REGAL

Publicist.

Brandy Alexander Souffle

2 envelopes unflavored gelatin
2 cups cold water
1 cup sugar
4 eggs, separated

1 8-ounce package cream cheese
3 tablespoons brandy
1 cup whipped cream
3 tablespoons creme de cacao

Soften gelatin in 1 cup water. Stir over low heat until dissolved. Add remaining water. Remove from heat. Blend in ¾ cup sugar and beaten egg yolks. Return to heat. Cook 2 or 3 minutes, until slightly thickened. Gradually add to softened cream cheese. Mix until well blended. Stir in creme de cacao and brandy. Chill until slightly thick. Beat egg whites to soft peaks. Add remaining sugar. Beat until they form stiff peaks. Fold mixture into cheese and fold whipped cream into cheese. Wrap 3-inch collar around top of 1½-quart souffle mold. Pour mixture into mold and chill overnight.

NOTE: This should not be blended in a food processor but with an electric mixer.

LESLEE REIS

Chef-owner of Leslee's, Cafe Provencal.

Black Raspberry Ice Cream with Black Raspberry Coulis

Ice Cream:
2 pints black raspberries
¼ cup sugar
9 egg yolks
¾ cup sugar

2 cups heavy cream
2 cups half and half
1 tablespoon vanilla extract

Puree black raspberries with sugar in food processor. Strain. Beat egg yolks till pale yellow and slowly beat in sugar. Beat until ribbon is formed.

195

Add heavy cream and half and half that have been scalded, slowly to eggs and sugar. Mix in well. Over moderate heat cook, stirring continually, until mixture coats spoon well but does not boil. Cool down, stirring, in bowl of ice cubes. When cool add vanilla and the raspberry puree. Chill well. Freeze according to machine directions. Makes one quart.

Black Raspberry Coulis:
1 pint black raspberries   **2 tablespoons framboise liqueur**
sugar to taste (about 2-3 tablespoons)

Puree all together and strain. Use sparingly as sauce for the ice cream.

"One sure way to heaven."

DON REUBEN

Lawyer, dog breeder, lecturer, writer, civic leader.

Jeannette's Chocolate Bread Pudding

1 pint milk   **1½ cups stale bread crumbs**
4 tablespoons chocolate   **2 egg yolks**
1 tablespoon butter   **¼ teaspoon vanilla**
⅓ cup sugar

Beat the two egg yolks until frothy, pour over 1½ cups stale bread crumbs. Set aside. Scald one pint milk, add 4 tablespoons chocolate that has been melted over hot water. Add one tablespoon butter, ⅓ cup sugar. Pour over bread crumb mixture and turn into a greased baking dish. Bake at 350 degrees for 30 minutes. May be topped with whipped cream.

LINDA JOHNSON RICE

Johnson Publishing Co. executive, patron of the arts, civic and charity leader.

Bread Pudding

2 tablespoons butter
7 cups sliced bread toasted and cut in cubes
2½ cups milk (whole milk or half and half)

2 eggs
1 cup sugar
¼ teaspoon cinnamon
⅓ cup raisins
1 tablespoon vanilla extract

In 1-quart saucepan, heat milk and butter until very warm; pour over bread cubes. In large bowl, combine sugar, cinnamon and eggs, mixing until well blended. Stir in raisins and vanilla flavor. Add bread to sugar mixture, mix until well blended. Spoon bread mixture into greased 8-inch square or round baking dish. Set baking dish into shallow pan. Pour 2½ cups hot water into pan. Bake at 350 degrees for 50 to 60 minutes or until knife inserted in center comes out clean.

Remove the dish from the water in the pan. Cool slightly before serving. Serve with whipped cream or leave it plain. 4 to 6 servings.

JAMES AND DARYL RILEY

President, Weber Cohn and Riley ad agency, James is active on Fair and Tourism boards. She is volunteer with youth groups.

Butter Pecan Dessert

1 10-ounce package Lorna Doone
   cookies
1 stick butter, melted
2 packages instant vanilla pudding

2 cups milk
1 quart butter pecan ice cream, softened
1 large carton Cool Whip
4 Heath bars, crushed

Crush cookies and mix with melted butter. Press into 9 by 13-inch pan. Prepare pudding as directed, using only 2 cups milk. Add softened ice cream. Spread on cookie crust. Top wtih Cool Whip and crushed Heath bars. Refrigerate overnight. Serves 12.

JIMMY RITTENBERG

Manager of Faces Night Club.

Tummy-Buster Sundae

1 scoop strawberry ice cream
1 scoop vanilla ice cream
1 scoop chocolate ice cream
1 scoop pistachio almond ice cream
1 scoop pralines and creme ice cream

melted marshmallows
whipped cream
hot butterscotch sauce
freshly roasted pecans
½ frozen Heath bar, crushed

Layer ice cream in large bowl with melted marshmallows and whipped cream, smother with hot butterscotch sauce, sprinkle with pecans and top with crushed Heath bar!

DAN AND DANIELE ROBERTS

He is a publicist and she works for Air France.

Lemon Crepe Souffle on Raspberry Coulis

Coulis:
1 package frozen raspberries, defrosted

To prepare the coulis, pass raspberries through a strainer to remove all seeds.

Crepes:
1 tablespoon milk
3 tablespoons water
1 whole egg
4 tablespoons flour

1 tablespoon sugar
pinch salt
1 generous teaspoon oil
pinch grated lemon zest

To prepare crepes, combine milk and water in a cup. Mix well other ingredients in a small bowl. Then add milk-water mixture a little at a time to avoid lumps forming. Cook in the usual manner. Yields 6 crepes, each about 6 inches in diameter.

Pastry Cream:
¾ cup milk
3 drops vanilla extract
3 egg yolks
6 tablespoons sugar

3 tablespoons flour
3 tablespoons lemon juice, grated zest
(combined)

To prepare the pastry cream, bring the milk and vanilla to a boil then keep hot. Meanwhile, in a small bowl work together with a spatula the egg yolk and sugar until the mixture becomes pale and forms a ribbon. Add the flour and mix. Add the warm milk to the egg-sugar-flour mixture, mix and return to the heat. Add the lemon juice and grated zest and bring the mixture to a boil, stirring constantly to avoid scorching. When the pastry cream is thick, transfer it to a bowl and let it cool, mixing occasionally.

Meringue:
6 egg whites
large pinch each: salt, cream of tartar

9 tablespoons sugar

When pastry cream is completed (but not more than 25 minutes before you want to serve dessert), preheat the oven to 500 degrees F. Meanwhile, beat the egg whites with salt until frothy. Add the cream of tartar, continue beating until stiff. Add the sugar, beat until shiny and firm. Add one quarter of this meringue to the pastry cream and mix thoroughly. Then add this mixture to the remaining meringue by carefully folding it in.

To serve, place three crepes each on two large greased sheet pans. Divide the mixture between the six crepes and fold the crepes in half, enclosing the mixture. Place the stuffed crepes in the oven with the fold toward the back of the oven. (Otherwise the meringue may brown too quickly). Bake 5-7 minutes. Meanwhile, divide the coulis on six large plates. When the crepes are done, carefully transfer one at a time with a spatula from the pan to a plate. Sprinkle confectioners sugar on each crepe and serve immediately. Serves 6.

BRINA RODIN

Actress and poetess.

Chocolate Austrian Cookies

Cookies:

¾ cup butter, softened
1¼ cups flour
¼ cup unsweetened Dutch cocoa
1 cup ground pecans, divided (reserve
  scant ¼ cup for sprinkling on tops of
  frosted cookies)

6 tablespoons sugar
¾ cup strained apricot jam
¼ cup orange marmalade which has
  been pureed in blender or worked
  through a sieve
chocolate frosting (below)

Put butter, flour, cocoa, ¾ cup of the pecans and sugar in a small bowl and combine with hands or with a wooden spoon. When dough is well mixed, wrap it in plastic wrap and refrigerate it for at least 15 minutes. Remove dough from refrigerator and divide into two parts. Place one of these between 2 sheets of waxed paper which have been lightly floured and roll dough to a ⅛-inch thickness. Remove top paper.

Cut out circles on dough, using a 2-inch round cookie cutter. Use a spatula dipped in flour to transfer each one to an ungreased cookie sheet. Repeat rolling and cutting with second half of dough. Cookies may be placed next to each other on cookie sheet, but they should not touch. Bake cookies in a 350 degrees oven for about 12 minutes, or until cookies are done. Transfer cookies to rack using spatula.

Mix apricot jam and marmalade together in a small dish. Spread a thick layer over one cookie. Place another cookie over this one for sandwich effect. Spread chocolate frosting over top of "sandwich" almost to the edge. Sprinkle cookie tops with reserved ¼ cup ground nuts. This excellent, sophisticated cookie improves if left to ripen for 24 hours.

Frosting:

¼ cup semi-sweet chocolate bits
1 ounce unsweetened chocolate
1 tablespoon butter
1 tablespoon corn syrup
pinch salt
½ cup confectioners sugar

¼ cup evaporated milk or more if
  needed for thinning
½ teaspoon creme de cacao (optional)
¼ teaspoon vanilla, or more to taste if
  creme de cacao is omitted.

In top of double boiler, melt semi-sweet and unsweetened chocolate. Stir in butter, corn syrup, and salt, mixing well. Sift confectioners sugar into melted chocolate, stir, and then add evaporated milk and stir again. Mix in creme de cacao and vanilla and add more evaporated milk if mixture is still too thick for spreading easily. It may also be necessary to add milk midway in the frosting process.

JIMMY ROHR

Chef-owner of Jimmy's Place Restaurant.

Caramel Apples with Rum and Ice Cream

6 small or 4 large baking apples
1½ sticks sweet butter
1⅓ cups sugar

1 teaspoon lemon juice
12 scoops coffee ice cream
1½ tablespoons dark rum

Peel, core and slice apples fairly thin. Melt butter in skillet and add sugar and lemon juice. Cook over medium heat until sugar turns to a light brown caramel. Add peeled sliced apples and cook 2 to 3 minutes. Add rum and serve immediately in bowls over two scoops of ice cream. Serves 6.

CAY ROHTER

Civic and charity leader.

Shortbread

¼ cup confectioners sugar
¼ cup superfine granulated sugar
⅓ cup rice flour

1⅔ cups unbleached flour
1 cup butter, at room temperature

Heat the oven to 325 degrees.

Mix confectioners and granulated sugars together in a small bowl. Mix the flours together in a separate bowl. In a large mixing bowl, thoroughly cream butter and the sugar mixture. Gradually add flour mixture to butter mixture, and mix with your hands until dough is smooth. Do not overwork.

Pat the dough into the shortbread mold, working it to the edge and making sure, by the use of hand pressure, that it is also worked into the design at the base of the mold.

Bake for 45 minutes, or until shortbread is slightly browned and still somewhat springy to the touch.

Let cool on a wire rack for about 15 minutes. Then gently run a knife around perimeter of mold to loosen shortbread. Invert mold on rack, and lift it from shortbread.

To serve, cut into 8 pie-shaped pieces.

DON ROSE

Political consultant, restaurant critic, writer.

Don's Favorite Chocolate Ice Box Cake

1 6-ounce package sweet (not milk)
 chocolate
1½ tablespoons water
1 egg, separated

1 tablespoon confectioners sugar
½ cup heavy cream
6 ladyfingers, halved lengthwise (a few
 more may be necessary)

Melt chocolate with water. Beat in egg yolk, then sugar until smooth. Whip cream and fold in. Beat egg white until stiff and fold in until color is uniform. Line an 8-inch loaf pan with waxed paper, then line bottom and sides with ladyfinger halves. Pour in chocolate mixture. Refrigerate overnight. Unmold and serve, topped with more whipped cream if desired.

JACK ROSEN

Premium sales tycoon, sportsman.

Phyllis' Banana-Split Cake Supreme

3 bananas
½ gallon ice cream, Neopolitan,
 chocolate or preference, softened
1 cup chocolate chips
1⅓ cups graham cracker crumbs
⅓ cup butter

½ cup butter
2 cups confectioners sugar
½ cup evaporated milk
1 teaspoon vanilla
1 can whipping cream

Cover bottom of 9 by 13-inch springform pan with graham cracker crumbs. Sprinkle ⅓ cup melted butter over it. Press firmly in bottom. Bake 350 degrees for 8 to 10 minutes. Cool completely. Place sliced bananas on bottom and cover with softened ice cream. Freeze.

Mix confectioners sugar, evaporated milk, butter and chocolate chips in a Corning Ware container. Set in microwave oven till melted. Stir till thick. Add vanilla and cool ½ hour. Pour this fudge topping over cake and chill till firm. Then cover with whipped cream and freeze. Decorate as desired.

MADELINE AND MICHAEL ROSENBERG

Patrons of the arts, philanthropists, civic leaders.

Michael's Favorite Cookies

1 cup butter
½ cup light brown sugar
1 teaspoon vanilla

¼ teaspoon salt
2½ cups sifted all-purpose flour
½ cup ground pecans

Combine butter and sugar until light and fluffy. Blend in vanilla and salt. Add flour and nuts. Beat thoroughly. Chill dough for about 2 hours. Using about 1 teaspoon of dough, shape into individual round cookies. Bake on ungreased cookie sheet at 350 degrees for about 15 minutes. Roll in confectioners sugar when cool. Makes approximately 4 dozen.

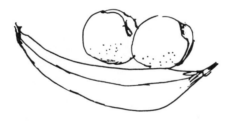

TONY ROSSI

Saks designer salon manager, socialite.

Italian Cheesecake

Sweet dough:
1⅛ cups flour
⅜ cup sugar
⅛ teaspoon salt
½ cup butter

⅛ teaspoon grated orange rind
1 egg yolk
¼ teaspoon vanilla extract
fine dry bread crumbs

Sift the flour, sugar, and salt together onto a pastry board or into a bowl. Make a well in the center of the mound and place in it the butter, orange rind, and the egg yolk and vanilla combined. With your fingers work those ingredients quickly into the flour mixture to produce a thick smooth paste. Shape it into a ball, wrap in waxed paper, and chill for 30 minutes.

Filling:

1½ pounds (3 cups) ricotta cheese, sieved

1 cup sugar

1 teaspoon vanilla extract

½ cup slivered almonds

1 tablespoon orange-flower water

½ teaspoon finely grated orange rind

⅛ teaspoon ground cinnamon

4 eggs

¼ cup finely chopped mixed glazed fruits

Preheat oven to 400 degrees. Butter an 8-inch cake pan and line it with the dough rolled ⅛ inch thick. Sprinkle it lightly with bread crumbs. Cut extra dough in ¼ inch strips and reserve for lattice-work topping.

In a mixing bowl thoroughly combine the cheese, sugar, vanilla, orange-flower water, orange rind, and cinnamon. Beat in the eggs, one at a time, and blend in the glazed fruit. Pour the mixture into the prepared pan and bake in the preheated oven for 20 minutes. Return it to oven for 20 minutes longer. Turn off the heat and continue to cook cake in oven with the door open. Decorate with slivered almonds. Cut cake in wedges to provide 6 to 8 servings.

CONG. DANIEL ROSTENKOWSKI

Veteran congressman, head of Ways and Means Committee.

Laverne's Creamy Cheesecake

Filling:

2 8-ounce packages Philadelphia cream cheese

1 3-ounce package Philadephia cream cheese

1 cup sugar

2 eggs

1 pint sour cream

1 teaspoon vanilla

graham cracker crust

Line bottom of springform pan with graham cracker crust. Add chopped walnuts for variation, if desired. Beat ingredients together until smooth. Pour over graham cracker crust. Bake 45 minutes in preheated 300 degree oven. Let cool in oven (overnight is acceptable). Refrigerate.

Glaze Topping:

2 pints fresh berries (blueberries or
　strawberries)
2 tablespoons cornstarch

½ cup sugar
½ teaspoon grated lemon rind
½ cup water

Combine cornstarch and sugar. Gradully add water and mix until smooth over low heat. Add lemon rind and 1 cup fruit packed down. Cook for 5 minutes and strain. Cut balance of strawberries or use whole blueberries and place over top of cake. Pour cooled glaze over fruit and refrigerate.

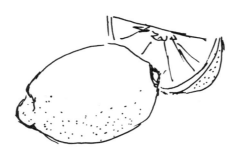

JUDGE ILANA ROVNER

Judge and former deputy governor of Illinois.

Lemon Cream Pie

One 9-inch pie tin
1 tablespoon unflavored gelatin
1 cup water
1 6-ounce can frozen lemonade,
　thawed

½ cup sugar
1 cup heavy cream, whipped
1 baked 9-inch pastry shell or graham
　cracker crust
small carton heavy cream for topping

Dissolve gelatin in ¼ cup cold water, add ¾ cup boiling water. Heat and stir until dissolved. Stir in lemonade and sugar. Stir until dissolved. Whip with electric mixer until fluffy. Fold in whipped cream. Turn into pie shell. Chill until firm. Top with whipped cream. (May be served as pudding in dessert glasses; top with fruit, if desired).

ARTHUR AND MARY RUBLOFF

He is premier Chicago realtor, philanthropist. Both are active socially; civic leaders.

Easy Cheesecake

1 cup confectioners sugar
1 8-ounce package cream cheese

1 envelope Dream Whip
1 graham cracker prepared crust

Cream sugar and cheese. Prepare Dream Whip per instructions. Fold gently into cheese mixture. Pour into graham cracker crust. Chill well before serving. You may add fresh blueberries, strawberries or kiwi on top or top with sour cream.

NANCY RUSH

Actress.

Seven Layer Bars

½ cup butter
1½ cups graham cracker crumbs
1 14-ounce can sweetened condensed
  milk

6 ounces semi-sweet chocolate morsels
1¼ cups flaked coconut
1 cup chopped nuts

Preheat oven to 350 degrees (325 for glass dish). In a 13 by 9-inch pan melt butter in the oven. Sprinkle the graham cracker crumbs over the butter, pour sweetened condensed milk evenly over crumbs. Top evenly with chocolate, coconut, and nuts; press down gently. Bake for 20 or 30 minutes, until lightly browned. Cool thoroughly before cutting.

DAVID RUSS

Interior designer.

Ginger's Melon Tart

Pastry:

6 tablespoons softened butter
¼ cup sugar
¾ teaspoon vanilla
⅛ teaspoon salt

1 cup flour
1 egg, beaten
butter for greasing

Cream butter and sugar until light and fluffy. Beat in vanilla and salt. Gradually stir in flour. Stir in egg until mixture is crumbly. Press mixture one-eighth inch thick over bottom and sides of buttered 9-inch tart pan with removable bottom. Trim edge. Bake at 400 degrees for 6 minutes or until golden brown; cool on wire rack 15 minutes.

Filling:

8-ounce package cream cheese, softened
1 egg, beaten
2 tablespoons sugar

¼ teaspoon vanilla
⅛ teaspoon almond extract

Beat cream cheese, egg and sugar until light and fluffy. Beat in vanilla and almond extract. Spread filling over pastry. Bake at 350 degrees for 13 to 15 minutes or until filling is barely set and light brown. Cool on wire rack for 30 minutes.

Topping:

3 cups cantaloupe or honeydew melon balls (or sliced strawberries and kiwi fruit)

¼ cup melted apricot preserves

Arrange fruit over filling. Brush with melted preserves. Serves 8.

SHIRLEY AND PATRICK RYAN

He is head of Combined Insurance and active in civic and business groups. She is dedicated charity volunteer.

Cherry-Berries on a Cloud

6 egg whites
½ teaspoon cream of tartar
¼ teaspoon salt
1¾ cups sugar
2 cups chilled heavy cream
2 3-ounce packages cream cheese,
   softened

1 cup sugar
1 teaspoon vanilla
2 cups miniature marshmallows
Cherry-Berry Topping

Heat oven to 275 degrees. Butter a 13 by 9 by 2-inch baking pan. In a large mixer bowl, beat egg whites, cream of tartar and salt until foamy. Beat in 1¾ cups sugar 1 tablespoon at a time, and continue beating until stiff and glossy. Do not underbeat. Spread in the pan. Bake 1 hour. Turn off the oven; leave meringue in oven with the door closed 12 hours or longer.

In a chilled bowl, beat cream until stiff. Blend cream cheese, 1 cup sugar and the vanilla. Gently fold the whipped cream and marshmallows into the cream cheese mixture; spread over the meringue. Chill 12 to 24 hours. Cut into serving pieces and top with Cherry-Berry Topping. 10 to 12 servings.

Cherry-Berry Topping:
1 21-ounce can cherry pie filling
1 teaspoon lemon juice
2 cups sliced fresh strawberries or

1 16-ounce package frozen strawberries,
   thawed

Stir together cherry pie filling, lemon juice and strawberries.

MARVIN AND JUDITH SACKS

He is an attorney. She is a para-legal. Both are active in civic, social affairs.

Chocolate Suicide

Crust:

12 ounces Oreo cookies   ½ cup butter

Crush Oreo cookies in food processor or blender. Melt butter and mix together. Pat this mixture in a 9 by 13-inch pan, then chill while preparing the following sauce.

Sauce:

½ cup butter   1 12-ounce can evaporated milk
1 cup sugar   1 6-ounce package chocolate chips

Combine this mixture in a saucepan. Bring to boil and continue cooking, stirring constantly until mixture thickens (about 15 minutes). Cool completely.

Filling: *Topping:*

½ gallon ice cream, any flavor   large carton Cool Whip

Soften ice cream. Slice ice cream and spread on top of cookie mixture. Put in freezer for about ½ hour. Then spread with sauce and top with large carton of Cool Whip. Chopped nuts optional. Return to freezer. Will keep in freezer up to 3 months.

LUCY SALENGER

Consultant on Illinois film production, former head of state film bureau.

Latticed Strawberry Rhubarb Pie

1¼ cups sugar   2½ cups fresh strawberries
⅛ teaspoon salt   2 tablespoons margarine
⅓ cup flour   1 tablespoon sugar
2½ cups fresh or sugarless frozen   1 9-inch frozen pie shell
  rhubarb, cut in 1-inch pieces

Combine 1¼ cups sugar, salt, and flour. Arrange half of strawberries and rhubarb in pastry-lined pie pan. Sprinkle with half of sugar mixture. Repeat with remaining fruit and sugar mixture; dot with butter. A lattice top crust shows the colors of the strawberries and rhubarb. Brush the top of the crust with milk and sprinkle sugar over this. Bake in 425 degree oven for 40 minutes.

JOAN SALTZMAN

Caterer.

Chocolate Mousse Cake

2 packages Nabisco chocolate wafers
½ stick unsalted butter, melted
2 12-ounce packages Nestle's semi-sweet
   chocolate morsels
6 tablespoons hot instant coffee

4 tablespoons sugar
6 egg yolks
2 teaspoons vanilla
6 egg whites stiffly beaten
3 cups heavy cream stiffly beaten

Crumble 1 package chocolate wafers into fine crumbs and add melted butter. Mix well and pat crumbs against sides and bottom of 9-inch springform pan. Melt chocolate morsels in a double boiler and add instant coffee and sugar. Whisk until smooth. Set aside to cool. Beat egg yolks, gradually adding sugar until mixture is lemon colored. Stir in vanilla. Add chocolate to yolk mixture and blend until smooth. Fold in beaten egg whites. Fold in whipped cream. Pour ½ mixture into springform pan. Layer chocolate wafers to cover top of mixture completely. Pour remaining chocolate mixture into pan. Cover and refrigerate at least one day before serving, or freeze. When ready to serve, top with additional whipped cream or chocolate leaves.

RYNE SANDBERG

Cubs Golden Glove second baseman, winner of the 1984 National League Most Valuable Player Award.

Cindy's Chocolate Chip Cookies

2¼ cups unsifted flour
1 teaspoon vanilla
1 teaspoon baking soda
2 eggs
1 teaspoon salt

6 to 12 ounces chocolate chips
1 cup softened butter
1 cup nuts
¾ cup sugar
¾ cup brown sugar, packed

Preheat oven to 375 degrees. In small bowl combine flour, baking soda and salt, set aside. In large bowl, combine butter, sugar, brown sugar and vanilla extract; beat until creamy. Beat in eggs. Gradually add flour mixture; mix well. Stir in chocolate chips and nuts. Drop by rounded measuring teaspoons onto ungreased cookie sheet. Bake 8 to 10 minutes.

TERRY SAVAGE

Financial authority, TV personality.

Terry's Apple Pie

Filling:
1 prepared pie crust
6 to 8 apples, sliced

1 cup sugar
1 tablespoon cinnamon

Fill pie crust with apples. Cover with sugar and cinnamon.

Topping:
1 cup flour
1 cup sugar

1½ sticks butter, cut small

Mix all together and sprinkle over pie. Bake in 375 degree oven for 50 minutes.

JENNY SCHMITZ

Socialite, patron of the arts.

White Grape Mousse

1½ pounds white seedless grapes,
   halved
¼ cup brown sugar, or more, to taste

3 to 4 tablespoons light rum
1½ cups sour cream
1½ cups heavy cream

Mix together grapes, sugar, rum, and sour cream. Chill well. Whip the heavy cream until stiff and fold it carefully into the grape mixture. Chill again before serving. Serves 6.

ELSA SCHRAGER

Philanthropist, world traveler, socialite.

Fleur's Orange Pie

Meringue Pie Shell:
4 egg whites
1½ cups sugar
1 teaspoon water

1 teaspoon vanilla
1 teaspoon white vinegar

Beat egg whites with water, vanilla and vinegar until soft peaks form when beater is slowly raised. Slowly beat in sugar till soft peaks form. Spread meringue in 12-inch pie plate; bake 1 hour in 300 degree oven. Cool on wire rack away from drafts.

Filling:
10 navel oranges
½ cup sugar
3 tablespoons cornstarch

1 teaspoon vanilla
1½ cups heavy cream
Toasted coconut (optional)

Peel oranges into sections, place into strainer. Pour sugar over oranges and drain overnight. Combine juice from oranges, cornstarch and cook until mixture thickens, stirring constantly. Let cool. Add orange slices to cornstarch mixture with vanilla. Beat heavy cream and spread over pie. Sprinkle with toasted coconut. Or coconut can be folded into whipped cream.

ELI SCHULMAN

Restaurateur for 40 years. Owns Eli's Place for Steaks. Sells cheesecake all over U.S.

Eli's Chocolate Chip Cheesecake

Crust:
1 8½-ounce package chocolate wafers,
   crushed into fine crumbs
¼ teaspoon nutmeg

1 6-ounce package ground walnuts
¼ cup sugar
⅓ cup melted butter

Combine cookie crumbs, nutmeg, walnuts, sugar and melted butter. Press into a 9-inch springform pan. Refrigerate while making batter. Pour batter into crust and bake in preheated, 350 degree oven for 1 hour. Allow to rest in oven about 1 hour, then cool in refrigerator.

Filling:

3 eggs
1 cup sugar
3 8-ounce packages cream cheese at
   room temperature

1 cup sour cream
1 teaspoon vanilla
⅛ teaspoon salt
12 ounces mini-chocolate chips

Beat eggs and sugar together at high speed of electric mixer. Add cream cheese and beat until smooth. If you don't have an electric mixer, it will be easier to beat softened cream cheese first, then cream with sugar and add eggs. Beat in sour cream, vanilla and salt. Add chocolate chips. Stir in.

NOTE: Because of competition, Mr. Schulman declined to give the actual recipe for his cheesecake. This cake is almost as good. (By adding 4 tablespoons flour with the sour cream, you'll get a more cakelike product. If desired, the crust, which is a thick cookie crust, can be halved.)

MIKE AND JOY SEGAL

He's an insurance executive. Both are active in charities, civic affairs.

Chocolate Mini-Chip Brownies

4 eggs
2 cups sugar
1 cup flour

2 sticks butter
4 squares unsweetened chocolate
1 12-ounce package mini-chips

Melt the 2 sticks of butter and 4 squares of chocolate in a small saucepan. Mix eggs and sugar. Then add melted mixture and flour. When this is well mixed, pour into greased 9 by 13-inch pan. Then sprinkle entire mini-chip package onto this chocolate batter mixture. Bake at 325 degrees for 40 minutes.

JERRY AND BARBARA SEIGAN

He's a lawyer. She is homemaker, sports and exercise enthusiast, charity volunteer.

Layered Ice Cream Cake

4 pints ice cream, your favorite flavors
1 package Oreo cookies, crushed
¼ cup margarine, melted

6 Heath candy bars, crushed
1 bottle maraschino cherries sliced in half

Combine 1 cup cookie crumbs (reserve rest for later) with ¼ cup melted margarine. Press into bottom of 8-inch round springform pan. Slice and layer first pint ice cream on crumbs (work quickly). Sprinkle some cookie crumbs and candy crumbs over ice cream. Press some cherry halves into crumbs. (If ice cream gets mushy, place in freezer until hardened and then continue with next step). Prepare the next three pints of ice cream the same way. But with the last pint just sprinkle with cookie crumbs. Put in freezer until ready to serve.

NOTE: You can be creative. Sliced fruit, chopped nuts, sliced bananas, or chocolate can be added.

SHARON SHARP

Deputy Director, Marketing, for State of Illinois.

Bourbon-Praline Sauce

½ cup butter or margarine
½ cup firmly packed brown sugar
½ cup heavy cream

¼ cup molasses
¼ cup bourbon
¾ cup pecan halves

In medium saucepan over medium heat melt butter. Add sugar and cream; stir with whisk or wooden spoon until sugar dissolves. Add molasses; cook and stir about 5 minutes or until sauce thickens and is a dark caramel color. Remove from heat; stir in bourbon and pecans. Cool. Cover. Refrigerate up to 2 weeks. Makes about 2 cups.

"Superb served warm over ice cream, toasted pound cake, waffles, crepes or fruit."

PHIL SHEN

Restaurateur, owner of the Abacus.

Peking Apple Tart

1 large apple, preferably Delicious
¼ cup cornstarch
¾ cup flour
1 cup water

6 to 8 ounces sweet bean paste
2 cups oil
2 tablespoons sugar
½ cup confectioners sugar

Slice apple into ½ inch discs perpendicular to core. Use only the mid-section of the apple. Remove seeds and core from slices.

Heat 2 ounces of oil in saucepan on low. Stir in sweet bean paste and sugar until sauce is homogeneous. Cool to room temperature.

Heat oil in wok to 350 degrees. Prepare a batter by mixing cornstarch, flour and water; dip apple slices into batter and fry in oil until golden.

Spread a layer of sweet bean sauce between two layers of apples. Sprinkle confectioners sugar over the top and serve. Serves 4.

HAROLD SHERMAN

President, United Savings of America.

Bananas Foster

2 tablespoons butter
¾ cup dark brown sugar
3 tablespoons banana liqueur
dash cinnamon

2 bananas, peeled and sliced lengthwise
   and in halves
1 shot warm brandy
4 large scoops vanilla ice cream

Melt butter in chafing dish or skillet. Add brown sugar. Blend with wooden spoon. Cook over medium low heat until mixture starts to caramelize. Add liqueur. Add bananas. Add cinnamon. Cook over slow fire until bananas get very soft and mixture thickens. Add warm brandy. Light with match and while flaming, spoon over vanilla ice cream in sherbet glasses. Serves four.

BILLY SIEGEL

Owner of That Steak Joynt Restaurant.

Chocolate Mousse Riley Simmons

6 ounces semi-sweet chocolate
1 ounce (1 square) unsweetened
  chocolate
2 ounces cocoa paste

½ cup cold coffee
4 egg yolks
1 cup sugar
1 quart heavy cream

Place chocolate, cocoa paste and coffee in top of double boiler over simmering water and heat until chocolate is melted and well blended. Beat yolks and sugar. Add chocolate mixture and beat well. Whip the cream. Mix it well with chocolate mixture. Put in a 2-quart mold and place in freezer or refrigerator to harden. Serve with whipped cream sprinkled with grated chocolate.

JOSEPH AND KAY KIMBERLY SIEGEL

Both are commodities traders, active in charities. She is a former movie star, on committee for Australia's 1988 Centennial.

Pears in Orange Sabayon

6 ripe pears (Bosc preferred)
large bowl acidulated water (water with
  a little lemon juice added)
3 cups water
1½ cups sugar

1 vanilla bean
1 whole cinnamon stick
½ cup finely diced mixed candied fruit,
  soaked in orange liqueur (optional)
Orange Sabayon

Carefully peel pears and drop immediately in large bowl acidulated water. (If you wish to fill pears with optional candied fruit, core and halve before placing in water.)

Combine 3 cups water, sugar, vanilla bean and cinnamon stick in 3-quart saucepan; bring to boil over high heat. When sugar is dissolved, add pears. Reduce heat to medium and poach until tender, about 25 minutes. Allow pears to cool in their poaching liquid. Poaching may be done several hours or day before serving.

Drain pears and arrange on platter; chill. If desired, fill halves with candied fruit. Serve with Orange Sabayon. Serves 6.

Orange Sabayon:
4 large egg yolks
¾ cup orange liqueur

⅓ cup sugar
1 cup heavy cream

Combine yolks, liqueur and sugar in top of double boiler and whisk until well blended. Place over simmering water and whisk constantly until mixture thickens and coats a metal spoon, about 20 minutes. Do not boil or mixture will curdle. Transfer to bowl and cool. Whip cream and fold in thoroughly cooled Sabayon.

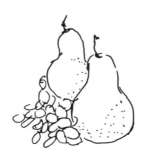

GARY SILBER

Award-winning photographer.

Chocolate Mousse

1 pound dark sweet chocolate, cut into pieces
3 ounces butter, cut into pieces
½ cup sifted confectioners sugar
3 egg yolks

¼ cup Amaretto
1 teaspoon instant coffee powder
2 cups heavy cream
3 egg whites

Melt chocolate and butter in top of double boiler set over simmering water. In large bowl, combine sugar, yolks, Amaretto and coffee. Blend chocolate mixture into this. In another bowl, whip cream until stiff, gently fold into chocolate mixture, blend well. Beat egg whites until soft peaks form, fold into chocolate cream. Refrigerate overnight. Serves 10 to 12.

JUDGE SEYMOUR SIMON

Lawyer, judicial expert, civic leader.

Roz' Apple Pie

4 cups apples
½ to ¾ cup sugar
1 tablespoon flour
¼ teaspoon cinnamon or nutmeg

½ teaspoon salt
2 tablespoons butter
pastry for 2-crust pie

Line a 9 ½-inch pie pan with pastry. Wash, pare, core and slice the apples. Add the sugar with the flour, and seasonings. If the apples are dry add 1 or 2 tablespoons of water. Pour this apple mixture into the pastry. Cut the butter into bits and put them on top of the apples. Moisten the edges of the under crust with water. Cut a few small gashes in the center of the upper crust. Then put it over the apples. Press the edges of the two crusts together; flute and trim. Bake at 425 degrees for 40 to 45 minutes.

If desired, ⅓ cup of grated cheese may be sprinkled over the top of the pie crust just before placing it in the oven.

ALBERT AND CYNTHIA SIMPSON

He is a real estate developer. She is a writer and charity worker.

Somemores

1 1.45-ounce Hershey milk chocolate
   bar, cut up

2 graham crackers per sandwich
1 marshmallow per sandwich

Make a sandwich of chocolate and crackers. Toast marshmallow to a golden brown. Place marshmallow into sandwich between chocolate and crackers. It is ready to eat as soon as chocolate begins to melt. Yummy. You'll say, "Can I have some more?"

"That fabulous, coveted memory of a gooey treat from childhood . . . remember? The one every Scout and camper learns about over an open campfire."

GORDON SINCLAIR

Restaurateur, owner of Gordon, Sinclairs, American Grill.

Mother's Scottish Shortbread

2 cups butter
1 cup sugar

4½-5 cups flour

Beat butter and sugar well. Slowly add flour. Press into jelly roll baking pan. Prick all over with fork. Bake in oven at 300 degrees for 30 minutes. Turn down to 250 degrees for 30 minutes. Cut in desired shapes with sharp knife when still hot. Serves 24.

BOB SINGER

Advertising and public relations expert.

Heavenly Cheesecake

¼ cup (½ stick) butter, melted
1 cup fine graham cracker crumbs
1 teaspoon cream of tartar
6 eggs, separated
3 tablespoons sugar
2 8-ounce packages cream cheese

1 3-ounce package cream cheese
1½ cups sugar
3 tablespoons flour
½ teaspoon salt
1 pint sour cream
1 teaspoon vanilla

Mix melted butter and graham cracker crumbs, and press all but ¼ cup on bottom of pan. Add cream of tartar to egg whites and beat until stiff peaks form. Set aside. Beat cheese until soft, add remaining sugar, flour and salt. Add egg yolks one at a time, beating well after each addition. Add sour cream and vanilla; mix well. Fold in egg whites. Pour mixture into 9-inch buttered springform pan. Sprinkle with reserved ¼ cup crumbs. Bake for 1 hour and 15 minutes or until firm at 325 degrees. Turn off heat, open oven door, and leave cake in oven 10 minutes. Remove from oven and let stand on a rack away from drafts until cool. Chill before serving.

ROSS AND MARTHA SIRAGUSA

Business tycoons, socialites.

Soft Rice Custard

3 cups cooked rice
4 cups milk (divided)
⅔ cup sugar
½ cup golden raisins

2 eggs, beaten
2 tablespoons margarine or butter
1 teaspoon vanilla

Combine rice, 3½ cups milk, sugar and raisins. Cook over medium heat, stirring occasionally until thick and creamy, about 15 minutes. Blend remaining milk and eggs. Stir into rice mixture. Cook 2 minutes longer, stirring constantly. Add butter and vanilla. Turn into serving dishes. Serve warm or cold.

JOYCE SLOAN

Second City's matriarch.

Taffy Apple Pie

Crust:
2 cups graham cracker crumbs
1 teaspoon cinnamon

1 stick melted butter

Mix together and press into a 9-inch pie plate. Bake for 40 minutes at 350 degrees.

Filling:
2 14-ounce cans condensed milk
5 Granny Smith or Delicious apples,
   peeled and sliced thin

1 cup unsalted peanuts, chopped

Remove labels from cans, boil cans in water for 3 hours. This caramelizes the milk. Let stand for one hour. Mix apples with one can milk, pour into pie shell. Pour second can milk on top of that. Sprinkle with peanuts. Do not bake.

KAY SMITH

Famous painter of the American scene.

Plum Cake

½ cup butter
1 cup sugar
1¼ cups flour, sifted
½ teaspoon salt
½ teaspoon cinnamon

¼ teaspoon baking powder
10 or 12 plums, cut in half
1 egg, slightly beaten
1 cup heavy cream

Sift all dry ingredients together—cut in butter. (Hold back ⅓ cup mixture after blended with butter). Pat butter and dry ingredients mixture onto sides and bottom of 8 by 8 by 2-inch pan. Cut plums in half. Place cut side down in pan. Sprinkle ⅓ mixture over top. Bake in preheated 375 degree oven for 15 minutes. Combine slightly beaten egg and heavy cream, stir lightly. Pour over top of crumb-baked mixture. Bake 25 to 35 minutes in 375 degree oven.

MARY ELLA SMITH

Teacher, fiancee of Mayor Harold Washington.

"Dump" Cake

2 cups all-purpose flour
2 cups sugar
¾ cup salad oil
2 eggs
1 can apple-pie filling
1 cup chopped walnuts

¾ cup raisins
2 teaspoons baking soda
1 teaspoon salt
1 teaspoon vanilla
1 teaspoon cinnamon

"Dump" all ingredients together. Stir well, do not beat.Bake in a greased and floured bread pan (10″ x 14″) at 350 degrees for 50 minutes. Cool. Cut into squares. Serve with ice cream or whipped cream.

SIR GEORG AND LADY VALERY SOLTI

He is the brilliant musical director of the Chicago Symphony Orchestra. She is active in London's charitable and social scene.

Summer Pudding

2 tablespoons water
5 ounces sugar
1 pound soft red fruit (blackberries, blackcurrants, raspberries, red currants)

4-6 ounces white bread, cut in small slices

Stir the water and sugar and bring slowly to boil. Add fruit and stew gently until soft. It is very important not to overcook the fruit; it should be soft but still retain its shape and not lose very much juice. 5 minutes is long enough. Keep your eyes on the fruit during this process!

Cut crusts from bread and line a 1½-pint pudding basin. Pour on fruit and cover with more slices of bread. Place a saucer with a weight on top of the pudding and leave overnight in a cool place.

Turn out the pudding into a dish and spoon the excess juice over the top to make it an even color. Serve with cream. Serves 4 to 6.

STACEY SOODIK

Actress and playwright.

Soodik Women's Chocolate Chip Cheesecake

1½ cups finely crushed Oreos (about 18 cookies)
¼ cup butter, melted
3 8-ounce packages softened cream cheese
1 14-ounce can sweetened condensed milk

3 eggs
2 teaspoons vanilla extract
1 cup mini chocolate chips
1 teaspoon flour

Preheat oven to 300 degrees. Combine crumbs and butter; pat firmly on bottom of 9-inch springform pan. In large mixer bowl, beat cheese until fluffy. Add condensed milk and beat until smooth. Add eggs and vanilla; mix well. In small bowl, toss together ½ cup chocolate chips with flour to coat; stir into cheese mixture. Pour into prepared pan. Sprinkle remaining chips evenly over top. Bake 1 hour or until cake springs back when lightly touched. Cool to room temperature. Chill. Remove sides of pan. Garnish as desired. "We like fresh hulled strawberries." Refrigerate leftovers if there are any.

JUDITH SPACEK

Career-woman, charity worker.

Dream Bars

1 cup graham cracker crumbs
½ cup softened butter
1 cup flaked coconut
6 ounces butterscotch chips

6 ounces chocolate chips
1 14-ounce can condensed milk
1 cup pecans or walnuts, chopped

Mix graham cracker crumbs with butter and line the bottom of a 9 by 13-inch pan with the mixture. Add the rest of the ingredients in order, in layers. Bake at 350 degrees for 35 minutes.

BARRY AND COOKIE STAGMAN

He is fashion expert and manufacturers' rep. She is active in charities, civic work.

Better Than Sex Chocolate Cream Bars

Brownies:

"Make your life a little easier by using your favorite boxed brownie mix (with or without walnuts) as your brownie base." Bake as directed in a 9 by 13-inch pan sprayed with PAM. Let cool 20 minutes.

Cream Filling:

½ cup salted butter

2 cups confectioners sugar

1 teaspoon vanilla

2 tablespoons milk

Cream butter. Add sugar, milk and vanilla. Beat until smooth. Pour over cooled brownie base. Refrigerate for 30 minutes.

Topping:

Melt 6 ounces semi-sweet chocolate chips with 4 tablespoons butter. Spread over chilled filling. Refrigerate for 30 minutes. Cut into squares.

BENE AND EDYTHE STEIN

He is head of Golf Mill Theaters and both are active in Variety Club charity endeavors.

Fudge Ribbon Cake

Cake:

1 8-ounce package cream cheese, softened

1 3-ounce package cream cheese, softened

1¾ cups sugar, divided

3 eggs

1½ teaspoons vanilla, divided

2 cups regular flour

1 teaspoon baking powder

1 teaspoon salt

½ teaspoon baking soda

½ cup butter or margarine

3 ounces unsweetened chocolate, melted

1⅓ cups milk

In a small mixer bowl, blend cream cheese at medium speed until softened. Add ¼ cup sugar, blending well. Add 1 egg and ½ teaspoon vanilla; beat at medium speed until thoroughly mixed. Set aside.

In large mixer bowl, combine remaining sugar, eggs and vanilla with ingredients through milk. Blend at low speed until moistened: beat 3 minutes at medium speed, scraping bowl occasionally.

Grease bottom of 13 by 9-inch pan and pour in half of chocolate batter. Spread batter to edges. Pour cream cheese mixture over batter, spreading to cover. Pour remaining chocolate batter back and forth over cream cheese to cover. Bake in 325 degree oven for 35 to 40 minutes or until top springs back when touched lightly in center. Cool completely in pan and frost with chocolate frosting.

Chocolate Frosting:

¼ **cup milk**
¼ **cup (½ stick) butter or margarine**
1 **ounce unsweetened chocolate, melted**

2½ **cups confectioners sugar**
1 **teaspoon vanilla**

In medium saucepan, heat milk, butter and chocolate until mixture boils. Remove from heat. Add confectioners sugar and vanilla; beat until smooth and creamy. If too thin, let cool slightly; if too thick add a few drops of milk.

MANFRED AND FERN STEINFELD

He is head of Shelby Williams Manufacturing Co. and both are active in charitable work.

Grandmother's Cookies

½ **stick butter, softened**
1 **cup brown sugar**
½ **teaspoon baking soda**

1 **egg**
2 **cups flour**
½ **cup raisins**

Pour hot water over raisins and allow to stand until raisins plump up. Drain well. Cream butter and sugar. Add remaining ingredients. Drop by teaspoonfuls onto ungreased cookie sheet. Bake 350 degrees for 10 to 15 minutes or until lightly browned.

VARIATIONS: instead of raisins indent middle of cookies and add drops of jam before baking or add chocolate chips to batter. Yields 2 to 3 dozen cookies.

GARDNER AND HANCHEN STERN

Patrons of the arts and civic leaders.

Crescent Cookies

2 sticks softened or melted butter
2 level cups unsifted flour
¼ cup confectioners sugar

1 teaspoon vanilla
½ to 1 cup ground nuts

Mix well. Roll, cut in strips and form crescents. Bake in 350 degree oven about ten minutes (should not get brown.) Roll in more confectioners sugar and let cool. One half of this recipe makes about three dozen small cookies.

LEE STERN

Owner of the Chicago Sting Soccer Team.

Norma Stern's Healthful Dessert

1 large navel orange
1 large banana
1 box strawberries

1 tablespoon sugar
Grand Marnier

Peel and section orange. Slice banana and strawberries. Mix together and sprinkle with sugar. Refrigerate until ready to use. Top with a dash of Grand Marnier. Serves 4.

ETTA AND LARRY STEVENS

Jewelry designers and radio talk show hosts.

Easy-Time Cherry Squares

1½ cups sugar
1 cup butter
4 eggs

2 cups all-purpose flour
1 tablespoon lemon extract
1 can cherry pie filling

Gradually add sugar to butter in large mixing bowl, creaming at medium speed until light and fluffy. Add eggs, one at a time, beating well after each. Then at low speed add flour and extract. Pour batter into well greased 15 by 10-inch jelly roll pan. With knife mark batter into 20 squares. Place 1 heaping tablespoon pie filling in center of each square. Bake at 350 degrees for 45 to 50 minutes. While warm, sift confectioners sugar over cake. Cool, cut into squares. Makes 20 servings.

MRS. THOMAS STEWART JR.

Civic leader, charity volunteer.

American Chocolate Cake with Fudge Frosting

Cake:
2¾ cups plus 2 tablespoons cake flour
2 cups sugar
1¾ cups solid vegetable shortening
½ cup unsweetened Dutch-process
   cocoa, such as Droste
4 tablespoons plus 2 teaspoons
   powdered milk

2½ teaspoons baking powder
1 teaspoon baking soda
1½ teaspoons vanilla extract
1 teaspoon salt
6 egg whites, at room temperature
Fudge Frosting (recipe follows)

Preheat the oven to 350 degrees. Lightly grease and flour two 9-inch round cake pans.

In a large mixer bowl, combine flour, sugar, vegetable shortening, cocoa, powdered milk, baking powder, baking soda, vanilla, salt and 1 cup water. Beat, beginning on low speed and gradually increasing to high, until smooth and light, about 4 minutes.

Add egg whites and ½ cup water. Beat until very smooth and light in texture, about 4 minutes. Divide batter between pans; smooth tops evenly.

227

Bake in center of oven 30 to 35 minutes, until the cakes are puffed and a tester inserted in the center comes out clean. Let cakes cool in pans for 10 minutes. Invert to unmold onto a wire rack; let cool completely, about 3 hours. (The cake layers may be baked a day ahead. Store at room temperature in plastic wrap.)

To assemble cake, generously cover top of one layer with frosting. Place second layer on top and frost top and sides with remaining frosting. To give frosting a shiny glaze, dip knife in warm water and lightly swirl in a decorative pattern. Store under a domed cake cover or large bowl until ready to serve. Serves 12.

Fudge Frosting:

4 ounces unsweetened chocolate, coarsely chopped
2 tablespoons solid vegetable shortening
4 cups confectioners sugar
¼ teaspoon salt
½ cup plus 2 tablespoons milk
1 teaspoon vanilla extract

In the top of a double boiler, combine chocolate and shortening. Warm over low heat, stirring, until smooth. Immediately remove from heat.

In a large bowl, combine confectioners sugar, salt, ½ cup milk and vanilla. Stir until smooth.

Scrape melted chocolate into sugar mixture and beat with a spoon until well blended. Let frosting stand for 1 minute; it will thicken considerably. Beat in remaining 2 tablespoons milk until smooth. Cover with plastic wrap and hold at room temperature until ready to use.

LIZ AND JULES STIFFEL

Civic and charity leaders, patrons of the arts.

Scrumptious Chocolate Souffle

Souffle:

4 ounces unsweetened chocolate
⅔ cup sugar
4 tablespoons strong cold coffee
6 egg yolks
4 tablespoons unsalted butter
4 tablespoons flour
1½ cups milk
¼ teaspoon salt
1 teaspoon vanilla
8 stiffly beaten egg whites

Melt together chocolate, sugar and coffee. Add slightly beaten egg yolks. Cool.

Make sauce of butter, flour, and milk. When thick add salt and vanilla. Mix the above in 2 steps. Then fold in stiffly beaten egg whites. Pour into buttered and sugared 2-quart casserole. Take a large spoon and run a groove about 1½ inches deep all around the top. Bake at 375 degrees and serve at once with sauce.

Brandy Sauce:
2 cups confectioners sugar
4 tablespoons butter
2 egg yolks
2 egg whites, beaten

1 teaspoon vanilla
1 cup whipped cream
1 tablespoon brandy

Cream confectioners sugar and butter. Beat egg yolks, add to creamed butter and sugar. Then fold in beaten egg whites, vanilla, whipped cream and brandy.

JOCELYN AND JAMES STOLLER

Real estate entrepreneurs, patrons of the arts.

Ice Cream Dessert Sauce

fresh fruit (strawberries, blueberries, or raspberries)

one pint vanilla ice cream
⅔ cup Cointreau

Melt ice cream. When melted, add Cointreau and mix. Serve fruit at room temperature with sauce.

JAMES AND DORIS STRAUSS

He is a packing house tycoon. She is an antiques expert and charity volunteer.

Almond Rum Torte

Torte:

8 eggs, separated
½ pound almonds, grated
1 cup sugar
½ cup bread crumbs
2 teaspoons flour, mixed with

½ teaspoon baking powder
juice and rind of 1 lemon
1 glass raspberry jelly
1 cup chopped walnuts

Beat the yolks with sugar until light. Add the almonds, bread crumbs and lemon. Then fold in lightly the beaten whites and the flour and baking powder, mixed. Bake in a springform pan for 1 hour in a moderate 350 degree oven. Allow cake to cool somewhat, then cut crosswise into two layers and put in a filling of 1 glass raspberry jelly and 1 cup chopped walnuts. Spread top and sides with:

Icing:

2 cups confectioners sugar
4 tablespoons heavy cream

2 tablespoons rum
walnut halves for garnish

Stir until smooth. Decorate with half walnuts.

DR. JEROME AND JOSIE STRAUSS

Both are active in civic, charitable groups.

Apricot Souffle

6 ounces dried apricots
1 cup water
5 egg whites
¼ cup granulated sugar

¼ cup sifted dark brown sugar
dash salt
½ teaspoon vanilla

Simmer apricots in 1 cup of water until mushy. Puree, retaining the syrup. Oil 1½-quart souffle dish and sprinkle lightly with sugar. Preheat oven to 350 degrees. Beat egg whites until stiff but not dry. Add granulated sugar, a tablespoon at at time, and beat between additions. Add brown sugar and beat lightly again well mixed. Fold in the apricot puree slowly and gently. Add salt and vanilla. Pour mixture into prepared dish. Sprinkle a little more sugar on top. Place dish in shallow pan of hot water and bake 30 minutes. Serve at once.

BETTY STUART-RODGERS

Photography expert, author.

President Eisenhower's Birthday Cake

½ cup butter
2 cups sugar
⅔ cup cocoa
½ cup water
3 egg yolks
1 teaspoon vanilla

2½ cups sifted flour
1 teaspoon baking soda
1½ teaspoons baking powder
¼ teaspoon salt
1 cup sour milk
3 egg whites

Cream butter and sugar. Dissolve cocoa in boiling water and mix until smooth. Cool. Add egg yolks and vanilla to creamed mixture; beat thoroughly. Add cooled cocoa solution. Sift together sifted cake flour, baking soda, baking powder, and salt. Have ready sour milk at room temperature. (You can mix 1 tablespoon vinegar with 1 cup sweet milk to sour it.)

Add sifted dry ingredients alternately with milk in thirds, beating until smooth after each addition. Fold in egg whites, which have been beaten stiff. Turn batter into two greased and floured 9-inch pans.

Bake at 375 degrees for 25 to 30 minutes. Remove cake from oven and turn out onto rack. When layers are cool, put them together with your favorite frosting and ice cake.

LAURIE AND LOUIS SUDLER JR.

Real estate tycoons, patrons of the arts.

Apple Dessert

5 Golden Delicious apples
orange juice
rind of 1 orange, grated
butter
sugar

orange flavoring
candied orange peel
ginger
1 tablespoon dark rum

Peel and core the apples and cook in a little orange juice until soft. Put in blender—add a little butter and sugar to taste and orange flavoring if you like—and blend. Then stir in grated orange rind. Chill thoroughly and serve in champagne glasses with candied orange peel or ginger sprinkled on top and approximately 1 tablespoon of dark rum.

JOHN AND BONNIE SWEARINGEN

He is chairman of Continental Ill. Corp. of Continental Bank, oilman, collects limericks. She is a former movie star and stock broker, now socialite, charity volunteer.

Chewy Brownies

2 squares bittersweet chocolate
2 sticks butter
2 cups sugar
2 eggs

1 cup flour
1 cup chopped nuts
1 teaspoon vanilla

Melt chocolate with butter in a double boiler or on low heat. Remove from heat. Add sugar and beaten eggs. Stir quickly. Fold in flour, vanilla and nuts. Bake at 300 degrees for 45-55 minutes in a greased 9 by 6-inch pan. Do not over cook. Cool 1 hour and cut into squares.

Fabulous Coffee Mousse

1 cup strong coffee
1 pint heavy cream, whipped

48 marshmallows

Add marshmallows to coffee and simmer until melted. Cool and fold in whipped cream. Pour into ring mold and chill. Unmold and fill center with more whipped cream and shaved chocolate. Serves 8.

"It tastes as if you've worked all day!"

Chocolate Mousse Sada

1½ cups Hershey's chocolate syrup
2 tablespoons brandy
2 envelopes gelatin dissolved in ⅓ cup
  water

1 cup boiling water
3 egg whites
2 cups heavy cream
2 tablespoons cocoa

Pour chocolate syrup into a mixing bowl. Stir in brandy. In a saucepan, mix dissolved gelatin into boiling water. Cool saucepan by dipping it into a large pan of cold water. Keep stirring until syrupy. Stir gelatin into chocolate syrup. Whip egg whites to soft peaks and gently fold into chocolate mixture. Whip cream stiff. Sprinkle cocoa through a fine sieve into whipped cream and then fold it in. Whip again a few seconds. (Do not overbeat or it will collapse.) Fold the whipped cream into the chocolate mixture. Transfer to individual serving dishes, chill, and serve. Serves 8.

PHIL AND DONNA TEINOWITZ

He is a real estate developer and both are patrons of the arts. She is a nurse.

Peach Cobbler

½ cup all-purpose flour
¼ teaspoon salt
5 tablespoons frozen, unsalted butter
4 tablespoons frozen shortening

4 or 5 tablespoons ice water
8 large ripe peaches, skinned and pitted
1 cup sugar
¼ cup unsalted butter

Preheat oven to 450 degrees. Lightly grease a 1½ to 2-quart dish. To make cobbler batter, place flour and salt in a food processor. Add butter and shortening and process to the size of small peas. Add 4 tablespoons ice water and process until dough begins to cling together (10 seconds or so). If more water is required, add it. Gather dough into ball. Wrap in plastic wrap or wax paper and refrigerate until ready to use.

Roll out the pastry into a large ragged circle. Since handling this large circle of dough can be difficult, dust it with flour and roll up on your rolling pin (window shade fashion). Unroll over the prepared dish. Carefully slip it down into the dish so that you have lined the bottom and sides, allowing the excess to hang over.

Cut each peach into 8 or 9 slices and heap into the dish. Cover with sugar and dot with butter. Flop the loose ends of the pastry over the top. Any extra loose pieces of dough you have can be used to fill in empty spaces. Put in preheated oven and turn down to 425 degrees. Bake for 45 minutes. Let cool and serve with vanilla ice cream, whipped cream, or plain light cream.

MIKE TEMKIN

Radio show producer.

Mandel Bread

3 eggs
½ cup Mazola oil
2 teaspoons baking soda
1 cup sugar
3 cups sifted all-purpose flour

1 teaspoon vanilla
½ teaspoon almond extract (optional)
1 cup chopped nuts
cinnamon

Beat together by hand the eggs and oil. Add baking soda, sugar, flour, vanilla and almond (optional). Add chopped nuts. Grease a cookie sheet lightly. Shape batter by spooning four long bars on cookie sheet. Sprinkle bars with cinnamon or cinnamon and sugar. Bake for ½ hour at 350 degrees. Cut into slices, turn over and bake additional (approximately) ten minutes.

"If you like them drier, bake a little longer. I love the cookie dry and hard; it makes for better dunking."

DANIEL TERRA

U.S. Ambassador-At-Large and creator of Terra Museum of Art; art collector, philanthropist.

Double Orange Cake

Cake:
6 eggs
1 cup sugar
¼ cup melted butter

3 tablespoons orange juice
1 orange rind, grated
1 cup sifted cake or all-purpose flour

Line 2 9-inch cake pans with waxed paper. Butter and flour. Preheat oven to 350 degrees. In bowl over boiling water, whip eggs and sugar until frothy. Remove from heat; continue to whip until thick, lemon-colored and tripled in volume. Fold in remaining ingredients. Bake 30 to 40 minutes. Cool on rack.

Orange Mousse Filling:
½ cup sugar
⅔ cup strained orange juice
4 egg yolks, beaten
⅓ cup water

1 envelope unflavored gelatin
1 tablespoon grated orange peel
4 egg whites
⅓ cup sugar

Soften gelatin in water. Combine sugar, orange juice, egg yolks and gelatin mixture in top of double boiler and cook over simmering water, stirring, until thick. Remove from heat. Stir in grated orange peel. Chill. Whip 4 egg whites with sugar and fold into cooled gelatin mixture. Refrigerate.

Orange Butter Cream:
4 teaspoons sugar
4 egg yolks
¾ pound butter, softened

3 teaspoons Grand Marnier
1 teaspoon grated orange rind

Beat sugar and egg yolks together until light and fluffy. Beat in butter, adding to sugar and egg yolk mixture in pieces. Beat well. Add Grand Marnier and orange rind. Beat again and set aside.

Orange Syrup:
½ cup sugar
1 cup water

3 teaspoons Grand Marnier

Bring all to boil and boil 5 minutes. Cool.

Assembly:

Cut cake layers in half. Place first layer on serving plate, sprinkle with syrup, and cover with orange mousse. Repeat twice, top with last layer. Refrigerate until firm. Remove from refrigerator, cover top with Orange Butter Cream. Decorate with thin orange slices and confectioners sugar if desired.

STANLEY TIGERMAN
Award-winning architect.

Grandma's Strudel

Dough:
¼ teaspoon salt
1½ cups flour
1 egg, slightly beaten

⅓ cup warm water
½ cup butter, melted

Mix salt, flour and egg. Add the water, mix dough quickly with a knife, then knead on board, stretching it up and down to make it elastic, until it leaves the board clean. Toss on a small, well-floured board. Cover with a hot bowl and keep it warm ½ hour or longer.

See that the room is free from drafts. Have materials for filling ready before stretching dough. Work quickly. Lay dough in center of a well-floured tablecloth on table about 30 by 48 inches. Flour dough. Roll into a long oval with rolling pin. Brush dough with ¼ cup of the melted butter. With hands under dough, palms down, pull and stretch the dough gradually all around the table, toward the edges, until it hangs over the table and is as thin as paper. Cut off dough that hangs over edge and drip ¼ cup more butter over surface of dough.

Sprinkle apple filling over ¾ of the greased, stretched dough. Fold a little of the dough at one end over the filling. Hold the cloth at that end high with both hands and the strudel will roll itself over and over, like jelly roll. Trim edges again. Twist roll into greased 11 by 16-inch pan or cut into 3 strands and lay them side by side by pan.

Brush top with more melted butter. Bake in hot oven 400 degrees ½ hour; reduce heat to 350 degrees and bake ½ hour or longer, or until brown and crisp, brushing well with butter from time to time during baking; using altogether about 1 cup melted butter for the strudel with its filling.

Filling:

2 quarts cooking apples, cut fine
1 cup seeded raisins
½ cup currants
¼ pound almonds, blanched and
  chopped

1 cup sugar mixed with 1 teaspoon
  cinnamon
½ cup melted butter

Combine all ingredients except butter. As rapidly as possible, spread apple filling evenly over ¾ of the stretched, buttered strudel dough. Drip some melted butter over the filling. Roll up, trim edges, then place in pan. Brush with rest of the butter from time to time while baking. Serve slightly warm.

Stanley's grandmother was chef at the Belden-Stratford Hotel circa 1935.

DR. CARL TINTARI

Dentist, authority on cosmetic dentistry.

Texas Cake

Cake:

1 teaspoon baking soda
2 cups all-purpose flour
2 cups sugar
2 sticks (½-pound) margarine
1 cup water

¼ cup cocoa
½ cup buttermilk
2 eggs
1 teaspoon vanilla

Put baking soda, flour and sugar in large bowl; mix and set aside. Boil two sticks margarine, water and cocoa. Pour second mixture over dry ingredients; stir. Add buttermilk, eggs, and vanilla; beat two to three minutes. Pour into greased and floured 17 by 11-inch jelly roll pan or cookie sheet. Bake at 400 degrees for 25 to 30 minutes. Frost at once.

Icing:

1 stick margarine
¼ cup cocoa
6 tablespoons homogenized milk (not
  low-fat)

16 ounces confectioners sugar
1 teaspoon vanilla
1 cup chopped nuts if desired

Boil margarine, cocoa and milk. Pour over confectioners sugar, add vanilla and beat well. Add nuts, if desired. Pour in middle of hot cake and spread to sides. This recipe, from Dr. Tintari's mother, Mary, will serve a crowd.

JOHN AND WEQUE TRUTTER

He is an executive with Illinois Bell and both are patrons of the arts.

Snowflake Bavarian

1 envelope unflavored gelatin
5 tablespoons sugar
2 eggs, separated
1 cup milk

2 tablespoons almond liqueur
½ teaspoon vanilla extract
1 cup (½ pint) heavy cream, whipped
⅔ cup flaked coconut

In medium saucepan, mix unflavored gelatin with 3 tablespoons sugar; blend in egg yolks beaten with milk. Let stand 1 minute. Stir over low heat until gelatin is completely dissolved, about 5 minutes. Stir in liqueur and vanilla. Pour into large bowl and chill, stirring occasionally, until mixture mounds slightly when dropped from spoon. In medium bowl, beat egg whites until soft peaks form; gradually add remaining sugar and beat until stiff. Fold egg whites, then whipped cream and coconut into gelatin mixture. Turn into 5-cup mold or bowl; chill until firm. Garnish, if desired, with cranberries. Makes about 10 servings.

LYNN AND ALLEN TURNER

Both are active in the arts community and he is a partner with Pritzker and Pritzker legal firm.

Banana Whipped Cream Pie

Crust:
1½ cups graham cracker crumbs
¼ cup sugar

⅓ cup butter, melted
¼ teaspoon each, cinnamon and nutmeg

Mix all of above together. Press into bottom and sides of 9-inch pie pan. Chill while preparing filling.

Filling:
4 large bananas
25 large marshmallows
¼ cup milk

1 cup heavy cream, whipped with ½
    small package unflavored gelatin

Using 2-quart saucepan, add marshmallows to ¼ cup milk. Heat on low setting until marshmallows have melted. Gently fold together melted marshmallows and whipped cream. Layer pie crust with bananas, then marshmallow-whipped cream mixture two layers deep. Chill and serve.

JOANNE UNKOVSKOY

Public relations head for Neiman-Marcus.

Paska

Paska is the traditional Easter dessert of Old Russia. The tall, molded pyramid is a noble sight, decorated with Easter symbols cut from candied fruit and wreathed at the base with flowers and Easter eggs.

2 pounds ricotta cheese
4 egg yolks
1 cup butter
2¼ cups sugar
1 teaspoon vanilla

grated rind of ½ lemon
1 cup heavy cream
½ cup raisins
½ cup citron

Prepare a mold by smoothly lining with cloth any container with holes in the bottom. (Our testers used a 2-quart flower pot lined with cheesecloth). Blend cheese with egg yolks until just smooth. Cream butter, then add sugar, vanilla, lemon rind, raisins and citron, and cream thoroughly. Combine with cheese mixture, then blend in cream. Pour mixture into mold and set over a bowl to drip for 24 hours. Discard drippings periodically. Paska becomes firmer with time. Unmold and decorate as desired. Good with pound cake or Kulich. Serves 8 to 10.

VALERIE VALENTINE

Active in Greek cultural activities.

Valentine Kisses

5 egg whites
1 cup sugar

1 tablespoon vanilla
1 tablespoon vinegar

Beat egg whites until stiff. Add sugar gradually, then vanilla and vinegar. Use lightly greased cookie tins. Drop kisses onto tins ½ inch apart. Preheat oven to 450 degrees. Turn off when ready to put kisses in oven and let remain in oven overnight. Do not open oven door until next morning.

GEORGE AND LILY VENSON

Community activists.

Grecian Walnut Cake

Cake:

1 cup finely ground zwieback
1 pound walnuts chopped coarsely
1½ cups granulated sugar
7 eggs, separated
grated rind of 1 orange

½ teaspoon nutmeg
½ teaspoon cinnamon
1 teaspoon baking powder
confectioners sugar

Mix zwieback and walnuts in bowl. Mix with sugar. Beat egg yolks until thick and set aside. Beat egg whites in large bowl until they form soft peaks. Fold yolks into whites, alternating with zwieback mixture. Add cinnamon, nutmeg, orange rind and baking powder. Pour into well-buttered 13 by 9 by 2-inch aluminum pan. Bake in 425 degree oven for 15 minutes. Reduce temperature to 275 degrees and bake 45 minutes longer. Cake is done when cake tester inserted in center comes out clean. While cake is baking, prepare syrup.

Syrup:

2 cups sugar
1¼ cups water
¼ cup honey
1 cinnamon stick

5 whole cloves
finely grated rind of 1 orange
finely grated rind of 1 lemon
juice of 1 small lemon

Combine sugar, water, grated rinds, cloves and cinnamon stick in saucepan. Bring to a boil and reduce to medium heat; simmer, uncovered, for about 10 to 15 minutes to thicken syrup. Remove from heat. Discard spices. Stir in honey and lemon juice. Pour cooled syrup over hot cake, using enough to lightly saturate cake. With sharp knife, cut cake into diamonds but leave in pan. Drizzle remaining syrup over cake and cool in pan. Sprinkle top with confectioners sugar before serving.

WILLIAM VON DAHM

President of own ad agency, authority on marketing, promotion.

Pears with Raspberry Puree

1½ cups sugar
1 tablespoon sugar
1½ cups water
2 tablespoons cold water
½ teaspoon vanilla extract

3 peeled ripe pears, halved
1 package frozen raspberries, defrosted
1 teaspoons cornstarch
kirsch
blanched, slivered almonds

Combine sugar and water and boil five minutes. Add the vanilla and pears and simmer until the fruit is tender. Drain and chill. Combine the raspberries with one tablespoon sugar. Mix the cornstarch with two tablespoons cold water and combine with the raspberries. Simmer three minutes and mash through a sieve. Chill and add kirsch to taste.

Spoon over the pears and sprinkle with almonds. Serves 6.

FORMER GOV. DANIEL AND ROBERTA WALKER

Developers of BW Oil Change franchises, both are active in banking, real estate development, the arts.

Pears with Raspberries

4 fresh pears
2 cups white wine
1 teaspoon sugar

pint fresh raspberries or
one package frozen raspberries

Peel and core pears. Poach for 2 to 3 minutes until tender in white wine with sugar added to liquid. Cool and serve covered with fresh raspberries or frozen raspberries, pureed, or raspberry liqueur.

241

NORMAN WALLACE

Veteran pianist-around-town, composer.

Applesauce Pie

24 graham crackers, rolled
¼ pound sweet butter, melted

1 can or jar applesauce
meringue or whipped cream (optional)

Mix crumbs and butter and line pie plate. Add applesauce and bake ½ hour at 350 degrees. Use meringue or whipped cream on top. I prefer meringue. Bake meringue, not the whipped cream!

"You can also use a lemon cream filling. Either way it's delicious and can be eaten warm or cold."

RIC WANETIK

Vice-President, advertising, of Marshall Field's.

Chocolate Drop Cookies

½ cup butter
1 cup sugar
1 egg
½ teaspoon vanilla
1 cup and 2 tablespoons sifted all-purpose flour
½ teaspoon salt

½ teaspoon baking soda
15 to 20 solid frango mint chocolates, each chopped into 8 small pieces (refrigerate chocolates for one hour before to make chopping easier)
½ cup chopped pecans if desired

Cream butter, add sugar. Beat in egg, vanilla. Sift and stir in flour, salt, soda. Carefully stir in chocolate and add pecans. Preheat oven to 375 degrees. Drop batter from a teaspoon on a greased cookie sheet. Bake for 10 minutes or until done. Makes four dozen 2-inch cookies.

DR. THOMAS WARD

Dentist, real estate developer.

Stephanie's Forgotten Torte

5 egg whites
¼ teaspoon salt
½ teaspoon cream of tartar
1 teaspoon vanilla

1½ cups sugar
½ cup chopped walnuts (optional)
strawberries and ice cream

Beat egg whites until frothy. Sprinkle salt and cream of tartar over top and beat until stiff. Gradually beat in sugar, 2 tablespoons at a time. Add vanilla and continue beating until stiff and peaked. Fold in walnuts, if desired. Pour into well buttered 9-inch springform pan. Place cake in oven preheated to 450 degrees. Turn off heat at once. Bake cake overnight in stored up heat. Remove following morning. Cover with strawberries and ice cream just before serving. Serves eight.

This Swedish treat from Tom's mother, Marie Anderson Ward, is better served 2 days after it is baked.

CAROL AND IRWIN WARE

Owners of the Ware Fur Salons; importers, designers of furs. Both are active in charity endeavors.

Chocolate Souffle Rothschild

3 tablespoons butter or margarine
⅓ cup sugar
⅓ cup flour
1 cup cream
3 well beaten eggs
2 ounces (2 squares) melted
   unsweetened chocolate
1 teaspoon vanilla

4 egg whites
extra granulated sugar
extra butter for coating pan
whipping cream and confectioners
   sugar for serving
a little Grand Marnier or any liqueur
   you like

Melt butter, blend in sugar and flour, mix well. Add cream, cook and stir constantly over medium heat. Beat in egg yolks. Cook exactly one minute more. Cool slightly. Stir in vanilla, and melted chocolate; beat egg whites stiff.

If you have a decorative souffle dish that is oven-proof use it—otherwise any 1½-quart souffle dish. Butter it well. Coat with your extra granulated sugar. Gently spoon mixture

243

into dish. Put in pan in 1 inch of hot water. Bake at 350 degrees for 30 minutes or until firm. Sprinkle with sifted confectioners sugar and serve at once with slightly sweetened whipped cream, which can be flavored with the liqueur of your choice.

RICHARD AND GERTRUDE WAXENBERG

He is 5-Way Chili entrepreneur, sportsman. She is county government executive, active in local charities.

Gert's Trifle

leftover cake for 6 servings
1 package vanilla pudding, any kind
1½ cups rum or brandy

fresh or canned fruit for 6 servings
dash nutmeg

Use leftover cake—angel food, pound, whatever. Place about a tablespoonful in bottom of individual ramekins, or if you wish, in a bowl. Make a recipe of your favorite vanilla pudding and season it with a little nutmeg. Pour enough rum or brandy over cake to soak it. Combine some sliced bananas, cut-up purple plums and peaches (if canned, drain well). Berries are good, too. Pour warm pudding over fruit. Chill and serve with whipped cream. Serves 6.

EDWARD AND LAWRIE WEED

He is an advertising, marketing expert. She is with Bruce Gregga Interiors. Both socialites.

Johnnie's Rich Date Drops

1½ cups chopped walnuts
2 teaspoons imitation maple flavoring
1 cup butter, softened
½ cup white sugar
1 cup brown sugar, packed
2 eggs

1 teaspoon vanilla
¼ teaspoon salt
2¼ cups flour
1 tablespoon baking soda
2 cups chopped dates

Combine chopped nuts with maple flavoring. Set aside. Cream butter and sugars until light and fluffy. Add eggs and vanilla and beat well. Add sifted dry ingredients (salt, flour, baking soda) and mix. Stir in dates and nuts. Drop by teaspoonfuls onto ungreased cookie sheet. Bake 10 to 12 minutes in 350 degrees oven until golden brown. Makes 6 dozen.

KITTY AND HARRY WEESE

Prominent architects and civic leaders.

Chewy Chocolate Pudding

Pre-heat oven to 325 degrees. Butter a 4-cup ring mold.

½ cup butter
1 cup sugar
2 eggs
¼ cup plus 1 tablespoon flour

¼ teaspoon salt
2 ounces baking chocolate
½ teaspoon vanilla
½ teaspoon baking powder

Melt chocolate in small pan over hot water. Cream butter and sugar. Add beaten eggs, mix well, add flour, salt, chocolate, vanilla, then baking powder. Pour into buttered mold. Bake ½ hour. Serve hot with whipped cream. This is a Weese family favorite.

JOAN AND CHARLES WEGNER III

He is head of Jel-Sert, a sportsman, civic leader. Both are socialites, world travelers, philanthropists.

French Eclair Cake

Cake:
1 box honey graham crackers
2 packages French vanilla instant
   pudding

1 8-ounce container Cool Whip

Prepare pudding per instructions, fold in Cool Whip. Butter 9 by 13-inch casserole dish and completely cover bottom wtih one layer whole graham crackers side by side. Spread ½ pudding over crackers. Top with another layer of whole graham crackers side by side. Pour over remaining pudding mix and top with third layer of whole graham crackers.

Frosting:

2 ounces Nestle's Choc O' Bake or
   bittersweet chocolate, melted
1½ cup confectioners sugar

2 teaspoons white corn syrup
1 teaspoon vanilla extract
3 tablespoons milk

Beat all ingredients, spread frosting on top layer of graham crackers and refrigerate.

"This must be made one day before serving. Something wonderful happens to this recipe when it stands overnight."

JOAN WEINSTEIN

Owner of Ultimo fashion salon.

Disgustingly Good Chocolate Pie

Crust:

25 vanilla wafers, finely crushed
½ cup finely chopped pecans

¼ cup melted butter

Mix well and press into pie plate. Bake 15 minutes in 300 degree oven and cool.

Filling:

¾ cup butter
1 cup plus 2 tablespoons granulated
   sugar
2 squares melted chocolate

1 teaspoon vanilla
3 eggs
whipped cream

Cream butter with sugar. Add melted chocolate and vanilla. Add well-beaten eggs one at a time. Mix well. Fold into cooled pie crust and refrigerate overnight. Cover with mounds of fresh whipped cream before serving.

"Caution: may be habit-forming."

BERNARD AND LOIS WEISBERG

He is an attorney, civic leader. She is head of special events for Mayor Washington.

Chocolate Sauce

1 package or less bittersweet chocolate
  morsels
a little water

2 or more tablespoons (to taste) cold
  Turkish coffee

Stir chocolate over hot water in double boiler until it melts. Add a little water to thin chocolate. Add coffee. Serve hot over ice cream.

JUDY WEISS

Cooking and baking authority, cateress, teacher.

Brownie Bottom Cheesecake

"This dessert consists of three layers, the bottom being a brownie, the center a cheesecake and the top a chocolate sour cream topping. But it only takes a maximum of 30 minutes to put together."

Brownie layer:
2 ounces unsweetened chocolate
¼ pound unsalted butter
2 eggs
1 cup sugar

¾ cup sifted flour
1 teaspoon baking powder
¼ teaspoon salt

Preheat oven to 350 degrees; grease bottom of 9-inch springform pan. Melt chocolate and butter together; allow to cool. Sift dry ingredients together. Then beat eggs and add sugar until batter is a creamy lemon yellow. Pour chocolate and butter mixture into egg batter, then incorporate dry ingredients until just mixed. Pour brownie layer into springform pan, clean pan sides.

Cheesecake layer:
16 ounces cream cheese
½ cup sugar
3 eggs

1 teaspoon bourbon (may substitute
  vanilla)

Cream cream cheese, adding eggs one at a time and scraping bottom and sides of bowl with rubber spatula. Add sugar and bourbon and mix until batter is creamy smooth. Pour cheesecake mixture on top of brownie layer and place pan in oven for 45 minutes. Allow to cool on rack.

Chocolate Sour Cream Layer:
16 ounces sour cream
¼ cup sugar

⅓ cup powdered cocoa
1 teaspoon bourbon (or vanilla)

Combine all ingredients. Spread on cooled cheesecake with a spatula and return cake to oven for 5 minutes. Allow Brownie Cheesecake to cool, cover and refrigerate overnight.

ROBERT AND FLO WEISS

Civic and charitable leaders, patrons of the arts.

Incredibles

1 cup butter
1 cup brown sugar
1 teaspoon vanilla
2 cups flour

dash salt
14-ounce bag Kraft caramels
2 6⅜-ounce packages Heath bars
⅓ cup evaporated milk

Cream butter, sugar, and vanilla. Add flour and salt. Mix well. Spread in ungreased 10 by 15-inch pan. Bake at 325 for 10 minutes.

Meanwhile, melt Kraft caramels with ⅓ cup evaporated milk. Carefully spread on top of base. Place Heath bar pieces on top of caramel. (Break or cut each ½ bar into 6 pieces.) Bake for 15 minutes more. Cool. Then refrigerate. Cut into squares when cold. Put in freezer. Best when served frozen.

SKIP AND FRANKIE WELFELD

He is head of N.H. Rosenthal Furs. She is fashion expert, former model.

Mud Pie

Pie:
**1 large package chocolate Oreo double
 stuffs (Skip's most favorite cookies)**
½ cup melted margarine

½ gallon softened vanilla ice cream
1 package ground pecans

Crush entire package of cookies and add melted margarine to ¾ of the crushed cookies. (Remainder of cookies to be used for topping.) Mix cookies and margarine and pat into bottom of 9 by 13-inch pan. Freeze for 20 minutes. Spoon in softened ice cream and top with remaining cookies. Sprinkle nuts over entire top and freeze. Serve with hot fudge sauce.

Hot Fudge Sauce:

small package semi-sweet chocolate chips
⅓ cup kirsh or brandy or both

3 tablespoons cream
2 teaspoons instant coffee powder

Mix in double boiler on very low heat until melted. Serve immediately.

JACK WETZEL

Male model, sportsman, socialite; active in local charities.

Egg Nog Cake

1 package yellow cake mix
1 small package instant vanilla pudding
4 eggs
¾ cup salad oil

¾ cup Harveys Bristol Cream Sherry
1 teaspoon nutmeg
confections sugar or vanilla or orange-flavored glaze

Put all ingredients in a bowl and mix at high speed with an electric mixer for 5 minutes. Pour into greased and floured bundt pan. Bake 45 minutes to an hour at 350 degrees, till tester or toothpick comes out clean. Cool cake for at least 20 minutes on rack. Invert, remove and sprinkle with confectioners sugar when completely cool or drizzle with vanilla or orange-flavored glaze. Good with fresh fruit or ice cream.

"If I can't find my electric mixer, I wear a sling when I serve the cake to show how much beating is required!"

JERRY AND SUE WEXLER

Real estate tycoons. She is the mother of movie star Daryl Hannah.

Wexlers' Sweet Tooth

5 or 6 chocolate-covered toffee bars,
    crushed
1 package chocolate wafers, crushed
1 quart vanilla-chocolate chip ice cream,
    softened

hot fudge sauce
whipped cream if desired

In a 9-inch pie pan make a layer of crushed candy bars mixed with cookie crumbs. Add a layer of softened ice cream. Keep in freezer. When ready to serve, cut in slices and top with hot fudge sauce and whipped cream if desired.

JASON AND JAMIE WILD

Child models and actors.

Sweet Tooth Soother

1 stick butter
1 cup graham cracker crumbs
½ cup semi-sweet chocolate morsels
½ cup milk chocolate morsels

1 cup coconut, shredded
1 cup chopped pecans
1 cup condensed milk

Pre-heat oven to 350 degrees.

Slowly melt butter in 8 by 8-inch baking pan.

Press graham crackers into butter evenly on bottom of pan. Sprinkle morsels on top, then coconut, then pecans. Pour milk over layers. Bake for 30 minutes. Slightly cool and cut into squares.

250

LOIS KAY WILLARD

Head of Gemini Sales and Supply, lady farmer, civic leader.

Joannie's Persimmon Pudding

Pudding:

2 cups persimmon pulp, put through a
   colander
3 eggs
1¼ cups sugar
1½ cups all-purpose flour
1 teaspoon baking powder
1 teaspoon soda
½ teaspoon salt

½ cup melted butter
2½ cups rich milk
2 teaspoons cinnamon
1 teaspoon ginger
½ teaspoon freshly grated nutmeg
1 cup raisins
1 cup nut meats

Topping:

2 cups freshly whipped heavy cream or
1 cup standard cream or hard sauce

Preheat oven to 325 degrees. Place the two cups of pulp in a large mixing bowl, and beat in all the other ingredients. Bake the pudding in a greased 9 by 13-inch baking dish until firm, about one hour. Wait until completely cool before adding a generous dollop of whipped cream. (Cream or hard sauce can be substituted.) Serve promptly. Serves 8.

DR. PHILIP AND CONNIE WILLIAMS

He is an active physician. Both are members of local health and charitable groups.

Pecan Pie

⅓ cup butter and margarine (half of
   each)
¾ cup firmly packed brown sugar
3 eggs, slightly beaten
1 cup corn syrup or maple syrup

1 cup whole, small pecan halves
1 teaspoon vanilla
¼ teaspoon salt
1 unbaked 9-inch pie shell

Cream butter/margarine mixture and sugar. Add beaten eggs. Stir in syrup, pecan halves, vanilla and salt and fill pastry-lined pan. Bake pie at 425 degrees about 45 minutes. An inserted knife comes out clean when pie is done. Cool and serve with or without whipped cream.

DORI WILSON

Publicist, former model, active socially, aids local charitable endeavors.

Hot Fruit Compote

12 dried macaroons, crumbled
4 cups canned fruits, drained (peaches,
    pears, apricots, pineapple or cherries)
½ cup almonds, slivered and toasted

¼ cup brown sugar
½ cup sherry
¼ cup melted butter

Butter a 2½ quart casserole. Cover bottom with macaroon crumbs. Then alternate fruit and macaroons in layers, finishing with macaroons. Sprinkle with almonds, sugar and sherry. Bake in a 350 degree oven for 30 minutes. Add melted butter. Serve hot. Serves 8.

TED AND BARBARA WILSON

Publicists, patrons of the arts.

Floating Island

4 egg yolks
¼ cup sugar
⅛ teaspoon salt
2 cups milk
1 teaspoon vanilla, rum or sherry or

a little grated lemon rind
4 egg whites
⅛ teaspoon salt
3 tablespoons sugar
½ teaspoon vanilla

Beat slightly egg yolks, add ¼ cup sugar, ⅛ teaspoon salt and milk. Place the custard over a very slow fire. Stir it constantly. Take care that it does not boil, or stir over simmering water until it begins to thicken. Cool custard. Add vanilla, rum or sherry or a little grated lemon rind. Chill it thoroughly. Place in baking dish.

Whip egg whites and salt until stiff. Add sugar and vanilla. Heap egg whites on custard. Place dish in a hot oven 500 degrees for 2 minutes until tips of meringue are brown. Serve the custard hot or cold.

BESS WINAKOR

Writer, publicist, supporter of the arts.

Bess's Best Chocolate Mousse

3 eggs, separated
¾ cup plus 1 tablespoon superfine
    sugar (If you can't find superfine
    sugar, regular sugar will do)
3 tablespoons Harvey's Bristol Cream
    Sherry

1 teaspoon vanilla
4 ounces unsweetened chocolate
4 tablespoons soft butter
3 tablespoons coffee
½ cup heavy cream

Beat the egg yolks with the ¾ cup sugar, Harvey's Bristol Cream and vanilla in the top of a double boiler until the mixture is slightly thick and pale yellow. (A small electric hand mixer is best for this.) Place the egg yolk-sugar mixture over simmering water and continue to beat it with the hand mixer about five minutes, until it is a bit foamy. (If the egg yolk-sugar mixture begins to crust against the edge of the double boiler top, your water is too hot.) Then take the egg yolk-sugar mixture off the water and let it cool to room temperature. Meantime, melt the chocolate. Then remove the chocolate pan from the heat and stir in the butter a little at a time. Stir the chocolate-butter mixture into the egg yolk-sugar mixture until everything is smooth and creamy. Then stir in the coffee.

Beat the egg whites until they are foamy. Sprinkle the additional 1 tablespoon of sugar over the egg whites and continue beating until stiff peaks form. Fold and stir the egg whites into the chocolate mixture until there are no white streaks. Then whip the cream and fold it into the chocolate.

Chill the mousse in a big bowl for several hours or overnight, and serve with additional whipped cream.

Serves 6 and recipe can be doubled.

DR. PETER AND MARY WARD WOLKONSKY

Social leaders, active in supporting the arts, charities, cultural affairs.

Mary's Berries

1 pint strawberries
½ pint raspberries
¼ pint red currants
1½ cups confectioners sugar
3 tablespoons Curacao or other orange
   liqueur

½ cup heavy cream
6 egg yolks
¼ bottle non-vintage champagne

Wash and dry strawberries, raspberries and red currants. Sprinkle with ½ cup of confectioner's sugar and Curacao. Allow to marinate for an hour or so. Transfer to shallow, heat-proof dish. Lightly beat whipping cream.

Make a sabayon sauce by whisking egg yolks with 1 cup of confectioners sugar to the consistency of thick cream. Gradually add non-vintage champagne. Place bowl over a pan of simmering water and whisk until the mixture doubles in bulk and is thick and fluffy.

Fold in the whipped cream and spread on the fruit. Sprinkle generously with confectioners sugar and put under a medium hot boiler until the sabayon topping is golden. Serve at once.

WILLIAM AND ELEANOR WOOD-PRINCE

Society, cultural leaders; active in supporting the arts, charities.

Grapes A La Wood-Prince

2 pounds seedless white grapes
kirsch

sour cream

Peel off the skins of the grapes and refrigerate grapes. Half an hour before serving as dessert, spoon onto four dessert plates. Sprinkle grapes with kirsch and place a tablespoon of sour cream on side of plate. Serve with vanilla wafers if desired.

MARVIN AND ESTHER WORTELL

He is president of Triton Industries. She is nutritionalist and teacher.

Healthful Peanut Butter-Cereal Balls

½ cup honey
½ cup natural peanut butter
½ cup oatmeal
½ cup Grape-Nuts flakes
½ cup raisins

½ cup chopped nuts
¼ cup wheat germ
(More honey may be added to your
   taste.)

Combine all ingredients in large bowl. With greased hands, roll into small balls. May then be rolled in coconut or Grape-Nuts for coating. Keep in refrigerator.

CONG. SIDNEY YATES

Veteran representative from Chicago, patron of the arts.

Addie's Forgotten Cookies

1 6-ounce package chocolate chips (mint
   or butterscotch may be used)

2 egg whites
⅔ cup granulated sugar

Preheat oven to 350 degrees. Beat the two egg whites until stiff. Begin adding the sugar a teaspoon at a time while beating constantly. After all sugar is added, continue beating a short while, being certain stiff peaks will form.

Fold in the chocolate chips. Drop by half teaspoonfuls onto cookie sheet which has been covered with waxed paper. Put in oven and turn oven off immediately. Do not open door for at least 8 hours! Makes 2 dozen.

"Make these in the evening and leave until morning. Good for a reception or tea party."

WILLIAM AND JANE YLVISAKER

He is head of Gould, active on the polo field. Both are social lions here and in Palm Beach, supporting arts and charities.

Hazelnut Meringue Cake with Apricot Cream

4 egg whites
9 ounce castor sugar
vanilla essence
½ teaspoon vinegar
4½ ounces browned ground hazelnuts
4 ounces dried apricots, soaked in water overnight

½ lemon, juice and rind
¼ pint water
4 ounces granulated sugar
¼ pint heavy cream
strawberries or raspberries for decoration

Prepare two 8-inch round cake tins by rubbing the sides with butter and dusting with flour and lining the bottom with a disc of bakewell paper. Set the oven at 375 degrees. Whisk the egg whites until stiff, then gradually beat in the castor sugar. Continue beating until very stiff, adding the vanilla and vinegar. Lastly fold in the prepared nuts. Fill the prepared tins and bake for about 30-40 minutes.

Have ready the soaked apricots. Stew gently in their liquid with strip of lemon rind to flavor. When tender rub through a fine seive or strainer. Allow to cool. Dissolve sugar in water, add lemon juice and boil for 3 minutes. Whip cream, sweeten to taste and mix in a little of the apricot puree. Spread between cake layers, adding a few berries if desired. Dust cake top with confectioners sugar. Dilute the remaining apricot puree with the sugar syrup and serve this sauce separately. Decorate cake with berries.

MRS. JOHN YORK

Active in local charities, civic affairs.

Lemon Cream with Fruit

3 eggs
2 egg yolks
½ cup sugar
grated rind of one lemon
¾ tablespoon unflavored gelatin

¼ cup lemon juice
2 cups heavy cream
1 pint blueberries, raspberries or
    strawberries

Beat eggs and egg yolks until frothy. Add sugar while beating at a slow rate, and continue to beat until mixture is thickened. Add the grated rind.

Combine the gelatin and lemon juice in a heatproof measuring cup. Place the cup over hot water and stir until gelatin dissolves. Add it to the egg mixture and beat well.

Whip the cream until stiff and fold into the egg and lemon mixture. Pour the mixture into a one-quart mold and chill for about 4 hours. Unmold and serve with blueberries, raspberries or strawberries. Serves 6.

LINDA YU

TV Personality.

Dr. Richard Baer's Chocolate Fix

4 ounces sweet butter, softened
2 ounces unsweetened chocolate
⅔ cup sugar
2 eggs, lightly beaten
½ cup flour
1 teaspoon vanilla extract

pinch salt
1 pint chocolate ice cream
1 cup peanut butter
3 ounces semi-sweet chocolate
11 by 14-inch jelly roll pan

Melt unsweetened chocolate in top of a double boiler. Beat together sugar and butter until creamy and light. Add eggs, flour, vanilla, salt. Stir in melted chocolate. Butter the pan.

Carefully spread brownie mixture in bottom of pan. Bake 10 minutes at 400 degrees. Cut into two even pieces. Wrap each in foil and freeze 2 hours.

Next, soften ice cream just until spreadable. Spread it on one side of a brownie layer. Spread peanut butter on side of other brownie layer. Put together like a sandwich. Wrap in foil and freeze at least 3 hours.

Melt remaining chocolate in top of double boiler. Cut frozen brownie "sandwich" into bars or smaller pieces. Dip into melted chocolate. Place on foil for few minutes until hardened. Freeze until ready to serve or eat them up all at once.

MARTHA ZAFER

Real estate authority.

Ravani (Greek Sponge Cake)

Cake:
6 eggs
1½ cups sugar
1 stick butter
½ cup lukewarm milk

lemon rind
1 teaspoon vanilla
2¾ cups sifted flour
3 teaspoons baking powder

Beat eggs and add sugar until well mixed. Melt butter and add milk until well mixed. Pour butter-milk mixture slowly into egg-sugar mixture and stir. Add lemon rind and vanilla, mix. Sift flour and baking powder together. Add flour to wet ingredients, stir and fold until well mixed. For a fluffier cake, use a wooden spoon. Bake in a 12-inch round cake pan at 350 degrees for 30 to 35 minutes. Remove from oven and pour cold syrup over hot cake.

Syrup:
3 cups water
3 cups sugar
½ lemon

1 stick cinnamon
6 whole cloves

Combine all ingredients and bring to boil in heavy saucepan. Boil for 1 hour at low heat or until the consistency of syrup. Remove the half lemon and stick of cinnamon from syrup and let it cool. Pour cool syrup over hot cake.

And now a luscious listing of sweet tooth favorites . . .

SUSAN ANDERSON
WBBM-TV personality.
Haagen-Dazs ice cream

MRS. LESTER ARMOUR
Society leader, supporter of Rehab Institute.
Cappuchino ice cream

ERNIE BANKS
Cub baseball great.
Honey Vanilla Natural ice cream

CHARLES BANE
Attorney.
Eileen Bane's Blueberry Bites

WILLIAM C. BARTHOLOMAY
Socialite, sportsman.
Ice cream topped with raspberries

CELESTE BECKER
Photographer.
Ice cream with macaroons

JAMES BELUSHI
Comedian and actor.
Key Lime pie

CARDINAL JOSEPH BERNARDIN
Archbishop of Chicago Archdiocese.
Cheese and fresh fruit

TYBE AND MILT BLINK
Patrons of the arts.
Strawberry Fluff

259

BECKY BISOULIS
Award-winning fashion designer.
Yogurt with peaches and Grand Marnier

BEVERLY DOWIS BLETTNER
Socialite, leader in charitable organizations.
Fresh strawberries with sour cream and brown sugar

DAVID BORTMAN
Attorney.
Yogurt with fresh bananas and peaches

HARRIET BRADY
Philanthropist, investor.
Blueberry pie ala mode

JULIE BURMAN
Dancer, Hubbard Street Dance Co.
Mrs. Field's oatmeal raisin cookies

JANE BYRNE
Former mayor of Chicago.
Old-fashioned strawberry shortcake

KATHY BYRNE
Daughter of former Mayor Jane Byrne, caterer, fashion consultant.
Creme Brulee with strawberries

HARRY CARAY
Sports announcer, "Mayor" of Rush Street.
Ice cream with Elmer's topping

JOSEPH CARLUCCI
Owner of Carlucci restaurant.
Torta Di Ciocolato

JANET CONNOR
Special events coordinator for Marshall Field's.
Gourmet ice cream

LOU CONTE
Artistic director, founder of Hubbard Street Dance Co.
Fannie May peanut clusters

DON CRAIG
WBBM-TV newsman.
Tapioca pudding

LINDSAY CROUSE
Actress.
Cheese and fresh fruit

JUDGE WALTER AND MARIE CUMMINGS
Socialites, patrons of the arts.
Chocolate mousse a la coconnas

JIMMY DAMON
Singer.
Rum-raisin ice cream

MERRI DEE
WGN radio personality.
Lemon meringue pie

CHARLOTTE PARK DOYLE
Active on the social and charity circuit, savvy businesswoman.
Ice cream with fresh fruits

GEORGE DUNNE
President, Board of Commissioners of Cook County.
Cappuchino ice cream

JOHN EDMONDSON
President of Charles A. Stevens, lyricist.
Key Lime pie

EDDIE EINHORN
President of the Chicago White Sox.
Fresh raspberries

DON EPHRAIM
Media attorney.
Pineapple upside-down cake

CHARLES O. FINLEY
Insurance executive and former owner of the
Oakland A's baseball team.
Frozen white grapes

CARLTON FISK
White sox catcher.
Apple pie

JAMES E. FLYNN
Travel authority. Vice president Sales, Central Region for
Royal Viking Line. Active in charitable promotions.
Breyer's vanilla ice cream

MICHAEL FOLEY
Chef and owner of Printer's Row Restaurant
Poached pears in wine

STANLEY FREEHLING
Investment banker.
Hot fudge sundae

DOM DI FRISCO
Public relations expert, leader in Italian-American
community.
Cheese and fresh fruit

MARTIN GAPSHIS
Printing magnate, patron of the arts.
Stilton cheese with apples, pears

JUDGE SUSAN GETZENDANNER
Lawyer, scholar, judge, patron of the arts.
Fresh raspberries

RONALD AND CHRISTINA KEMPER GIDWITZ
He heads Helene Curtis Industries. She is a top model.
Both are socialites, active on cultural scene.
Cricket's hot fudge sundaes

MACK GILMAN
Art gallery owner, champion fencer.
Rhubarb pie

SHECKY GREENE
Comedian.
Strawberry shortcake, hot fudge sundaes

JOE GUZALDO
Actor.
Chocolate-chip cheesecake

DARYL HANNAH
Movie star, rising actress, vegetarian.
Fresh fruit

HENRY HANSON
Senior editor, columnist for *Chicago Magazine*; cap collector; art expert.
Banana yogurt with banana chips

JOHNATHAN HARDING
Former Maître d' at 21, Zorine's.
Strawberries romanoff with crushed macaroon topping

DR. ROBERT HARRIS
Dentist, community leader.
Jo's strawberries verona

SHARON HART
Fashion designer.
Poached pears stuffed with chestnut puree

BOBBY HULL
Hockey superstar.
Lemon-strawberry cake roll

WALTER JACOBSON
WBBM-TV newsman, commentator.
Chocolate . . . anything chocolate

HELMUT JAHN
Famous architect.
French tortes

MARTIN JANIS
Head of Martin Janis Public Relations firm, supporter of the arts.
Maple-flavored whipped cream

IRWIN JANN
Prominent lawyer, supporter of the arts.
Pistachio nuts and Bavarian pretzels with hot mustard.

GEORGE JEWELL
Caterer who trained at Buckingham Palace, socialite, patron of the arts.
Fresh figs dipped in chocolate

KANAE
Award-winning fashion designer.
Glazed oranges in their shells

BLAIR KAPLAN
Comedy writer.
M & M's plain

TIM KAZURINSKY
Movie, stage and TV comedian.
Marsha's English trifle

VICKI AND RICHARD KOHN
Business executives, civic and charity leaders.
Champagne and raspberries

JOHN KRAMER
General manager of the Chicago World Fair 1992 Authroity.
Fresh fruit

SHERRY LANSING
Movie Producer.
Chocolate chip ice cream

AUSBY LEE
Award-winning interior designer.
Poached pears with raspberry sauce

SHERREN LEIGH
Publisher, *Today's Chicago Woman*
Fresh raspberries

MICHAEL AND KATHERINE LEVENTHAL
Owners and creative geniuses behind Ronsley
Florists and Design Center.
Fresh raspberries with dom perignon

JOHN J. LOUIS JR.
Former ambassador to England.
Watermelon sorbet

RUTH LOVE
Former Superintendent of Schools.
Butter-pecan ice cream

SHELLY MAC ARTHUR
Socialite, model.
Baked Alaskas in orange shells

DAVID MALL
Orchestra leader.
Banana split topped with hot fudge

DAVID MAMET
Pulitzer Prize-winning playwright.
Cheese and fruit

DR. ROBERT MENDELSOHN
Medical and nutritional authority.
Rice pudding made with brown rice

JACK MITSAKOPOULOS
President, Chicago Fish House.
Rice pudding like mama used to make

DEBORAH NORVILLE
TV personality.
Cheesecake or sacher torte

POTTER PALMER
Philanthropist, Rosehill Cemetery owner, socialite.
Haagen-Dazs boysenberry sherbet

FRANK PARKER
Tennis "great" and head of the McClurg Sports Complex.
French apple pie a la mode

HERBERT PASCHEN
Builder, contractor.
Pralines and cream ice cream

WALTER PAYTON
The Bears' great running back.
Mrs. Field's cookies

CLARA PELLER
Star of TV commercials.
"Desserts? Desserts? I love everything!"

PHILIPPE AND LYSSA PIETTE
He is an international investment consultant. She has an
importing firm.
Chocolate mousse

HARRY PORTERFIELD
WBBM-TV newsman
Hot apple pie a la mode

RHODA PRITZKER
Patron of the arts.
Cantaloupe

DONNA "SUGAR" RAUTBORD
Socialite, writer.
Poached pears in brandy

JERRY REINSDORF
Balcor Realty chairman and chairman of the White Sox.
New owner of the Bulls.
Chocolate chip cheesecake

BERNARD RICHTER
Palmer House Hotel executive.
English trifle

MARIA RODRIGUEZ
Fashion designer.
Flourless chocolate cake

JOHN ROGERS
Stockbroker.
Mrs. Field's cookies

MICHAEL ROMAN
Caterer, head of the Mixing Bowl.
Flourless chocolate cake

THOMAS ROSENBERG
Real estate developer, major power-house in national
and local Democratic circles.
Fresh raspberries

NORMAN ROSS
Bank executive, radio personality, Far East expert,
socialite.
**Peach halves stuffed with cream cheese and
raspberry jam**

MIKE ROYKO
Columnist for the Chicago Tribune.
Butter-pecan ice cream

BERNARD SAHLINS
Second City's patriarch.
Lemon meringue pie

VICTOR SKREBNESKI
World-class photographer.
Popcorn

MAUREEN AND EDWARD BYRON SMITH, JR.
Patrons of the arts, socialites, civic leaders.
Strawberries with raspberry sauce

W. CLEMENT STONE
Insurance tycoon, philanthropist.
Jessie's Concord grape pie

FORMER GOV. WILLIAM AND SHIRLEY STRATTON
Still a force in GOP politics, the Strattons are active in
civic, social and charitable affairs.
Bananas foster

MR. T (LAWRENCE TERO)
Movie and TV star.
Three pieces of apple pie a la mode

SAMANTHA THOMPSON
Student and daughter of Gov. and Mrs. James
Thompson.
Chocolate ice cream with chocolate chip cookies

TONY TONTINI
Maitre d' of The Dining Room in the Ritz-Carlton Hotel.
Fresh fruits with port

HARRY VOLKMAN
TV weatherman.
Lemon meringue pie

ALD. EDWARD VRDOLYAK
Lawyer, veteran alderman, political power-house.
**Fresh strawberries sprinkled with grand marnier
and topped with whipped cream**

BOB WALLACE
WBBM-TV newsman.
Bananas flambe over vanilla ice cream

WILLIAM WEISS
Chairman and chief operating officer Ameritech.
Hot fudge sundaes

GEORGE WENDT
TV and movie actor and comedian, Second City star.
Cherry pie a la mode

MIKE WILKIE
Entrepreneur, sportsman, socialite.
Fresh raspberries

DAKIN WILLIAMS
Brother of the late Tennessee Williams, author, actor.
Baked Alaska

OPRAH WINFREY
Tv Personality, talk-show host.
Chocolate chip cookies

HARRIET WOLFSON
Philanthropist.
Eggless cookies

Index